Sub-Regional Cooperation for Trade, Investment, and Employment in North-East India

Sub-Regional Cooperation for Trade, Investment, and Employment in North-East India

Edited by

ASHISH NATH

OXFORD
UNIVERSITY PRESS

OXFORD
UNIVERSITY PRESS

Great Clarendon Street, Oxford, OX2 6DP,
United Kingdom

Oxford University Press is a department of the University of Oxford.
It furthers the University's objective of excellence in research, scholarship,
and education by publishing worldwide. Oxford is a registered trade mark of
Oxford University Press in the UK and in certain other countries.

Published in the United States of America by Oxford University Press
546 Fifth Avenue, New York, NY 10036, United States of America.

British Library Cataloguing in Publication Data
Data available

Library of Congress Control Number: 2026937181

ISBN 9780197908921

DOI: 10.1093/9780197908938.001.0001

Printed on demand

The manufacturer's authorized representative in the EU for product safety is
Oxford University Press España S.A. of Parque Empresarial San Fernando de Henares,
Avenida de Castilla, 2 – 28830 Madrid (www.oup.es/en or product.safety@oup.com).
OUP España S.A. also acts as importer into Spain of products made by the manufacturer.

To my father and mother (the late Hari Kumar Nath and Rajlaxmi Nath), who taught me the first line of knowledge

Preface

The quest for growth and development has remained a priority over the years for the policymakers as well as academics throughout the world, though the strategy towards the attainment of the same changes with time. The Northeastern Region (NER) of India, comprising eight states, is located in South Asia and shares more international border with neighbouring countries than borders with its own country. The majority of the states of the region were carved from Assam. The territories were ruled by different kings and chiefs at various points in time. The states of the region are recognized as "North-East India" during the British Raj[1] for the ease of doing business during the nineteenth century. Subsequently, the states of the region became part of the Indian union. Assam was the first state of the region to become a constituent state of India in 1950.[2] Manipur and Tripura were made union territories of India in 1956, and both the states, along with Meghalaya, attained fully fledged statehood in 1972. Nagaland formally became the sixteenth state of the Indian union in 1963.[3] Mizoram[4] and Arunachal Pradesh[5] became the twenty-third and twenty-fourth state of the Indian union, respectively, in 1987. Sikkim[6] was added as a state of India in 1975 and integrated with the Northeastern states in 2002. The eight distinct states of North-East India have more than 200 different ethnic groups residing within them, and each of these ethnic groups has its own dialect and script. The region is of strategic importance not only to India but also to the other Asian countries from South and Southeast Asia for political and economic reasons. On the one hand, this region can become the gateway for India to expand its economic opportunities in the growing Asian market, and on the other hand, the South and Southeast Asian countries have the opportunity to enter the vast and growing Indian market through this region as well. However, there has been a delay in understanding the growth process of the region as the geographical location of the states of the region has 5437.15 km of international border with a number of neighbouring Asian countries and is connected to the other states of the country through a narrow stretch called the "Siliguri Chicken's Neck" with a width ranging between 22 and 35 km.

India (NER) shares a border with five[7] Asian countries and has blood, cultural, ethnic, and trade relationships with these border sharing countries. However, the NER of India has always remained involved in border and insurgency problems with its neighbouring countries. Interestingly, each and every state of the region shares a boundary with one or more of the Asian countries, and they have established different channels of trade among themselves. Arunachal Pradesh and Sikkim are the only two states of the NER that share an international border with three countries. On the one hand, Arunachal Pradesh shares the longest (1,817 km) international border with Bhutan, Myanmar, the longest stretch being with China, while Sikkim shares only 350.15 km with Bhutan, China, and Nepal. Assam shares 530 km with Bangladesh and Bhutan, while Mizoram shares 828 km with Bangladesh and Myanmar. However, Manipur, Meghalaya, Nagaland, and Tripura share 398 km, 443 km, 215 km, and 856 km, respectively, with a single country, Bangladesh.

As such, the development of the eight states of the region to a large extent depends on the neighbourhood policies of the countries with which they border not only for trade but also for supporting the people living along the international border areas. The people of both sides of the border share ethnic, blood, cultural, and many other relationships. These relationships between the two sides have given rise to formal as well as informal channels of trade. Policymakers believe that cooperation among countries helps to improve the growth prospect of the cooperating countries by engaging them in product development; technical know-how; and value-chain, marketing, and other value-added services. This is true for the Northeastern states of India as well, and these states can gain further by integrating themselves with the neighbouring countries. In order to improve the growth prospects of the Northeastern states of India, a number of agreements (including trade agreements and connectivity projects) have been initiated to boost relationships with the neighbouring countries over the past few years.

Cooperation for trade and investment is regarded as an important instrument for the growth-and-development process of an economy and is in fact, regarded as engine of growth. In many instances, trade has helped to reduce poverty as well. Trade has helped economies to improve their growth and, at the same time, economic integration with different countries has helped countries to push their existing growth patterns. However, the nature of integration varies from country to country and also from region to region. Asian economies have grown very fast during the past two decades. They received a boost in the era of globalization, which changed the growth-and-development landscape of many countries, especially developing countries of the world. This has led to the creation of regional blocks and cooperation to push further the development agenda. The cooperation at regional level, and even at the sub-regional level, has emerged as one of the potential tools for boosting the trade agenda apart from geopolitical aspects.

Scholars have noted that the prosperity by the Asian region is largely driven by intra-regional cooperation led by East Asian countries viz. China, Japan, and South Korea; the Southeast Asian countries of Indonesia, Thailand, and Malaysia; and India. India's engagement with the Asian countries, especially in the South and Southeast Asian region, began during the early 1990s with the declaration of the Look East Policy (LEP) in 1992. The declaration of the policy created enthusiasm in North-East India because of the region's geographical and cultural proximity to the selected Asian countries. The policy was renamed the "Act East Policy" in 2014 for effective implementation of the policy for realizing the developmental agendas into realities. Again, the region received priority with the declaration of India's "Neighbourhood First Policy" towards the management of relations with countries in its immediate neighbourhood. Every state of the NER has rich and distinct natural resources, which require complementary institutional arrangements for their efficient use for the region's development. Besides the cultural and social affinity, the regions hold strong prospects for tourism, people-to-people contact, and cultural collaborative programmes to bring closer ties and understanding between the regions. This compendium contains a set of contributions specific to the individual states of the NER and its relation with the neighbouring countries.

The book focuses on state-specific developmental strategy based on cooperation with the neighbouring countries for boosting trade, investment, and employment. It has eleven chapters, with nine state-specific chapters focusing on individual states' developmental strategy. The book starts with the India's region-making approach and sub-regional programme, examining the importance of sub-regional cooperation with reference to the NER followed by nine state-specific chapters. The final chapter examines cross-border trade in the form of "border *haats*" as instruments for addressing local needs and livelihood concerns of people living along the international border areas of the states of North-East India and neighbouring countries.

The introductory section is followed by the first chapter, "Region Making in India's New Sub-Regional Approach: An Epistemic Understanding" by Rakhee Bhattacharya. The chapter looks into the importance of the sub-regional approach of development and how the NER of India could benefit from this approach. India has placed herself in the forefront of development by negotiating bilateral, multilateral, sub-regional, and regional agreements. This has been made possible by India through developing confidence among the different countries throughout the world. In order to make an inclusive development for the NER, for the past few years, the Government of India has undertaken many connectivity projects with a view to developing sub-regional cooperation. The chapter stresses that the Act East Policy and the Neighbourhood First Policy create immense potential for engaging North-East India in the sub-regional programme of India. India's rise in the global and regional forum demands an attuning of its sub-regional policy in a more robust framework with strong rationale and change in the present thinking. This chapter sets the argument for the NER in general and states of the region in particular for engaging in cross-border cooperation with neighbouring countries.

Chapter 2 by Ashi Lama and Amitava Mitra discusses the Indo-Myanmar border trade in terms of the existing status and future prospects of border trade between the two countries through the Nampong–Pangsau corridor in Arunachal Pradesh. At present, the major trade partners of Myanmar are Thailand and China, but given the composition of trade in Myanmar, there is a strong possibility of increasing trade with Myanmar. However, the Nampong Land Customs Station (LCS) is non-functional, and the infrastructural facilities are also very low at the land port. There is huge diversification of trade towards informal channels, and there is a lot of scope to increase trade through the Nampong LCS, if it were to be made functional. Again, given the success of "border *haats*" in other Northeastern states, the Government of Arunachal Pradesh has constructed a "border *haat*" at Pangsau Pass on the Indian side. The *haat* is yet to be operationalized. The chapter also lists potential products that could be traded between India and Myanmar.

Informal channels of trade are prevalent in almost all the states of the NER. Tirap, Changlang, and Longding (TCL) are border districts of the state of Arunachal Pradesh and share international borders with Myanmar in the east. The border communities recognize their respective group across the border and are actively engaged in informal cross-border exchange. Myanmar and Arunachal Pradesh have historical connections and deep-rooted cultural and ethnic ties. The people of the TCL region are engaged in shifting cultivation, where infrastructure is very low. The third chapter of this book by Manngam Wangpan and Sailajananda Saikia examines the prevalence of informal trade in the TCL region and highlights the significance of the region in terms of economic and geostrategic area. This region is inhabited mostly by the tribes on both sides of the border, and they share blood relations. Cross-border movements are a normal phenomenon in the region. Though there are challenges, cross-border trade has the potential to make the TCL region a pivotal hub for trade and connectivity.

Assam is the largest state in the NER and shares borders with Bangladesh and Bhutan. The fourth chapter on Assam by Saswati Choudhury discusses how connectivity corridors can function in different ways to integrate the social and economic spaces of two regions to create agglomeration of development outcomes, which primarily have both forward and backward linkages. Given the geostrategic location of Assam, the state is well poised to meet the import demand of neighbouring countries and the region with development of its manufacturing capabilities, human resources, and infrastructure including logistics. The export potential of the state could easily make Assam the gateway to the Association of Southeast Asian Nations (ASEAN).

Manipur has a rich cultural heritage and a well-educated population. However, over the years, the growth of the state has stagnated due to internal instability and declining relationships with its neighbouring countries. The fifth chapter by Ch. Priyoranjan Singh posits that identity politics still festers and threatens the enabling strides the North-East has made in recent decades in economic development and growth. The lacunae of India's foreign trade policy towards Southeast Asia have boosted the informal trade between India and Myanmar. The demand for bilateral trade through Moreh-Tamu Custom Station increased over the years, but the COVID-19 pandemic of 2020 put a brake on the flow of goods. This land station offers ample opportunities for expansion of economic corridors through the Trilateral Highway to Southeast Asia. The Trilateral Highway at Myanmar and Thailand's Myawaddy-Mae Sot is emerging as a planned and coordinated economic hub. Given Manipur's contact and historical relations, the state offers many sectors for development of formal trade through the Trilateral Highway, including the scope for value chains for a number of products and services.

Similarly, the sixth chapter Saswati Choudhury on Meghalaya and Bangladesh cooperation puts forward the circumstances on which the state of Meghalaya came into existence. The chapter also points out how the Khasi, Jaintia, and Garo Hills were used for lucrative resources over the colonial era. The history of the formation of the modern boundary between the present-day Sylhet (now in Bangladesh) and Meghalaya (in India) can be traced back to the events of the 1780s. The partition of the state has increased the sufferings of the people living along the international border areas as most of them depend on the fields for their livelihood. As such, the need to develop the road network in order to improve the economic conditions of the people of the border areas was immediately recognized by the government after Meghalaya attained statehood in 1972. The opening of the cross-border trade, including border *haats* and schemes to facilitate the marketing of border products, has greatly increased the livelihood opportunities of the people there. The benefits from cross-border cooperation, including the initiatives taken by the governments, are discussed in detail in this chapter.

Mizoram is known for its lush green landscapes, vibrant culture, and rich heritage and shares borders with Myanmar and Bangladesh. Chapter 7 by Konthoujam Gyanendra Singh presents the current trade relations of Mizoram with Myanmar and Bangladesh through different trade points and the infrastructural bottlenecks associated with the trade. The trade point between Mizoram and Myanmar is at Zokhawthar-Rih sector, and different types of commodities are traded through Zokhawthar LCS. Similarly, the Lunglei, Mamit, and Lawngtlai districts of Mizoram share borders with Bangladesh, and Kawrpuichhuah LCS was notified as trading point. However, the LCS is not functional, and the existence of the same ethnic group on both sides of the border makes it easy to trade with each other for local consumption. The chapter also discusses in detail the benefits of Mizoram for cooperation and initiatives taken for engaging further with Myanmar and Bangladesh.

Chapter 8, authored by T. Zarenthung Ezung, looks into the challenges and prospects facing Indo-Myanmar border trade, locating Nagaland at the centre of discussion. Nagaland has a 215 km-long border with Myanmar, but trade between India and Myanmar through Nagaland has less impact on the markets as very few items or volumes are traded. There is regular inflow of Myanmar goods to the Indian markets. There are four international trade centres in Nagaland, and the chapter examines both formal and informal trade between the two countries by studying these centres, pointing out the challenges for expanding trade and suggesting various measures for improving trade. The comparison of the Naga people living in these two countries shows a very high inequality in terms of socio-economic conditions and, hence, cross-border trade between India and Myanmar through Nagaland state could play an important role in developing and raising the standards of living of the people in the border areas.

The trade prospects of Sikkim through sub-regional cooperation with Nepal and Bhutan, with whom the second smallest state of India shares an international border, is discussed in Chapter 9 by Gadde Omprasad. The chapter argues that imagining sub-regional cooperation without Sikkim would be incomprehensible as the state shares historical, socio-cultural, and religious linkages and ethnic similarities with the neighbouring countries. A number of connectivity projects were undertaken with Sikkim as the epicentre. So, it is important to locate Sikkim in the sub-regional cooperation with neighbouring countries by bringing the Darjeeling hills into its ambit not only because of the shared commonalities but also because the region facilitates physical connectivities. Sikkim's economy holds a transformative potential through the Trans-Himalayan Cultural and Eco-Tourism Circuit model for deepening sub-regional integration with Bhutan and Nepal.

Chapter 10 by the editor discusses how the sub-regional cooperation of Tripura with Bangladesh could drive the growth process of the state.

Tripura is the only state that has a border with a single country (i.e. Bangladesh) on three sides. Tripura and Bangladesh have cultural, blood, and ethnic relationships and have engaged in both formal and informal channels of trade. Again, the location of the state is strategic in the international context, being between Bangladesh, on one side, and Southeast Asia, on the other. The location and resource advantages of Tripura, along with socio-economic linkages with Bangladesh, could make the state a potential hub for trade with and through Bangladesh for the entire North-East of India. The past few years have witnessed an increase not only in trade volume between Tripura and Bangladesh but also in connectivity projects, which is expected to boost the growth process of the state further.

Border markets between countries are prevalent in many parts of the world. These markets generally improve the economic condition of the population living adjacent to the international border areas. Border markets have been functional in various parts of the NER for years and the past decade has witnessed renewed interest among the border-sharing countries to introduce border markets in the form of "border *haats*". The last contribution of this compendium is by Indranil Bose on "border *haats*". A border *haat* is a trade concept introduced between Bangladesh and the Northeastern states of India for improving the standard of living of the people living along the international border areas. This final chapter argues that border trade is not a new concept, and there are many instances to show that mechanisms are there to facilitate trade and exchange among people across the border. Indo-Bangladesh border *haats*, operational between select states of the NER and Bangladesh, is successful in many dimensions. The case of the Indo-Bangladesh border *haats* reveals that prudent measures on the part of governments can go a long way in transforming the worlds of people living in often neglected and remote border regions of developing countries.

The chapters together provide comprehensive and transformative thinking relating to different dimensions of sub-regional cooperation of the states of North-East India with their neighbouring countries. The analysis of the actors of the different states of the region during the past, and the implications for the future, are extremely important for understanding the behaviour and approach of the states of the region towards cooperation with the neighbouring countries. Though different states have diverse perspectives on cooperation, all the chapters unanimously propose that the states of the region would gain immensely through co-operation with their neighbouring countries.

Ashish Nath

Notes

1. https://indianculture.gov.in/north-east-archive/history-north-east.
2. https://assam.gov.in/about-us/394.
3. https://www.nagaland.gov.in/nagaland-profile.
4. https://aizawl.nic.in/tourism.
5. https://arunachal.mygov.in/arunachal-pradesh-statehood-day.
6. https://indianculture.gov.in/north-east-archive/history-north-east.
7. Bangladesh, Bhutan, China, Myanmar, and Nepal.

Acknowledgements

This book is the outcome of the thought process of the past four years. The Northeastern states of India are unique in themselves and the states of the region became a part of the Indian union with the passage of time. The NER of India comprises eight states, and the interesting fact is that each and every state shares an international boundary with one or more neighbouring countries. At the same time, the people living along the international border areas on both sides have blood and ethnic kinship among themselves, and consequently, different forms of cross-border trade developed between the people on both sides. The formal trade between the states of the region and the neighbouring countries is carried out mainly through the land ports. On the other hand, informal cross-border trade between the peoples living along the international border of all the states of the NER of India and the peoples of the corresponding neighbouring countries has developed not always for commercial purposes but for sustaining livelihood as well. At the same time, border *haats* have also been established to improve the livelihood of the people living along the vicinity of international border areas between Bangladesh and the states of Meghalaya and Tripura. Thus, given the geographical location, the states of the region have developed formal and informal trade relations with the neighbouring countries. However, resources differ between the states of the region and, to a large extent, the states can further push their growth and development process by expanding cooperation with the neighbouring countries. This has been the principal motivation behind the inception of this volume, which engages with the aspects of the growth strategy of all the eight Northeastern states of India separately with the help of the neighbouring countries.

I express my gratitude to the Coordinator, University Grants Commission (Special Assistance Programme-Departmental Research Support Level II) (UGC (SAP-DRS II)) and faculty members of the Department of Economics, Tripura University for giving me the opportunity to organize the UGC (SAP-DRS II) seminar, which inspired me to conceptualize the genesis of the book. The seminar was successful, to a large extent, from the initial funds received from the UGC (SAP-DRS II) earmarked for organizing the seminar. I must acknowledge the support and help received from the Indian Council of Social Science Research—North Eastern Regional Centre (ICSSR—NERC), Shillong and other organizations for extending financial assistance to organize that seminar as well.

My sincere appreciation goes to each and every contributor to this book, all of whom agreed to prepare the respective state's chapter as per the subject matter of the book.

I would like to express my gratitude to the publisher, Oxford University Press, for accepting this book for publication. In particular, I would like to thank Dhiraj Pandey for guiding me continuously since the conception of the published book came up. I am grateful to the reviewers for recommending the manuscripts for publication. I also express my gratefulness to Amrita Brahmo and the editorial team of Oxford University Press for guiding and shaping the book into its final form.

The regular support from my family members is invaluable and cannot be expressed in a few lines. My discussion with my elder son, Abheshek, a student at the London School of Economics and Political Science, has been one of my greatest sources of inspiration. He discussed the organization of the book and gave valuable suggestions whenever required. My younger son, Aniket Nath, always helped me to boost morale, and my wife, Sampa, provided me with unfailing guidance and unstinted support. Her quiet encouragement and willingness to give me the space and time needed to carry out this research have been indispensable.

Ashish Nath

Contents

Illustrations

Figures

Tables

Abbreviations

AA	Arakan Army
ADB	Asian Development Bank
ADCs	Autonomous District Councils
AEF	Act East Forum
AEP	Act East Policy
AFSPA	Armed Forces Special Power Act
AH	Asian Highway
AIDIA	Asian Institute of Diplomacy and International Affairs
AIIMS	All India Institute of Medical Sciences
APEDA	Agricultural and Processed Food Products Export Development Authority
ASA	Assam State Archive
ASEAN	The Association of Southeast Asian Nations
ATM	Automated Teller Machine
B20	Business 20
BADP	Border Area Development Programme
BBIN	Bangladesh, Bhutan, India, and Nepal
BCM	Billion cubic metres
BCIM	Bangladesh–China–India–Myanmar
BCIM EC	BCIM Economic Corridor
BCPL	Brahmaputra Crackers and Polymers Limited
BIG-B	Bay of Bengal Industrial Growth Belt
BIMARU	Bihar, Madhya Pradesh, Rajasthan, and Uttar Pradesh
BIMSTEC	Bay of Bengal Initiative for Multi-Sectoral Technical and Economic Cooperation
BNP	Bangladesh Nationalist Party
BoB	Bay of Bengal
BRI	Belt and Road Initiative
BRO	Border Roads Organization
BSCCL	Bangladesh Submarine Cable Company Limited
BSF	Border Security Force
BSNL	Bharat Sanchar Nigam Limited
BTA	Border Trade Agreement
BTAD	Bodoland Territorial Autonomous Districts
BTC	Bodoland Territorial Council
CEL	Centre for Endangered Languages

CENISEAS	Centre for Northeast India, South and Southeast Asia Studies
CFA	Centre for Financial Accountability
CLAWS	Centre for Land Warfare Studies
CLMV	Cambodia, Lao, Myanmar, and Vietnam
CoE	Committee of Experts
CTC	Crush, Tear, Curl
CUTS	Consumer Unity & Trust Society
DFTP	Duty-Free Tariff Preference
DGCI&S	Directorate General of Commercial Intelligence and Statistics
DGFT	Director General of Foreign Trade
DoNER	Ministry of Development of North Eastern Region
DPIIT	Department for Promotion of Industry and Internal Trade
DSP	Deep Sea Port
EBTC	Eastern Border Transportation Coalition
EHR	Eastern Himalayan Region
EPC	Engineering Procurement Contract
EPI	Export Preparedness Index
EPIP	Export Promotion Industrial Park
ERI–ASEAN	Economic Research Institute for ASEAN
EXIM	Export–Import
FDI	Foreign Direct Investment
FICCI	Federation of Indian Chambers of Commerce and Industry
FIEO	Federation of Indian Export Organizations
FMR	Free Movement Regime
FTA	Free Trade Agreement
G20	Group of Twenty
GBPS	Gigabits per second
GDP	Gross Domestic Product
GoAP	Government of Andhra Pradesh
GoI	Government of India
GPs	Gaon Panchayats
GR	Guaranteed Remittance
GSDP	Gross State Domestic Product
GST	Goods and Services Tax
GSTIN	Goods and Services Tax Identification Number
GSVA	Gross State Value Added
GVA	Gross Value Added
HDFC	Housing Development Finance Corporation
HDR	Human Development Report
HMC	*Haat* Management Committee
IANS	Indo-Asian News Service

IBEF	India Brand Equity Foundation
IBP	Indo-Bangladesh Protocol
ICAR	Indian Council of Agricultural Research
ICC	International Chamber of Commerce
ICD	Inland Container Depot
ICP	Integrated Check Post
ICSSR—NERC	Indian Council of Social Science Research—North Eastern Regional Centre
IDBI	Industrial Development Bank of India
IEC	Importer–Exporter Code
IHCAE	Indian Himalayan Centre of Adventure and Eco-Tourism
IISEC	Institute of Socio-economic Investigations
INA	Indian National Army
INC	India–Nepal Centre
ISAS	Institute of South Asian Studies
IST	Indian Standard Time
JWG	Joint Working Group
KLCL	Kommorrah Limestone Company Limited
KMTTP	Kaladan Multi-Modal Transit Transport Project
LCS	Land Customs Station
LEP	Look East Policy
LFPR	Labour Force Participation Rate
LSC	Lafarge Surma Cement Ltd
LUMPL	Lafarge Umiam Mining Pvt. Ltd
LUPL	Lafarge Umiam Private Limited
MCCL	Mawmluh Cherra Cements Ltd
MGC	Mekong–Ganga Cooperation
MoU	Memorandum of Understanding
MOVCDNER	Mission for Value Chain Development for North East Region
MSME	Micro, Small, and Medium Enterprises
MVA	Motor Vehicles Agreement
NABARD	National Bank for Agriculture and Rural Development
NADI	Natural Allies in Development and Interdependence
NEC	North Eastern Council
NER	Northeastern Region
NERAMAC	North Eastern Regional Agricultural Marketing Corporation
NERSDS	North-East Road Sector Development Scheme
NET	Northeast Today
NH	National Highway
NITI Aayog	National Institution for Transforming India
NRL	Numaligarh Refinery Ltd

NSCN	National Socialist Council of Nagaland
NSDP	Net State Domestic Product
NSO	National Statistical Office
ODA	Official Development Assistance
OGL	Open General Licence
OKDISCD	Omeo Kumar Das Institute of Social Change and Development
ONGC	Oil and Natural Gas Corporation Limited
OTPC	ONGC Tripura Power Company Private Limited
PAN	Permanent Account Number
PDR	People's Democratic Republic
PIB	Press Information Bureau
PM-DevINE	Prime Minister's Development Initiative for the North-East Region
PHC	Primary Health Centre
PMJDY	Pradhan Mantri Jan Dhan Yojana
PMSSY	Pradhan Mantri Suraksha Yojana
PRC	People's Republic of China
PTI	Press Trust of India
PwC	PricewaterhouseCoopers
RBI	Reserve Bank of India
RCEP	Regional Comprehensive Economic Partnership
RIS	Research and Information System for Developing Countries
Rs	Rupees
RTA	Regional Trade Agreement
SAARC	South Asian Association for Regional Cooperation
SAFTA	South Asian Free Trade Area
SAGQ	South Asian Growth Quadrangle
SASEC	South Asia Sub-regional Economic Cooperation
SBI	State Bank of India
SDC	Sikkim State Development Council
SEZ	Special Economic Zone
SHG	Self-help Group
SIMFED	Sikkim State Co-operative Supply and Marketing Federation Ltd
SIRD&PR	State Institute of Rural Development and Panchayati Raj, Sikkim
SWOT	Strengths, Weaknesses, Opportunities, and Threats
SRIT	Sikkim Research Institute of Tibetology
TBA	Three Brotherhood Alliance
TCL	Tirap, Changlang, and Longding
TLH	Trilateral Highway
TMT	Thermos-mechanically Treated

UGC (SAP-DRS II)	University Grants Commission (Special Assistance Programme-Departmental Research Support Level II)
ULFA	United Liberation Front of Asom
UN	United Nations
UNLF	United National Liberation Front
UNNATI	Uttar Poorva Transformative Industrialization Scheme
WTO	World Trade Organization

Contributors

Rakhee Bhattacharya, Professor and Chairperson (Economics), Special Centre for the Study of North East India, Jawaharlal Nehru University, New Delhi, India.

Indranil Bose, Associate Professor, Department of Political Science, St Xavier's College (Autonomous), Kolkata, India.

Saswati Choudhury, Professor and Acting Director, Omeo Kumar Das Institute of Social Change and Development, Assam, India.

T. Zarenthung Ezung, Professor, Department of Economics, Nagaland University, Nagaland, India.

Ashi Lama, Associate Professor, Department of Economics, Rajiv Gandhi University, Arunachal Pradesh, India.

Amitava Mitra, Former Pro Vice-Chancellor and Professor (Retired), Department of Economics, Rajiv Gandhi University, Arunachal Pradesh, India.

Ashish Nath, Professor, Department of Economics, Tripura University, Tripura, India.

Gadde Omprasad, Associate Professor, Centre for South Asian Studies, School of International Studies, Jawaharlal Nehru University, New Delhi, India.

Sailajananda Saika, Professor, Department of Geography, Rajiv Gandhi University, Arunachal Pradesh, India.

Ch. Priyoranjan Singh, Professor (Retired), Department of Economics, Manipur University, Manipur, India.

Konthoujam Gyanendra Singh, Professor, Department of Economics, Manipur University, Manipur, India.

Manngam Wangpan, Research Scholar, Department of Geography, Rajiv Gandhi University, Arunachal Pradesh, India.

1

Region Making in India's New Sub-regional Approach

An Epistemic Understanding

Rakhee Bhattacharya

Introduction: India and the Emerging World Order

India has emerged as a powerful Asian player in the contemporary world order. India's voice is considered to be significant in rebalancing the Global North–South dialogue in many key areas of climate change and green economy, social development and sustainable growth trajectory, technology and digital regulation, war and geopolitics, terrorism and global governance. Such global recognition is supported by India's rising geopolitical mastery and weighty performance on the domestic front in the past decade. Many significant changes in governance and policy reforms have supported the economic rise and stability of the country, which is endorsed by global acknowledgement. This uninterrupted effort has paid off, and a recent report of the World Bank has acclaimed India as one of the fastest-growing economies of the world in the post-COVID-19 period (post-2020) (World Bank, 2023), while the National Statistical Office (NSO) of India showed a rise of more than 100 per cent in India's per capita net national income at current prices from rupees (Rs) 86,647 in 2014–15 to Rs 1,96,716 for the year 2022–23 (NSO Report, 2023). This rising performance has pushed India into the group of largest world economies with the United States, China, Japan, and Germany; and the country claims to be emboldened to reach high middle-income status by 2047, the year of India's centenary of Independence (World Bank, 2023).

Rakhee Bhattacharya, *Region Making in India's New Sub-regional Approach* In: *Sub-Regional Cooperation for Trade, Investment, and Employment in North-East India*. Edited by: Ashish Nath, Oxford University Press.
 DOI: 10.1093/9780197908938.003.0001

Additionally, the success of hosting a year-long G-20 presidency in 2023 with the theme of "One Earth, One Family, One Future" has given this democracy more responsibility and authority at the global and regional levels. Similarly, India's push on specific strategies, especially during the COVID-19 period, with mindful support in the social sector to the neighbouring and smaller countries, reaffirmed goodwill and put the country in a position to negotiate for a fair and shared world order for seeking justice for vulnerable people, economies, and ecologies. It has reinforced India's confidence in nation-building project and underpinned its role in constructive transnational, sub-regional, and neighbourly relations.

As the nation becomes an acceptable and dependable partner in various bilateral, multilateral, sub-regional, and neighbourhood relations, India's commitments and responsibilities are unleashed at various levels for meaningful alliance on economic, governance, political, and climate change aspects. It also puts pressure on the achievement of a progressive and inclusive nation, making growth and development a reality in every part of the country. The latest report of the World Bank, cited by the Government of India, claims that out of 167 nations, India has become the fourth most "equal" country after the Slovak Republic, Slovenia, and Belarus with the Gini Index at 25.5 (Press Information Bureau, 2025). The policy reforms have systematically aimed at economic empowerment, digital and physical infrastructure, and social inclusion to address the issues of inequality and regional disparities. It must be noted here that India's economic development has been highly asymmetrical among people in the neoliberal period and also among the regions, with certain areas or groups of states regarded as "backward", such as the far-flung Northeastern Region (NER) or the Hindi Heartland Region of Bihar, Madhya Pradesh, Rajasthan, and Uttar Pradesh (BIMARU). The NER was particularly marked as "frontier", "underdeveloped", "isolated", "disturbed", and "secessionist" and was mostly kept outside the realm of any developmental policy reforms in the past. The current policy reforms have made a change in approach with the objective of remaking the region as core and integral to India while turning it into a land-linked and open-region borderland for external engagements with its neighbouring countries. This U-turn in the region-making approach has transformed the NER as a visible space with policy attention turned towards connectivity infrastructure, economic development, and livelihood opportunities. Simultaneously, attention is being paid to peace-building measures to transform this prolonged conflict-prone region into a region of stability, which serves as a precondition for any trans-regional, sub-regional, and neighbourhood engagement programmes.

At this juncture of transformation, there is a need for deeper intellectual debates on the conceptual reference to claim it as a paradigm shift in India's region-making approach. It is also important to understand whether this transforming region-borderland can play a sustainable role as a linking space in India's sub-regional programmes. This chapter explores the critical testable features of this new approach to sub-regional understanding. Sections 1.2 and 1.3 attempt to understand such a transformative narrative and the various counterforces on the ground to reflect on the implications and challenges of this new regional approach. The final two sections propose a sustainable framework for the NER to work towards a brighter contour of India's new sub-regional programme and explore an epistemic debate in the existing understanding of sub-regionalism with reference to the NER.

The Making of the NER: Determinants of Peace and Progress in the Post-2014 Era

Region making, according to the *Encyclopaedia Britannica*, is termed with single or multiple features or an approach that considers human space with ethnic, cultural, linguistic, climatic, topographical, and economic specificities within a defined administrative unit and political geography. The intellectual discourse therefore draws logical reference to such selected features of cohesiveness and homogeneity in region making that facilitate convenience and become integral to various national and international programmes of engagements and strategies. The NER is one such unique cohesive construct in the modern Indian subcontinent that was produced first during a colonial cartographic and border-making exercise for administrative, political, and economic convenience. Unfortunately, on the ground, the features of multiplicity and diversity have resisted such a cohesive construct of the North-East of India and have produced many fault-lines and fragilities in India's post-colonial nation-building project. The region was eventually affixed with "durable disorder" syndrome after a large set of debates on issues of perpetual conflicts and underdevelopment. Henceforth, in both policy and academia, India's region-making project in the North-East remained a perpetual challenge. However, in 2014, a renewed roadmap was drawn for accountable political and developmental outcomes and a large set of policies was charted out for the NER. Such policies have made a two-fold intervention on restoring peace and development in the region. The region has been under critical narratives of conflicts and violence, with multiple armed movements, over the entire post-colonial period and was understood as a "disturbed" and "secessionist" frontier that derived support through cross-border connections from the neighbouring nations. Numerous ethno-insurgent groups have consistently challenged the idea of the North-East within India's nation state framework and made national–territorial security a consequential subject in this region. The astonishing complexity, penetration, and compliance to such armed groups have allowed many unlawful activities to be sustained, grow, and become institutionalized in the region. With its vast functional area across the valley and hills, this has affected the everyday life and livelihood of common people and disrupted businesses and industry, both large and small. A prolonged method of violence and extortion by the armed groups became integral to the region, with a sense of legitimacy among the social and ethnic forces.

As a counter-insurgency measure, the NER was covered under an exceptional Armed Forces Special Power Act (AFSPA). This act empowered armed forces with unlimited power to deal with violence, which subsequently militarized and engulfed the region for several decades. The AFSPA defined the region for about six decades from 1958, within a frame of exception, and penetrated deeply the lives and psyche of the people. There was an official and complete closure of international borders for ensuring territorial security, which made the region severely isolated and cut off. During the early neoliberal period of 1990s, however, India aimed to transcend the region's extraordinary situation, largely driven by a security narrative. A developmental paradigm was invoked and an attempt was made to create cross-border economic engagement. However, the strategy did not succeed, and the idea grew that such a neoliberal developmental paradigm was embedded within India's securitist approach (Bhattacharya, 2018). It therefore failed to resonate with the confidence and consensus of the people and the stakeholders. Multiple insurgency operations and their cross-border connections nevertheless remained forceful as a counterforce to such a developmental idea, and the region continued to be afflicted by persistent violence, *bandhs*, blockades, bloodsheds, and terror strikes, which reinforced it as "disturbed" and "secessionist" over the entire period of the 1990s and 2000s.

The post-2014 approach, however, is claimed to be a break from the past. To restore peace in this troubled region, there has been a gradual shift to a humanistic and comprehensive approach through dialogue and support measures over the past ten years. Through multi-level political negotiations, an attempt has been made to ensure that the region has more access to the Delhi power corridor and to understand and address the decades old antipathy. Most significantly, an attempt was made to repeal the controversial AFSPA in a phased manner to gain the confidence of the people, and Tripura was the first state to remove this law completely in 2018. Apart from some areas of Assam and Manipur, 75 per cent of the region covered under the AFSPA has now been allowed to claim a security policy that is more human-centric. As this draconian law is slowly and carefully being phased out from the states of the region, it is losing its relevance in the social forces. New political promises and consensus are being built to provide essential support in bridging the decades' old colossal gap between the coercive state and the antagonized society of the NER. The state made several attempts to create dialogue with the armed groups to bring about ceasefires, surrender, and a peace agreement. Over the past five years, around 8,900 cadres of the militant groups of the region surrendered and joined the mainstream. Around twenty peace accords have been signed to send a signal that there is change with more stability (Hindustan Times, 2024). Some of the most prominent and oldest armed groups, such as the National Socialist Council of Nagaland (NSCN), the United Liberation Front of Asom (ULFA) in Assam, and the United National Liberation Front (UNLF) in Manipur, which have stirred up the region for around half a century, have ended their operations. The violence in the region has gone down by 73 per cent over the past ten years. These are major accomplishments that aim to erase a prolonged militarization of the region, making the contemporary security approach more pragmatic, people-centric, and constructive, with state and society converging to break from the rapturous past.

Peace and progress are deeply interconnected, and India's North-East has shown clear links between the two post 2014. India's policy invoked a well-framed development paradigm in the region to address its decades-old issues of regional underdevelopment and geographical isolation. Multiple projects on connectivity infrastructure, agriculture, livelihood, and trade were strategically unfolded through the Act East Policy (AEP). This policy decisively centralized the region with a developmental approach, and outcomes over the past decade have been phenomenal. Road infrastructure has made revolutionary progress against the inaccessibility of the region due to mountain and river systems. Road projects have been invigorated at the policy level since 2014–15 not only to transform the perceived sense of isolation but also to be used as a technology for integration (Bhattacharya and Deka, 2021). In 2017, an important North-East Road Sector Development Scheme (NERSDS) replaced a two-decade-old Special Accelerated Road Development Programme—North-East that was introduced in 2005 to counter geographical isolation and to mainstream the region in the national discourse. The NERSDS aimed to have built 19,903 km of roads by 2025, and some of the most difficult connections have already been made, such as Asia's 9.15-km Dhola–Sadiya road bridge over the river Lohit-Brahmaputra, built in 2017 to connect the most remote and most cut-off, mountainous Eastern Arunachal Pradesh with Assam. In 2018, another milestone over the River Brahmaputra was achieved with a 4.94-km Bogibeel road-cum-rail bridge to connect Assam, connecting its southern and northern towns of Dibrugrah and Dhemaji and the central part of Arunachal Pradesh. The riverine Dhubri–Phulbari road bridge over Brahmaputra is on the way to making connections between the inaccessible interiors of Meghalaya and Assam. The 166.8-km strategic Shillong–Silchar Highway is envisioned as an access-controlled greenfield expressway to connect Mawlyngkhung near Shillong in Meghalaya to Panchgram near Silchar in Assam and is expected to reduce the travel time between Shillong and Silchar significantly. The data of the Union Ministry of Road Transport and Highways, Government of India shows that from 2015 to 2019, the total growth rate of roads in the North-East was 7.32 per cent against the All India growth rate of 4.40 per cent (Bhattacharya and Deka, 2021). Similarly, the other important modes of connectivity (i.e. rail links, air links, and water links) are making immense changes in the region. This new multi-modal connectivity infrastructure has undoubtedly become a prominent marker of a regional entity, making the 28-km Siliguri road corridor, the sole post-colonial life-line of the people of the NER less consequential, while the strategic significance of this narrow corridor remains high in India's national security. Much other cross-border connectivity infrastructure is strategically recreating the vast international borders of the North-East as the "keys to cooperation dynamics" in a sub-region consisting of Bangladesh, Myanmar, Bhutan, the NER of India, and Nepal. This tight, geographically integrated sub-region, as argued by Lama, along with the two neighbouring Indian states of Bihar and West Bengal, form the core interface to provide points of connection to other neighbouring countries, and this is seen as one of the most attractive geographies of contemporary Asia (Lama, 2017). This transformation therefore is expected to create a cascading and spiralling impact through cross-border trade, circulation, and exchange for economic expansion. There is a focus on the regional development of the NER, with parallel emphasis on social mobility and progress. The Prime Minister's Development Initiative for the North-East Region (PM-DevINE), which was launched in 2023, aims to finance social development, livelihood, and community capacity-building projects in the region. The policy has also focused on human development by ensuring schemes such as the Pradhan Mantri Jan Dhan Yojana (PMJDY) (a revolutionary financial inclusion programme) and the Pradhan Mantri Suraksha Yojana (PMSSY) (a tertiary health-care programme), which have improved health-care quality and lives for millions in the North-East. The establishment of the North-East's first All India Institute of Medical Sciences (AIIMS) in Guwahati and three medical colleges at Nalbari, Nagaon, and Kokrajhar are creating a high-quality health infrastructure. Such a multi-pronged approach to restoring peace, development, and social progress has to a significant extent broken the prolonged vicious cycle of conflict and underdevelopment. It is slowly creating a new "virtuous cycle" of peace and progress to ensure economic progress, social well-being, and community trust (Stewart, 2004). Such "fusion of security and development", as argued by Mark Duffield elsewhere, conceptually nullifies any destructive force and defensive military approach that threatens progress. Being mutually inclusive and integrative, idea of fusion acknowledge the universalism of life and solidarity among people (Duffield, 2005) and has global acceptability (Tschirgi,

2005). This dual-policy approach to security development furthermore creates a foundation for impressing the NER on the mainstream imagination and produces epistemic rethinking on regional construct and its sustainability with legitimate political, economic, and social fabrics. However, it is always important to test the robustness of such an approach through a critical understanding in the academic field.

Lines, Fault Lines, and Unruly Edges

For any understanding of a sustainable regional and sub-regional frame, a careful analysis is needed because of the opposing and alternative power forces that distract from any constructive approach. For example, the diverse communities in the NER in the past mostly responded differently to any constructive policy approach to peace and development, making the region a fragile frontier in sub-regional engagement. There are several factors other than the notion of underdevelopment that transcended the idea of peace, eluded universalism, and created grounds for multiple resistance and violence. A captivated notion of identity, for example in the NER, always exaggerates intra-ethnic violence. This is also drawn from a sense of autonomy and territoriality having cross-border associations. Communities who are central in any territorial space in the NER are unified (or divided) through a certain set of historical and cultural norms and derive certain controlling power and legitimacy over the land and resources to deny any state craft of region making. According to Sahasrabuddhe (2008), this is a threat, and such a regional complex as a social system ingrained in identity matrix often dates back to premodern history and the long history of interdependence as the beginning of the regionalization process. This may include both state and non-state actors. At this level, the region turns into an active subject with distinct identity, legitimacy, and decision-making structure. The dividing line between separate and "imagined" national communities within the region also begins to disappear. It gives rise to an entity that would be larger than the nation state in territorial terms but by no means having the same degree of homogeneity or sovereignty. This entity demonstrates a sense of authority, power, and resistance and tends to decentralize at local and micro-regional levels. It is not devised to suggest progression but causes a decreasing sense of region or even dissolution of a region (Sahasrabuddhe, 2008). A sudden and extraordinary bout of violence in Manipur for the past more than two year amidst the transforming narrative of the North-East is the best case to study to understand how ethno-contesting forces on the ground can be unleashed to distract from any constructive approach to region making. It goes far deeper than the security–development matrix that is currently devised for regional construction and poses a critical challenge to such a shifting paradigmatic frame. The challenge is largely embedded within the historical context, ethno-social structure, and power relations and tends to produce unruly edges, making the idea of the NER inconsequential in India's nation state framework.

The ethno-social structure in the NER is ethno-spatially derived and, thus, easily spills across the borders to challenge any sustainable region-making approach. It further threatens sub-regional construct across the bordering and neighbouring nations. From the early 1990s, the NER was reframed as an open connecting borderland for India's sub-regional programme, and Manipur–Myanmar was at centre-stage for the constructive India–Association of Southeast Asian Nations (ASEAN) cross-border engagement. Given the strategic location, Myanmar and India's Manipur were seen as the "gateways" to Southeast Asia, and the first official cross-border route was announced in 1996 through Moreh-Tamu Land Customs Station (LCS) as part of India's sub-regional programme with Southeast Asia, followed by the Border Trade Agreement signed with Myanmar. The small border towns Moreh and Tamu, sometimes referred to as twin towns, became the first spotlights for official border trade. By 1997, official border trade through this transit earned Rs 87 crore, and the initial agreement of twenty-two tradable duty-free items gradually increased to sixty-two listed items with the hope of creating a vibrant trading relationship with Myanmar and beyond. To symbolize India's attention to such cross-border engagement, the Indo-Myanmar Friendship Gate was constructed in Moreh, which was followed by a 160-km India–Myanmar Friendship Road project in 2001. This turned into an ambitious 1,360-km trans-boundary Trilateral Highway Project in 2002 to connect India, Myanmar, and Thailand and then to other Southeast Asian countries. This was the impetus for India's new sub-regional programme beyond the South Asian Association for Regional Cooperation

(SAARC). Finally, India's most prominent initiative for a sub-regional programme, the Bay of Bengal Initiative for Multi-Sectoral Technical and Economic Cooperation (BIMSTEC), was formalized in 2004 with the member nations of Bangladesh, Bhutan, India, Myanmar, Nepal, Sri Lanka, and Thailand. The NER became central for connecting these South and Southeast Asian nations for constructive sub-regionalism within the BIMSTEC forum, which consists of about 1.73 billion people and has a combined gross domestic product of US dollars (USD) 5.2 trillion, with multiple trade and economic possibilities. The forum simultaneously aimed to stabilize relations between the NER and Myanmar and Bangladesh. By the early 2010s, the political transition had begun in Myanmar and Bangladesh to restore democracy and BIMSTEC became live and relevant in policy and academic debates. By 2014, India's noteworthy AEP and Neighbourhood First Policy gave further impetus to it having the North-East as the "core" region; and the Manipur–Myanmar gateway remained significant. The strategic Trilateral Highway Project pushed the Indo-Myanmar Friendship Bridge in 2018 when the two nations operationalized the Land Border Crossing Agreement via Moreh. The Free Movement Regime (FMR), which has historical relevance, was pushed to allow mobility for people between the NER and Myanmar up to 16 km into each other's territory without any legal visa. This agreement supported the residents of various communities within this 16-km radius to cross the border with a border pass valid for up to one year. The arrangement supported local trade and travel to become more vibrant, while also bringing New Delhi closer to Southeast Asia. Subsequently, in 2020, the Motor Vehicle Agreement and a Memorandum of Understanding (MoU) were signed by both India and Myanmar to commence a bus service from Imphal to Mandalay.

Unfortunately, this ambitious sub-regional programme received a massive blow with the military coup in Myanmar in mid-2020. Myanmar has become a political hotspot in the sub-region since 2017, under Suu Kyi's tenure, with the Rohingya massacre and the marginalization of many ethnic groups, to global alarm and condemnation. Her claim over transitioning to democracy was questioned at many forums and was seen as "pseudo-democracy". However, the decade-old battle to restore democracy ended with a military take-over in 2021 and the annulment of the election outcome. With this, Suu Kyi's democratic voice became irrelevant to the evolving geopolitics of this sub-region. Unfortunately, this new political complexity has blurred India's excelling engagement programmes with Myanmar since 2017 and its geostrategic ambitions to get access to Southeast Asia and further to the Asia Pacific region via Myanmar. The recent rise of ethnic armed organizations and the Three Brotherhood Alliance (TBA) in Myanmar, which gives tremendous resistance against the junta military regime, has made Myanmar's political space more fractured and created deep repercussions in the neighbouring NER, especially in Manipur and Mizoram, with a continuous inflow of the hilltop ethnic groups. This inflow has been easier under the FMR but has added deeper ethnic fault lines in the region. Another threat is a rising cross-border drug trade which, to many, is now replacing the threat of armed militant groups. There is a persistent rise in trade of such products through the Manipur gateway, which is spilling across the states of the NER as connectivity has improved in the region in the recent times. Myanmar, according the Southeast Asia Opium Survey, has become the world's biggest opium producer with an 18 per cent increase in the land use pattern (1,16,000 acres) for growing illicit crop and a 16 per cent rise in production (The Shillong Times, 2023). These issues have re-ignited national–territorial security dynamics in this sub-region with a changed geopolitical calculus. There are new fragilities to the NER as an open borderland, which has triggered the need for remaking the 1,643-km border between Myanmar and the NER with fencing and closing the FMR to restrict such illegal mobility. Such new threats and remaking the border has halted cross-border constructive engagement, including India's much-hyped flagship connectivity project Kaladan Multi-Modal Transit Transport, which aimed to connect the port of Kolkata with the port of Sittwe in the Arakan State of Myanmar, connecting Mizoram by road and the Kaladan river which flows by Paletwa, a town in Myanmar. This project is important for India to enhance the road and maritime connection with Myanmar and with Southeast Asia to improve sub-regional engagement but has faced a deadlock as Paletwa, a small linking town in Myanmar, which borders Mizoram, was captured by the Arakan Army (AA) in 2024 (The Hindu, 2024). Such evolving cross-border complexities have escalated India's territorial security concerns and the prospects of sub-regional engagement and gateway diplomacy have become murky in the immediate future. It demands more intense diplomatic and geopolitical attention in the long run, while intellectual rethinking and conceptual debates on India's sub-regionalism also need to be highlighted. Recognition of the sense of the North-East as a region demands a much deeper attention to community relations and cross-border dynamics, and the place of the NER in India's sub-regional programme cannot blindly be acknowledged in policy decisions and academia.

Towards Brighter Contours for India's Sub-regionalism

However, India's rise in the global and regional forum demands an attuning of its sub-regional policy in a more robust normative frame with sound rationale and a smart shift in its contours. The Asian sub-regional programme in the 1980s found a new rationale of "collective self-reliance" and cooperation on aspects of sovereignty, equality, territorial integrity, and security as an alternative to the Global North. With rising economic globalism–liberalism by the 1990s, an interplay of "state and market" became critical in transnational relations on trade, mobility, and economy to compete with the Global North. In this interplay, the idea of a geographical borderland became important for creating more linkages of global, regional, and national stakeholders and markets. The sub-regional programme henceforth adopted a "process whereby a geographical area is transformed from a passive object to an active subject, capable of articulating transnational interests of an emerging sub-region" (Sahasrabuddhe, 2008). The impetus was derived from economic globalism and born out of the failure of SAARC to achieve its desired outcome on regional cooperation.

Increasing economic activity to counter the Global North has pushed India to adopt the "Gujral Doctrine", which suggests improving quality engagement with a region's immediate neighbours. By 2014, there was a visible paradigmatic shift in approach towards rebuilding neighbourhood relations and sub-regional activities in order to strengthen India's stature in the world. This shift in approach promoted more engaging neighbourhood relation. It invoked cordiality and friendly relations with smaller neighbours like Bhutan, Bangladesh, and Nepal to gain trust and goodwill. With the operationalization of India's Neighbourhood First Policy and the AEP in 2014, neighbourhood relations shaped India's political and economic power in the sub-region, particularly with Bangladesh. There were many disruptions in relations with Bangladesh due to many earlier Partitions that had led to perpetual border disputes between the two nations. This was finally addressed through bilateral agreement in 2015 by the passing of the Land Boundary Agreement Bill along with a transit routes permit. It is noteworthy that the highest connectivity network with Bangladesh has been made through the most isolated state of the NER, Tripura. Tripura's engagement with Bangladesh goes back to 1998, when the state was making efforts to address insurgency and underdevelopment. This landlocked state quietly emphasized improving its connectivity network through neighbouring Bangladesh to reduce the distance between it and mainland India. However, the Tripura–Bangladesh link did not gain momentum in the 1990s because India's policy attention turned towards the Manipur–Myanmar Gateway Project. A decade later, in 2008, when Bangladesh made the political transition to democracy, India's neighbourhood relationship with this nation was seen as important. Tripura became visible, and in 2012, this tiny state created history by hosting Prime Minister Sheikh Hasina. No head of Bangladesh had visited India's North-East since 1971, and her historic visit gave hope and vista to Tripura. This has subsequently supported India to rebalance bilateral relations with Bangladesh, and road connection was made between Dhaka and Agartala and rail connection between Akhaura and Agartala, with potential use of Chittagong Port for accessing the Bay of Bengal. Tripura gradually became pivotal in India–Bangladesh relations towards a "mutually constructive future". Thus, by the mid-2010s, the long-standing wire fencing project of the porous Indo-Bangladesh border was completed to turn a large space of illegality and vulnerability into a legal and vibrant cross-border relationship. The shared space and the fluid border that had produced multiple unruly edges for illegal relations among communities became largely transformed into a formal cross-border relationship, and the communities in the border villages henceforth learnt to live within the domain of the state boundary.

The Neighbourhood First Policy intensified this ongoing engagement. Multiple projects of cross-border connectivity have been completed. The Maitree Express, Bandhan Express, and Mitali Express were successfully opened to facilitate mobility between the nations. The 1.9-km "Maitre Setu" over the River Feni was made to link the small border town of Sabroom in Tripura with Ramgarh in Bangladesh. Sabroom has thus emerged as a new "trading lifeline" and "fully fledged logistic hub" of the North-East with an integrated check post. It gave access to the Chittagong port of Bangladesh for India's maritime connectivity network by reducing the distance from 1,600 km to less than 100 km. Tripura also hit the national news in 2023 by opening its waterway with Bangladesh over the rivers Gomati and Meghna via a 90-km water stretch from Sonamura to Daudkandi. This waterway was included in the second Addendum of the Indo-Bangladesh Protocol (IBP) routes of 2015 for the connectivity and economic opportunities of Tripura. In 1972, the original Inland Water Transit and Trade Protocol was signed by both the nations to open eight trans-boundary waterways at different locations in West Bengal and the Northeastern states. Such multiple connectivity projects have enhanced the geostrategic significance of Tripura and repositioned it as a core borderland in India's sub-regional programme in recent times. The first border *haat* along the Tripura–Bangladesh frontier was inaugurated at Srinagar in the south of the state in 2015. This weekly rural market accommodates about 500 people from both sides to facilitate trade and exchange for all locally produced goods such as agricultural and horticultural crops, spices, poultry, dairy products, cottage-industry items, furniture, handicrafts, and handloom products to benefit local communities and their livelihoods. Tripura's Industry and Commerce Department intends to open seven more border *haats* in Bamutia, Hiracherra, Amlighat, Hrisyamukh, Boxnagar, Rasyabari, and Akinpur. Tripura–Bangladesh trade volume has shown a persistent increase from Rs 4.12 crore in 1995–96 to Rs 330.60 crore in 2012–13 and to Rs 537 crore in 2018–19 (Deb, 2020). This market system has also helped to re-establish the lost social relations of the frontier communities. In 2015, India's new Foreign Trade Policy was unfolded with a Trade Facilitation Action Plan to augment logistics with efficient management of time and cost of doing business and easy access to trade-related information and infrastructure with all the "immediate and extended neighbourhoods and geographies". These provided the impetus to build deeper cultural and intellectual diplomacy. In February 2020, Tripura organized a two-day friendship festival in memory of the contribution of Tripura in the 1971 Bangladesh liberation war, giving a fillip to tourism by identifying important historical and archaeological sites. Sustained political interest in the theme of connectivity, mutual trust, and consensus have made this bilateral relationship successful, and Tripura has become a most significant and stable state in India's Neighbourhood First Policy, providing a new framework to India's sub-regional schema.

Sub-regional contours were also discussed by exploring the Assam–Bangladesh gateways. The Barak valley of Assam historically had trade and cultural connections with the Sylhet district of Bangladesh. In India's post-Independence period, the valley was pushed to the margin of the dominant narrative of Assam's political economy, and its potential was undermined. Karimganj, a small border town in this valley, which is situated on the bank of the Kushiara river and shares around 3 km of border with Bangladesh, has enormous locational significance. Other than a waterway, its road connection has the possibility of restoring the relationship with Sylhet via Sutarkandi, which is only 48 kms away. This small border town (renamed as Sribhumican) is now a district of Assam and connects Shahabajpur in the Sylhet district via railway through an old, abandoned station from the pre-Independence period at Mahisashan. This abandoned track used to join India to Myanmar through the Moreh-Tamu area, which is about 400 km away from Karimganj. The track could also connect Akhaura on Bangladesh side. So Karimganj in Assam could strategically be a connecting space for two important neighbours of India and Bangladesh and become a significant emerging border town of the NER to facilitate a circulatory network for trade and mobility across the borders and provide economic and livelihood opportunities to the local communities. Unfortunately, no political power in Assam has ever considered this valley seriously. There was an attempt to connect the Brahmaputra valley of Assam with Myanmar and China through Ledo, a border town of Upper Assam, by restoring the Stilwell Road of the colonial period. However, this never materialised due to Myanmar's political indecisiveness. Meghalaya is another state that, likewise, had deep historical connections with Sylhet besides Mymensingh and Rangpur of Bangladesh but became economically feeble with the closure of borders. The state is now proactively exploring possibilities to restore connections like the Tamabil–Dawki road passage for cross-border trade activities. Dawki is slowly growing as another border town of the North-East with new economic opportunities. Meghalaya could also promote its other border town Dolu in the Garo hills as a business hub with Bangladesh. These cross-border routes and connections with Bangladesh could ideally make the NER a linking space for sub-regional engagements. Revival of small border towns in this process could be catalysts for creating external linkages and ensure long-running economic sustainability and growth in this region.

Apart from such neighbourly relations, cross-border connectivity creates scope for a new sub-regional framework with like-minded nations that ensure trust and a degree of stability with similar ecosystems and worldviews. India already has a stable maritime and airways engagement with Southeast Asia and has gained enormously in the neoliberal period through foreign direct investment (FDI) inflow other than tourism and trade. This engagement, however, has subverted the NER while providing huge economic benefits to other Northern, Southern, and Western regions of India (Bhattacharya, 2015). To make the NER effective and inclusive in India's sub-regional programme, more contours need to be explored. In this regard, other than the Southeast Asia and Asia Pacific region, engagement with the smaller Eastern Himalayan neighbours of Bhutan and Nepal also provides another exciting sub-regional contour. The Eastern Himalayan Region (EHR) that includes India's NER shares not only contiguous geography but also common concerns, capacities, ecologies, and worldview. The Neighbourhood First Policy made a concerted effort to increase complementarity and capacity of the economy and development of this entire region and has found the right balance between functions and territory over the past one decade. In this context, an existing sub-regional construct of Bangladesh, Bhutan, India, Nepal (BBIN) has been re-examined more keenly, which complements the EHR on the rationale of contiguous area, shared history, economic practices, and infrastructural linkage. The BBIN was conceptualized in 1996 within the idea of a South Asian Growth Quadrangle (SAGQ) comprising BBIN with cooperation strategies. It was mooted under the ambit of Article 7 of the SAARC charter, which allows for action committees to be set up "comprising of Member States concerned with the implementation of projects involving more than two but not all member states" (Gambhir, 2020). The BBIN countries subsequently approached the Asian Development Bank (ADB) for improving trans-border economic cooperation in this sub-region, which led to the creation of the South Asian Sub-regional Economic Cooperation (SASEC) programme in 2001 to bring together the BBIN countries. Subsequently Maldives, Myanmar, and Sri Lanka were also included to "promote regional prosperity, improve economic opportunities, and build a better quality of life for the people of this sub-region". In 2016, the SASEC countries approved the strategic ten-year roadmap under the "SASEC Operation Plan 2016–2025" to expand the focus beyond intra-regional cooperation for developing linkages with Southeast and East Asia, thereby widening the scope of transport, trade facilitation, and energy cooperation. The SASEC programme is seen as far more successful than SAARC in achieving the objectives of economic integration, trade facilitation, and energy security; and by 2019, the member countries had successfully implemented fifty-five ADB financed investment projects worth more than USD 12.5 billion across transport, trade facilitation, energy, and economic corridor development (Gambhir, 2020). Unfortunately, the ongoing crisis in Myanmar halted these projects under SASEC and even under BIMSTEC. The focus therefore was shifted to the BBIN to ensure continuity in sub-regional engagement, while exploring shared and unique worldviews. This could constitute a cogent framework of the sub-region with ontological and ideological correlates derived from connected histories, cultures, and even food habits.

This proposed framework could be kept within the structure larger state affairs with the driving forces of economic complementarities, geographical proximity, political framework, infrastructural linkage, and market accessibility. The member states have already made certain important collaborations, having signed a Motor Vehicles Agreement (MVA) in 2015 for the regulation of passengers, personnel, and cargo vehicular traffic between the four South Asian neighbours. The scope of the BBIN initiative saw expansion at the second Joint Working Group (JWG) meeting held in 2015, where it covered areas of cooperation in water resources management and power/hydropower in addition to sub-regional connectivity. In 2020, BBIN states met to deliberate upon a proposed MoU for the implementation of the MVA. In 2022, these countries finalized passenger and cargo protocols. Other than physical connectivity, electricity grid connectivity across these nations also awaits a future for energy projects and sub-regional power trade (CUTS International, 2024). Having the advantage of accessibility to several ports (such as Chittagong and Mongla in Bangladesh, Haldia and Damra in India, and Sitwee in Myanmar), this sub-region could become very significant in India's engagement with its Asian neighbours. The focus on cross-border connectivity of the NER has given India an opportunity to build constructive engagement by circumventing political challenges posed by opposing neighbours such as Pakistan, Sri Lanka, China, and Maldives, which fractured Asian sub-regional initiatives and the ethos of regional cooperation in the past. Member nations like Bangladesh and Nepal at some points faced opposition from domestic stakeholders like the Bangladesh Nationalist Party (BNP) and the United Marxist and Leninist Party, which could be resolved gradually with India's rising power and commitment towards neighbouring nations. It therefore provides an interesting opportunity to the member states to make up for the "achievement deficit" encountered by earlier attempts at sub-regional forums. The BBIN framework is therefore acceptable and robust in both policy and theory to re-integrate the subcontinent, while bringing together the Bay of Bengal and the EHR for shared peace and prosperity, having the nuanced role of the NER as an open-region borderland. The scope of the BBIN is wide as the member Himalayan nations are on agreeable terms and show a readiness for engagement, provided that Bangladesh can play a constructive role. However, a most ill-fated political unrest in Bangladesh in 2024 has put this mammoth initiative at risk. The dramatic fall of Sheikh Hasina and her regime in 2024 has brought Bangladesh to a critical juncture, with immediate implications for India's ongoing constructive cross-border engagement and sub-regional programme. With Myanmar's extraordinary political turbulence, India had been engaging more confidently with Bangladesh and pushed Tripura–Bangladesh as a new gateway in India's sub-regional programme, However, such domestic political transformation in Bangladesh and its new and emerging geopolitical content has put India's policy at stake, at least for the immediate future. However this does not take away the scope of other sub-regional programmes. Though such a sudden U-turn in Bangladesh has produced immediate loss and rupture in India's cross-border engagement activities, it should not be discouraged from pursuing sub-regional engagement to make its NER relevant as a connecting and open borderland.

The Emerging Relevance of the NER in India's Sub-regional Epistemology

The idea of sub-regionalism is largely state-centric, and its institutionalization process is based on an efficiency matrix that often tends to ignore various local forces and the uniqueness around them. As the NER follows a peace and development trajectory, it assumes a central role as a regional epicentre for India's sub-regional engagement with neighbouring nations in the areas of economics, culture, and security. However, the epistemology needs to be grounded in the issue of sustainability and uphold the like-mindedness of the stakeholders. It also should be derived from the shared regional concerns and vulnerabilities in this contiguous geographical space. So, India's big engagement programmes on economy, energy, and security for an efficient sub-regionalism needs to pay parallel attention to common worldviews of the concerned nations to make it more people-centric and sustainable. Nevertheless, the success of India's sub-regional engagements largely depends on the political situation and the response of the partnering nations. As both Myanmar and Bangladesh are faced with domestic political deadlocks, India needs to explore the other neighbouring nations to continue its engagements. The EHR in this regard holds a special relevance as it is the home of a vast and diverse ecosystem and cosmology, grounded on close-knit communities, self-sufficient economies, and common resource systems, which could provide the groundwork for a strong, sustainable, indigenous economic network. It shares common knowledge and worldviews on economic complementarities with various local and diverse production networks, sharing geographical proximity and common climate, knowledge sharing, and ecological substances. Thus, the epistemology of the Eastern Himalayan sub-region could be derived from an endogenous and bottom-up approach based on a sustainability matrix drawing strength from the diversity and reason for its preservation. For example, agglomerating certain agro-industrial units that are rooted and endowed in this sub-Himalayan region and strengthening cross-border engagement could also sustain the sub-regional programme during a time of political distress for some nations.

Such an epistemology necessarily needs to be converged with the emerging realities and larger interest of India to make the NER a "natural gateway" to foster the complementarities, equity, and efficiency in the sub-regional programme and support the supply chain. Various contemporary phenomena of world geopolitics in the aftermath of the COVID-19 pandemic of 2020, the ongoing Ukraine–Russia war, and (most importantly) China's downturn syndrome and the tariff war of the United States have utterly disrupted the global supply chain. Global investors are henceforth looking for new geographies such as the China + one strategy, and India is gaining significance as an emerging Asian negotiator in this changing geopolitical strategy. It has successfully produced multiple cross-border linkages to attract investors for economic engagements. India has also boosted the manufacturing ecosystem with policy reforms to increase its relevance. The two most celebrated policies of Atmanirbhar Bharat and the Make in India programme have transformed its vast manufacturing sector to become a global supply-chain hub. Its regional development programme also shows a readiness for cross-border engagements and finds new relevance in global geopolitical understanding. During the Group of Twenty (G20) presidency programme in 2023, all the eight state capitals of the NER hosted B20 meetings and explored the possibility of global investment and business relations involving local stakeholders to create an engaging ecosystem. In this arena of shifting dynamics, the North-East has repositioned itself as an open borderland to support India's sub-regional programme with a closer network of production, mobility, business, and financial and human capital. Tea, which has a deep historical relevance, is one very important sector, with deep socio-cultural significance in this vast region and great allure for the external market. Currently, various types of tea are grown in this extended region that have increasing market value, and a well-laid cross-border agglomeration model for the tea industry in this sub-Himalayan region could create a gainful supply chain. The major tea-growing state of Assam and the new growers such as Nagaland, Manipur, Tripura, and Arunachal Pradesh of the NER could form a production agglomeration, a common marketing strategy, and a global network with the Terai in Nepal and North Bengal and Darjeeling areas of West Bengal and also with neighbouring Sylhet in Bangladesh to formalize an Eastern Himalayan Tea Region, which could potentially spread over 9 lakh hectares of geographical area with participation from local stakeholders. Similarly, agro-horticulture is another sector where the EHR has tremendous potential, varying from bamboo, cane, and rubber to betelnut and many varieties of spices. A core Eastern Himalayan Plantation Region could therefore be mapped out, spreading across this geographical area to scale up production and supply chain and to link to the external markets. Also, the rising demand for organic products among urban consumers creates a *niche* for an Eastern Himalayan Organic Region, where traditional skills and knowledge would be pertinent.

However, there are still a few challenges that the region needs to resolve. The most urgent is the construction of an integrated and regulated market system, without which supply chain and uninterrupted mobility cannot take place to make sub-regional engagement a success. The NER, with various complex interstate border systems, deep ethnic divides, and lack of political consensus, has failed to articulate an integrated and regulated market system in the past. This has ruptured free flow and circulation, even within the region, to a very large extent and has affected accessibility, scalability, and sustainability. In the early 1980s, there was an initiative to form a North Eastern Regional Agricultural Marketing Corporation (NERAMAC) to create a common agricultural marketing system. NERAMAC has currently made an effort to create a common market system for agriculture and horticultural products of the region and to connect to the national and global markets. Such a common regional market forum, along with connectivity infrastructure, is essential to create a sustained supply chain and expand beyond the region to promote various unique and diverse products at a global level.

Each sub-regional initiative is a building block to take cooperation and progress forwards, and the states need to decide the best time and strategy to derive the best from it (Pant and Yhome, 2020). The wide potential of BIMSTEC or SASEC remains as all the eight states of the North-East together share about 1,880 km of borders with the four important nations of Bangladesh, Bhutan, Nepal, and Myanmar making the blocks paramount to sub-regional understanding. India's statecraft in the revival of region making and its role in sub-regional engagement through the AEP and Neighbourhood First Policy therefore creates immense potential to recreate an epistemic logic in the dominant narrative of sub-regional engagements.

References

Bhattacharya, Rakhee (2015), "Look East to Act East Policy: Is It a Renewal of Hope for Northeast India?", *Eastern Quarterly*, 11 (I and II), pp. 3–17.

Bhattacharya, Rakhee (2018), "Insider or an Outsider: Where Is the Northeast in India's Act East Policy?", in Atul Sarma and S. Choudhury (eds), *Mainstreaming the Northeast in India's Look and Act East Policy*, Singapore: Springer Nature, pp. 45–62.

Bhattacharya, Rakhee and Nijara Deka (2021), "Road Matters at the Periphery: India's Post-Liberalisation Road Projects in the Northeast", *Journal of Economic and Social Development*, 23 (2), pp. 321–37.

CUTS (Consumer Unity & Trust Society) International (2024), "Energy Cooperation in the BBIN Region", Jaipur (https://cuts-international.org/IACP/base_energy_cooperation.html).

Deb, Ratan (2020), "Border Trade in NER in the Regime of 'Act East Policy': An Analytical Study", *International Journal of Creative Research Thoughts*, 8 (6), pp. 4501–08.

Duffield, Mark (2005), "Human Security: Linking Development and Security in an Age of Terror", Department of Politics and International Relations, Lancaster University, 21–24 September.

Gambhir, Mohak (2020), "Evolution of Regional and Sub-regional Cooperation in South Asia", Delhi: Centre for Land Warfare Studies (CLAWS).

Hindustan Times (2024), "73 Percent Reduction in Violent Incidents in North East during PM Modi's Tenure", 20 January.

Lama, Mahendra (2017), "Renewable Agenda", *Kathmandu Post*, 13 December.

NSO (National Statistical Office) Report (2023), "Second Advance Estimate of National Income 2022–23", NSO, Government of India (https://www.mospi.gov.in/sites/default/files/press release PressNoteNAD_28feb23final.pdf).

Pant, Harsh V. and K. Yhome (2020), "India's Subregional Connectivity Initiatives: Re-imagining the Neighbourhood", *India Review*, 19 (1), pp. 33–51.

Press Information Bureau (2025), "India's Story on Bridging Inequality: World Bank Places India among World's Most Equal Societies" (https://databank.worldbank.org/reports.aspx?source=2&series=SI.POV.GINI&country).

Sahasrabuddhe, Uttara (2008), "SAARC: A Study in the Context of Globalisation and New Regionalism", in P. L. Dash (ed.), *Emerging Asia in Focus: Issues and Problems*, Delhi: Academic Excellence.

Shillong Times (2023), "Myanmar-Based Narcotics Trade Replaces Insurgency as Threat in N-E", 17 December.

Stewart, Frances (2004), "Development and Security", Centre for Research on Inequality, Human Security and Ethnicity (CRISE), Working Paper No. 3, mimeo, London.

Tschirgi, Necla (2005), "Security and Development Policies: Untangling the Relationship", paper prepared for the Conference of the European Association of Development Research and Training Institute, mimeo, International Peace Academy, Bonn.

World Bank (2023), "India Overview: Development News", New Delhi: World Bank Group.

2

Border Trade between India and Myanmar through Arunachal Pradesh

Present Status and Future Prospects

*Ashi Lama and Amitava Mitra**

Introduction

Borderland between countries provides both opportunities and challenges. On the one hand, it can be a source of security threats, smuggling, and illegal migrations. On the other hand, it can be a resource for economic development (Sohn, 2014). Borders can be used to facilitate cross-border trade in goods and services, which can be beneficial for the people living on either side of the border. Border trade can also have substantial positive effects on the relationship between neighbouring countries (Das, 2014). It enables the people living across the border to dispose of their surplus output across the border and obtain goods from other side of the border and provides an alternative source of livelihood to border communities, which usually have limited livelihood avenues. Border trade can take place in two forms: formal and informal trade. Formal border trade is that which is regulated by state machinery and takes place through legal channels. Such trade is carried out by registered and licensed enterprises. On the other hand, informal border trade refers to unregulated economic activities, which are in the nature of extralegal trading, tolerated in practice even if illegal. It takes place as the state

* This chapter is based on a minor research project funded by the Indian Council for Research on International Economic Relations (ICRIER), New Delhi. The authors would like to acknowledge the financial support of ICRIER.

Ashi Lama and Amitava Mitra, *Border Trade between India and Myanmar through Arunachal Pradesh* In: *Sub-Regional Cooperation for Trade, Investment, and Employment in North-East India*. Edited by: Ashish Nath, Oxford University Press. © Oxford University Press 2026. DOI: 10.1093/9780197908938.003.0002 machinery is not present in all corners of society in developing countries (Taneja and Pohit, 2001). Border trade is facilitated by porous borderland; trade policies; friendly relations; and ethnic, cultural, and linguistic ties between the people living on both sides of the border. It usually takes place between the people residing within a few kilometres on either side of the international border. However, with proper border management, connectivity, and infrastructure facilities, border trade can be extended to normal international trade with a larger bilateral and multilateral trade pattern for greater economic integration and development.

Several studies have analysed the issues related to cross-border trade. For example, Taneja and Pohit (2001) examined the institutional mechanism and reasons for vibrant, informal cross-border trade between India and Nepal. The factors promoting informal trade were an efficient contract enforcement mechanism, information flows, risk sharing and risk mitigation, no paperwork, quick realization of payments, and no procedural delays. Singh (2007) found that the inefficiency and high transaction costs associated with formal trade has led to the promotion of informal border trade. The study revealed that there was a missing of link between the border trade and production structure in the NER of India, as a result of which larger gains accrued to traders outside the region. Aung (2009) reported that cross-border trade with neighbouring countries such as China, Thailand, and India has become an important source of income for Myanmar. However, due to various restrictions and constraints, cross-border trade has diverted towards the informal channels.

Kshetrimayum (2010) argued that Myanmar is important for India as it can serve as a gateway to the Association of Southeast Asian Nations (ASEAN)[1] for trade and economic integration. But there is a need to build up infrastructure facilities, improve security, and attract skilled human resource to boost trade with Myanmar and beyond it. Kudo (2013) reported significant growth in border trade between China and Myanmar, and the important drivers were roads and gates along the borders. The ethnic insurgency was found to impede the development of bilateral border trade. Das (2014) argued that border trade has substantial beneficial effects on the people living on either side of the border area and also has a positive impact on relationships between the neighbouring countries. Ge et al. (2014) revealed that multilateral and regional integration, market size, and institutional quality played a significant role in the promotion of border trade of China with its fourteen neighbouring countries. Dutta (2015) examined the nature of Indo-Bangladesh border trade through North-East India. The study showed that there was an opportunity for cross-border trade. But there is a need to enhance connectivity and commodity diversity in Assam, Tripura, and Meghalaya.

Singh (2007) and Reimeingam (2016) found that border trade between India and Myanmar through Moreh has benefited local people in terms of employment, infrastructure development, and trade and other relations. However, the trade through Moreh accounted for only 2 per cent of the total volume of Indo-Myanmar trade. The low volume of trade was attributed to strikes, insurgency, and an unstable currency exchange rate. Taneja et al. (2019) also reported that Indo-Myanmar border trade is quite low due to a restrictive trade policy framework under which border trade is permitted in a limited list of locally produced items. The study indicated that formal border trade between India and Myanmar has become almost negligible over the past two years due to trade diversion to informal channels. Shahriar (2020) analysed the nature of Indo-Myanmar border trade through the Moreh–Tamu region in the context of India's new foreign policy towards Southeast Asia and China's Belt and Road Initiative of 2013. The study showed that there was growing trade and economic engagement between India and Myanmar. The major obstacles to border trade between India and Myanmar were ethnic insurgency, weak borderland infrastructure, and Sino-Indian rivalry.

The Northeastern Region (NER) of India consists of eight states, namely, Arunachal Pradesh, Assam, Manipur, Meghalaya, Mizoram, Nagaland, Sikkim, and Tripura. The NER accounts for around 8 per cent of the country's total geographical area and is endowed with plenty of natural resources such as forests, rivers, coal, limestone, petroleum, copper, iron, and uranium. It is suitable to produce spices, fruits, vegetables, flowers, and herbs abundantly. Despite being rich in natural resources, the region is lagging behind on various fronts of economic development. The lack of essential infrastructure has rendered the region perpetually underdeveloped. The region suffers due to high transaction costs and inadequate transport systems for connecting it with the rest of India. It is connected to the rest of the country only by a narrow, 22-km land mass known as the "Chicken's Neck" corridor in West Bengal as 98 per cent of its border is shared with neighbouring countries. Inadequate connectivity and distant national markets are thus major constraints for the development of domestic trade in the region. However, due to its proximity to Southeast Asia, the region has a good advantage for cross-border trade, which can generate substantial gains for both producers and consumers. In fact, the region could serve as a gateway to Southeast Asian countries for cooperation in trade, investment, and security.

The region shares a 5,437.15-km international land border with five countries, namely, Bangladesh (1,880 km), Bhutan (516 km), China (1,300.35 km), Myanmar (1,643 km), and Nepal (97.8 km) and accounts for 36 per cent of India's total international land border (15,106.7 km). The cross border markets can be more cost-effective for the region for exporting surplus production than the national markets located at far distance (Das and Bordoloi, 2015). Thus, the geographical proximity of the region could emerge as a big opportunity to reap the benefits of cross-border trade with neighbouring countries. Further, the region assumes importance in the context of the Act East Policy (a revitalized version of the Look East Policy launched in 1992), which was introduced in 2014 to enhance India's economic and security integration with Southeast and East Asian countries. Among the South Asian countries, Myanmar is important for India as it is the only country with which India has both a land and maritime border. The country shares a long international land border of 1,643 km with Myanmar through the four Northeastern States of Arunachal Pradesh (520 km), Manipur (398 km), Mizoram (510 km) and Nagaland (215 km). However, the potential for cross-border trade with neighbouring countries has remained untapped for various reasons, such as inadequate connectivity, security challenges, and restrictive trade policy (CUTS and FICCI, 2017).

Arunachal Pradesh, the eastern-most state of India, is strategically located as it shares international boundaries with three countries: China in the north, Myanmar in the east, and Bhutan in the north-west. It consists of 2.55 per cent of India's landmass but accounts for 11.65 per cent of the country's total international land border. It shares a long international border with China (1,080 km) followed by Myanmar (520 km) and Bhutan (217 km). Its border with China accounts for 59.44 per cent of its total length of international border and borders with Myanmar and Bhutan account for 28.62 per cent and 11.94 per cent, respectively

(Ministry of DoNER, n.d.). The state is so strategically located that it accounts for 33.42 per cent of the total length (5,437.15 km) of international border of the NER, which is the highest among the states of the region. At present, Arunachal Pradesh has twenty-eight districts, out of which fifteen districts (54 per cent) have an international border. Two districts of the state (namely Tawang and Anjaw) have an international border with two countries. While Tawang share a border with China and Bhutan, Anjaw shares a border with China and Myanmar. The long international border poses both opportunities and challenges to the state. On the one hand, there is a security threat, with the operation of insurgency, smuggling, etc. On the other hand, it offers a good advantage for cross-border trade with Southeast Asian countries through Myanmar, provided political, economic, and cultural relations are used to generate businesses. Since the border with China in Arunachal Pradesh is closed for trade, the border with Myanmar could serve as a gateway for the state to expand trade with Southeast Asian countries.

The Nampong–Pangsau corridor, a border pass between India and Myanmar, is located near Nampong in the Changlang district of Arunachal Pradesh. The Pangsau Pass is situated at a distance of only 12 km from Nampong. Nampong is a small town on the eastern corner of the state and is administered by an additional deputy commissioner. It also has an Office of the Trade Development Officer, which regulates the informal cross-border trade between the people of two countries. The area is inhabited by the *Tangsa* tribe of Arunachal Pradesh who are of Mongoloid descent. The *Tangsas* are hard-working and peace-loving. They are experts in handicrafts, particularly in woodcarving. The majority of them are engaged in agriculture for their livelihood. They produce output mainly for self-consumption. However, a small proportion of surplus output (mainly vegetables) is sold in the local market. The proceeds from the sale of such vegetables are used to purchase manufactured goods from the market.

Given this background, this chapter attempts to examine the present status and future prospects of Indo-Myanmar cross-border trade through the Nampong–Pangsau corridor in Arunachal Pradesh. While a good number of studies (Singh, 2007; Kshetrimayum, 2010; Shahriar, 2020) have explored and analysed the Indo-Myanmar border trade through the Moreh–Tamu corridor, there is hardly any study that has explored the nature and status of cross-border trade through the Nampong–Pangsau corridor. Thus, the study fills this gap in knowledge and expand the literature on border trade. The study is based on both primary and secondary data. Secondary data were collected from the website of the Ministry of DoNER (n.d.), Commissionerate of Customs (n.d.) and GoAP (n.d.). Primary data were collected by conducting a field survey in the study area, Nampong, between March and June 2019. The survey was conducted with a structured questionnaire, which was designed to collect information related to traded items, prices, and values and the availability of infrastructure. A focus group discussion was also conducted with the stakeholders (including government officials, local people, and traders) to understand their perspectives on cross-border trade.

Trade Infrastructure at the Nampong–Pangsau Corridor

Nampong Land Custom Station (LCS) is located at Nampong, a census town in the Changlang district of Arunachal Pradesh, India near the Indo-Myanmar border. It is located close to Pangsau Pass (Indo-Myanmar border point) and is the last town in the eastern corner of India, sharing a border with Myanmar. Nampong is located along the historic "Stilwell Road" constructed during the Second World War period. The road was originally known as "Ledo Road". It was named Stillwell Road after the American General, Joseph Warren Stilwell undertook the responsibility of constructing the project in December 1942 to open links for the Allied forces from India to send reinforcements to Kunming in the Yunnan province of China and free Burma (Myanmar) from the control of Japanese forces (Pattnaik, 2017). The road starts at Ledo in Assam and passes through Nampong to Pangsau Pass. In the context of India's Act East Policy, the road is considered as a gateway for economic integration of North-East India with East and Southeast Asian countries (Pattnaik, 2016).

The Nampong LCS was notified by the Government of India, but it has been non-functional for many years. There is no official machinery and infrastructure at Nampong LCS except a semi-permanent building, which is maintained by the Department of Trade and Commerce,

Table 2.1 Facilities available at Nampong town

Facilities	Status/availability	Distance (in km) from Nampong
Rail station	No	Ledo (50)
Electricity	Yes	–
Telecommunication facility	Yes	–
Internet facility	Yes	–
Secured compound	No	–
Post office	Yes (sub-post office)	–
Bank facility	No	Jairampur (18)
At-the-market (ATM) facility	No	Jairampur (18)
Health centre	Yes (LCS has PHC)	–
Parking facility	No	–
Cold storage	No	–
Warehousing	No	–
Informal border market	Yes	–
Informal trade	Yes	–

Source: Authors' field survey, 2019.

Government of Arunachal Pradesh. Since there is no infrastructure facility at Nampong LCS, the study explored infrastructure at Nampong town for facilitating informal trade. The infrastructure available at Nampong sub-district headquarters is presented in Table 2.1.

Nampong is well connected by a two-lane metalled road (NH-153), and the road goes through Nampong up to the Indo-Myanmar border point (Pangsau Pass). The distance from Nampong to Dibrugarh (Assam) is 158 km, and it passes through several important towns of upper Assam, namely, Tinsukia, Digboi, Marghrita, Ledo (which is the starting point of historic Stilwell Road), Lekhapani, and Jairampur in Arunachal Pradesh. The nearest railway head is Lekhapani in Assam, which is located at a distance of 40 km and the nearest airport is Mohanbari airport in Dibrugarh (Assam), which is 143 km from Nampong.

Nampong is provided with electricity and telecommunication facilities, but service quality is reported to be very poor. It also has a primary health centre, which serves the people of the area by giving primary health facilities. There is a government higher secondary school, which provides education up to class twelve standard. However, the banking facility is found to be poor as it does not have a branch of any commercial banks and there is no automated teller machine (ATM) booth. So the people of the area have to depend on a branch of the State Bank of India (SBI) located at Jairampur, which is situated at a distance of 18 km.

The LCS at Nampong is non-functional as the Government of India did not operationalize it. From the discussion with the stakeholders, it appears that security concerns were the primary reason for non-operationalization of the LCS. However, informal cross-border trade on a limited scale has been taking place between the people living on either side of the border. Again, informal border trade is permitted in only certain notified items and on selected days or dates. But the volume of trade is very low due to restrictions on movement of people. In an attempt to promote cross-border trade, the Government of Arunachal Pradesh constructed a trade centre with stay facilities and shopping complex at Nampong to facilitate trade with the people living across the border.

Trends in Indo-Myanmar Border Trade

India shares a long international border with Myanmar. Its border with Myanmar is stretched over four states of North-East India, namely, Arunachal Pradesh, Manipur, Mizoram, and Nagaland. These states also share linguistic, ethnic, and cultural ties with Myanmar. However, despite sharing a long border and ethnic ties with Myanmar, the volume of border trade between the two countries is low and fluctuating. The lion's share in Myanmar's documented cross-border trade is accounted for by Thailand (51 per cent) and China (47 per cent) (Aung, 2009). But there are good prospects for cross-border trade between the two countries through North-East India. There are many border trade centres to facilitate trade between Arunachal Pradesh and the border-sharing countries. In the context of the Act East Policy, which aims to accelerate economic integration and promote trade with East and Southeast Asian countries, Myanmar is important to India because of its proximity to the prosperous economies of Southeast Asia and China. In other words, Myanmar is not only important for border trade but also could serve as a route for greater economic ties between North-East India and the countries to the east and

Table 2.2 LCSs at the Indo-Myanmar border

Serial no.	LCS in India	LCS in Myanmar	Status
1	Nampong (Arunachal Pradesh)	Pangsau	Non-functional
2	Moreh (Manipur)	Tamu	Functional
3	Zakhawthar (Mizoram)	Rih (Tiddim)	Functional
4	Avangkhu (Nagaland)	Somara	Bilaterally agreed but not yet notified

Source: Ministry of DoNER (2025), *NEC Yearbook 2025*, Government of India, March (https://www.mdoner.gov.in/static/uploads/2025/08/4ee337cea2a08143726ab363a3ceae91.pdf @ https://lpai.gov.in/sites/default/files/2022-07/LPAI_LCS_Evaluation_Report_Vol1.pdf).

south-east of Myanmar (Bezbaruah, 2007). Through Myanmar, India could reach the markets of Thailand, Laos, Cambodia, and Vietnam.

Border trade between India and Myanmar is governed by the Border Trade Agreement (BTA). The Indo-Myanmar BTA was signed between the Government of India and the Government of Myanmar on 21 January 1994 to permit locally produced commodities to be traded as per prevailing customary practices on both sides of the border. The agreement initially permitted trade in only twenty-two items,[2] which consisted of mainly agricultural produce and minor forest products. The list of tradable items was increased to forty items in 2008 and further to sixty-two items in 2012. The Indo-Myanmar border trade takes place through four LCSs as shown in Table 2.2.

The trend in the volume of Indo-Myanmar trade through the formal channel has been dwindling over the years. Initially, there was a sudden spurt in the volume of border trade between the two countries during the second half of the 1990s. The trade volume increased rapidly from rupees (Rs) 15 crore in 1995–96 to Rs 62.39 crore in 1997–98. After this, there was a sharp decline in the volume of border trade between the two countries. This was mainly on account of restrictions imposed by the Myanmar authorities, which required that exports from India should precede imports from Myanmar with effect from November 1997. The total volume of formal border trade sharply declined to Rs 8.62 crore in 1998–99 (Bezbaruah, 2007). The recent trend in volume of Indo-Myanmar trade is given in Table 2.3.

Table 2.3 Volume of Indo-Myanmar border trade (value in rupees crore)

Year	Export	Import	Total volume	Trade balance
2006–07	6.13	2.69	8.82	3.44
2007–08	4.94	1.35	6.29	3.59
2008–09	1.61	0.76	2.37	0.85
2009–10	24.5	8.32	32.82	16.18
2010–11	0.26	3.8	4.06	-3.54
2014–15	37.51	120.53	158.04	-83.02
2015–16	25.18	121.32	146.5	-96.14
2016–17	0.67	147.1	147.77	-146.43
2017–18	0.44	2.04	2.48	-1.6
2018–19	3.07	0.00	3.07	3.07
2019–20	358.17	1.45	359.62	356.72
2020–21	11.72	0.00	11.72	11.72
2021–22	5.28	0.37	5.65	4.91
2022–23	0.00	0.00	0.00	0.00
2023–24	0.00	0.00	0.00	0.00

Source: Ministry of DoNER (2025), *NEC Yearbook 2025*, Government of India (March), https://www.mdoner.gov.in/static/uploads/2025/08/4ee337cea2a08143726ab363a3ceae91.pdf, accessed 26 March 2026.

There was a continuous declining trend in Indo-Myanmar border trade during the period 2006–07 to 2008–09. The volume of border trade between the two countries declined to Rs 8.82 crore in 2006–07. It further declined to a low level of Rs 2.37 crore in 2008–09. After recovering to Rs 32.82 crore in 2009–10, it again fell sharply to Rs 4.06 crore in 2010–11. In recent years, there has been substantial growth in the volume of trade between the two countries, on account of a change in policy regime in India (a shift from border trade to normal trade through LCSs), duty-free tariff preference (DFTP) and the ASEAN–India Trade in Goods Agreement. The volume of trade had increased sharply to Rs 158.04 crore in 2014–15. But imports were higher than the exports, due to which India had a border trade deficit of Rs 83.02 crore. In 2016–17, the volume of trade declined to Rs 147.77 crore, but trade deficit widened to Rs 146.43 crore. Most of the trade takes place from the Moreh–Tamu sector. The imports from Myanmar consist of mainly areca nut. The volume of trade, however, declined sharply to Rs 2.48 crore in 2017–18, with a trade deficit of Rs 1.6 crore. The decline in trade volume was mainly due to a sharp fall in imports from Myanmar through the Moreh–Tamu sector. The data shows that there were no imports from Myanmar via this route during 2017–18. This was due to social and political unrest in Manipur. The state witnessed an economic blockade called by the United Naga Council against the creation of seven new districts.

Thus, it can be observed that the volume of formal cross-border trade between the two countries has been dwindling over the years and has declined to a very low level. At the same time, there had been drastic fluctuations in the trade volume. The analysis of trade balance showed that India had been enjoying positive cross-border trade balance. However, in 2010–11, India suffered negative cross-border trade balance with Myanmar. This was mainly due to a sharp fall in exports from Rs 24.5 crore in 2009–10 to Rs 0.26 crore in 2010–11. The decline in the volume of cross-border trade between the two countries can be attributed to the trade restrictions, trade in limited items, the poor state of infrastructure, transit trade, and insurgent activities. These constraints have led to the diversion of trade to the informal channels. The volume of informal border trade was estimated to be much higher than that of the formal trade (Bezbaruah, 2007). The goods traded through the informal channels are beyond the permitted items. At the same time, most of the products coming from Burma are not of Burmese origin (Das and Bordoloi, 2015).

Indo-Myanmar Border Trade through the Nampong–Pangsau Corridor

Nampong LCS is non-functional, and there are no custom officials present to record and monitor the border trade. So, whatever trade is taking place between India and Myanmar through the Nampong–Pangsau Pass is informal. However, the trade activities are regulated by the state government machinery, and the trade is allowed only in a list of permitted items. The informal border trade has been taking place between the two countries for many years. Informal border trade is permitted only on certain days or dates, and only local traders and people of Nampong residing within a radius of 16 km from Pangsau Pass are

Table 2.4 List of commodities traded between India and Myanmar through the Nampong–Pangsau corridor

Heads	Name of items
Export items	Bamboo, betel nuts and leaves, fresh vegetables, fruits, edible items, pulses and beans, garlic, soya bean, coriander seeds, cosmetics, resin, agricultural machines, broom, medicines, mosquito coils, tobacco, stationery items, leather footwear, blades, electronic items, ready-made garments, utensils
Import items	Local swords, clothes, Tangsa traditional dress, energy drinks, Burmese cigar, Burmese shoes, cosmetic cream

Source: Authors' field survey, 2019.

allowed by the government to visit Pangsau for trade. They are allowed to visit Pangsau only on tenth, twentieth, and thirtieth of every month (only three days in a month). They are not allowed to cross the border check gate with vehicles. They have to keep their vehicle at the check gate and have to walk with commodities up to Pangsau market, where they can dispose of their commodities and purchase Myanmar's goods. On the other hand, Myanmar traders and people are allowed to come to Nampong every Friday to sell their products and buy products from Nampong market. They are also not allowed to come with vehicles. Since Nampong is located 12 km inside the border point, they have to walk for 12 km with their commodities. The list of items exported and imported through the Nampong–Pangsau corridor (informal) is presented in Table 2. 4.

Table 2.4 shows that the bulk of the items exported and imported are primary products. Only a few of the items exported and imported through the corridor are manufactured items. This indicates that the border trade through this corridor could not take advantage of expansion in the list of tradable items for Indo-Myanmar trade. This may be due to restrictions on the movement of people across the border and also to low per capita income of people across the border. The major items traded between India and Myanmar through the formal channel is listed in Table 2.5.

The commodities traded through the informal route are limited and are similar to those traded through the formal channel. However, the

Table 2.5 Major items traded between India and Myanmar through the formal channel

Major commodities exported	Major commodities imported
Coal and limestone	Cement
Crushed stone	Refined palm oil
Boulder stone	Fresh ginger
Betel nut	Arecanut
Rice	Synthetic net fabrics
Diesel, petrol	Cotton waste
Tyres	Plastic furniture
Liquid petroleum gas	Melamine and plastic goods
Wheat flour	Ready-made garments
Pulses	Plywood
Bleaching powder, chemicals	Big cardamom
Fresh fruits (apples)	Dry fish
Dry chilli	Rope of jute
Bamboo	Fishing nets
Sanitari ware	Steam coal
Agarbati	Oil cake
Machinery products and parts	Silicon products
Textiles	Drinks, food items

Source: Commissionerate of Customs (n.d.), "Shillong Custom House" (https://shillongcustoms.gov.in).

commodities traded through the formal channel between the two countries are relatively large in number.

The volume of informal trade between India and Myanmar through the Nampong–Pangsau corridor is given in Tables 2.6 and 2.7.

The month-wise volume of trade from July 2018 to December 2018 is given in Table 2.6. In 2018, the volume of trade per month varied from Rs 4.18 lakhs in February to Rs 10.38 lakhs in June. On the other hand, the total volume of trade during the period from July to December 2018 was Rs 75.12 lakhs. On the other hand, the total volume of trade in 2019 (up to 20 November) was Rs 79.19 lakhs. The average volume of trade per month during the period from January to November 2019 was Rs 7.20 lakhs, which was lower than Rs 12.52 lakhs in 2018.

Table 2.6 Volume of informal trade across the Nampong–Pangsau corridor, 2018

Month	Amount (rupees)	Percentage
July 2018	17,05,200	22.70
August 2018	15,55,000	20.70
September 2018	11,23,650	14.96
October 2018	12,91,560	17.19
November 2018	10,13,340	13.49
December 2018	8,23,110	10.96
Total	**75,11,860**	**100.00**

Source: GoAP (Government of Arunachal Pradesh) (n.d.), "Indo-Myanmar Border Trade", Department of Trade and Commerce (https://aruntrade.gov.in/ind_my.html).

Table 2.7 Volume of informal trade across the Nampong–Pangsau corridor, 2019

Month	Amount (rupees)	Percentage
January 2019	4,47,735	5.65
February 2019	4,18,720	5.29
March 2019	7,65,195	9.66
April 2019	6,75,165	8.53
May 2019	9,04,860	11.43
June 2019	10,38,000	13.11
July 2019	6,62,000	8.36
August 2019	5,45,000	6.88
September 2019	10,32,000	13.03
October 2019	8,40,000	10.61
November 2019	5,90,000	7.45
Total	**79,18,675**	**100**

Source: GoAP (Government of Arunachal Pradesh) (n.d.), "Indo-Myanmar Border Trade", Department of Trade and Commerce (https://aruntrade.gov.in/ind_my.html).

The analysis shows that the informal border trade is permitted through Nampong–Pangsau Pass in certain notified items. The trade is highly restricted and is allowed in selected commodities and on selected days and dates. The imposition of too many conditions and restrictions was reported to be mainly a security consideration as the entire area is strategically located and is affected by insurgent activities. It is observed that trade activities are adversely affected due to restrictions owing to security concerns.

Recent Initiative: A Border *Haat* at *Pangsau* Pass

The Government of Arunachal Pradesh has constructed a "border *haat*" at Pangsau Pass on the Indian side. The *haat* was built at the cost of Rs 3.53 crore to facilitate cross-border trade among the people living close to the border and to simplify border trade in the area. The *haat* is expected to increase the opportunity for border trade and help the local communities to extract the benefits from cross-border trade. The project for the border *haat* was sanctioned in 2016 and completed in August 2019. However, it is yet to be commissioned due to lack of an approach road and water connection. It is expected to be commissioned soon as per the Department of Trade and Commerce, Government of Arunachal Pradesh, which is the nodal department to look after trade and commerce activities, including the border trade in the state. The border *haat* has forty-two shops, a warehouse, a dumping yard, a security barracks, a common toilet, and a parking space for trucks to cater for trade (Arunachal Times, 2019).

The Future Prospects of Indo-Myanmar Border Trade through the Nampong–Pangsau Corridor

The region has a good export potential, which could cater to Myanmar's requirements in spite of the fact that the NER of India is lagging behind in industrial activities. Some of the export potentials of the region are as follows:

- **Crude oil**: the region has four oil refineries, which are located in Upper Assam. Pangsau Pass (Indo-Myanmar border point) is only around 100 km away from Digboi, the oldest oil refinery of Assam. The region has a substantial exportable surplus of refinery products, which can be exported to Myanmar. Export to Myanmar will have a transport cost advantage over transporting to distant parts of the country.

- **Manufactured items**: the region can export some manufactured items such as bicycles, motor parts, fertilizers, medicines, and food products like Maltova and Horlicks and edible oils.
- **Power**: the region has huge hydro power potential. With the commissioning of the numerous power projects, it will have a huge power surplus, which could be exported to Myanmar.
- **Construction materials**: the region could export construction materials such as cement, iron bars, and bricks to Myanmar.
- **Heath-care services**: the region has good number of super-speciality hospitals in Guwahati, Dibrugarh, Imphal, and Shillong. Hence, it could trade in health-care services and cater to the health-care needs of the Myanmar people living near the borders. However, there is a need to soften the borders to increase the movement of people from Myanmar to make available such services.
- **Tourism**: the region has high potential for tourism and recreational services. In fact, tourism has been considered as the potential service activities on which the region can mutually trade with Myanmar owing to the common ethnicity on both sides of the border. The growth in tourism will definitely facilitate tourism-related services such as transport, communication, hospitality, and other related services in the region.

The export potential of Arunachal Pradesh includes apples, oranges, bananas, pineapples, ginger, flowers, and medicinal plants (GoAP, 2011). Some export potentials of Myanmar are as follows:

- **Rice and pulses**: Myanmar is traditionally a surplus producer of rice and pulses. The NER depends for these food items on supplies from Northwestern India, which involve a large transport cost. India itself is deficit in the production of pulses and has to depend on large imports to meet the domestic requirement. Thus, Myanmar could export pulses and rice to North-East India through cross-border trade.
- **Vegetables**: Myanmar is also a good producer of vegetable crops. Hence, it could export crops like onions to North-East India, for which the region depends on distant state like Maharashtra.

- **Forest products**: Myanmar has good reserve of high-value timber such as teak. Most of the forest-based industries in North-East India have suffered due to the ban on the felling of timber in the region by the Supreme Court. Hence, supply of timber products from Myanmar could help to revive those industries in the region.
- **Minerals**: Myanmar has deposits of various types of minerals such as marble and granites. There is a good market for such minerals in North-East India due to the boom in construction activities. The region has depended on such minerals from the western part of the country (Rajasthan), which involves high cost. Myanmar could export these minerals to North-East India through cross-border trade at low cost owing to transport cost advantages.
- **Semi-precious stones**: Myanmar is famous for precious stones such as jade and rubies. There is a good demand for these stones in North-East India and India due to a rise in per capita income.
- **Natural gas**: the coastal areas of Myanmar are rich in deposits of natural gas. There is a high demand for energy in India as its economy is growing rapidly. The supply of natural gas from Myanmar could be of great advantage to India. Despite having huge hydropower potential, the NER continues to suffer from power shortages due to untapped potential. Hence, the import of natural gas from Myanmar could be used in thermal power plants and other industries.

The export potential of India through the NER and the export potential of Myanmar show that they are complementary in nature rather than competitive. Hence, there is good potential for mutually beneficial border trade between the two countries through trade corridors in North-East India. In spite of challenges, the Indo-Myanmar border trade is crucial for India's Act East Policy (Das, 2016). There are great prospects for cross-border trade between India and Myanmar and other Southeast Asian countries through the Nampong–Pangsau corridor, which is connected by the Stilwell Road. The road starts at Ledo in Assam (India) and goes across Nampong in Arunachal Pradesh (India) and the Pangsau Pass. From Pangsau, it goes through Shindbwiyang, Myitkyina, and Bhamo in Kachin Province (Myanmar) and further links the Ledo–Burma road junction to the city of Kunming in the Yunnan Province of China. The road covers a distance of 61 km in India (Ledo–Pangsau Pass), 1,033 km in Myanmar, and 632 km in China. Thus, the total length of the road is 1,726 km.

India has renovated its portion of the Stilwell Road to two-lane highways, while China has renovated its portion of the road to six-lane highways. But the Myanmar segment of the road is reported to be in poor condition. Initially, Myanmar was sceptical about reopening the Stilwell Road because it ran across the insurgency-affected Kachin region, upon which the Military Junta did not have any control. However, in 2010, the Myanmar government assigned the contract to Yunnan Construction Engineering Group of China and the military-backed Yuzana group to reconstruct the 312-km road from Myitkyina in Myanmar to Pangsau Pass at the Indo-Myanmar border. However, the current status of the road is reported to be poor.

This construction would benefit India, China, and Myanmar for both bilateral as well as multilateral trade. Presently, the bulk of goods from the North-East is transported through the narrow Siliguri corridor to Kolkata, covering nearly 1,600 km, and then transhipped through the Strait of Malacca to Southeast Asia and China. The present route takes nearly seven days for the landing of cargo. If the Myitkyina–Pangsau Pass portion of the road were to be renovated, the same consignment through the Stilwell route could land in Myanmar and China in two days or even less (Pattnaik, 2017). This would significantly reduce the transport costs. The Ledo–Nampong corridor could be further connected to Muse, Lashio, Mandalay, and Yangon (Myanmar) through Asian Highway (AH)-14; Ruili, Wanding, and Kunming (China) through AH-3; Bangkok (Thailand), Kuala Lumpur (Malaysia), and Singapore through AH-2; and further to Phnom Penh (Cambodia) and Ho chi Minh city (Vietnam) through AH-1. This would greatly boost the trade between India and Southeast Asian countries through North-East India and accelerate the pace of economic development in the region.

Policy Suggestion

The findings and discussion lead to the following policy suggestions for promoting cross-border trade through the Nampong–Pangsau corridor:

1. The border trade between India and Myanmar through the Nampong–Pangsau route is highly restrictive in nature. Trade is allowed only in a few items and on certain days and dates. These restrictions should be relaxed to enhance the border trade between the two countries.
2. There is a need to boost production of exportable commodities in the state, particularly in the districts sharing an international border. This would increase the export of locally produced products and benefit the local people.
3. Trade infrastructure is essential for the promotion of cross-border trade. Hence, efforts should be made to operationalize the border trade *haat* and Nampong LCS with requisite facilities to promote formal border trade.
4. The Government of India should help Myanmar to improve the road from Pangsau to Myitkyina in Myanmar. This would provide connectivity to Southeast Asian economies and boost trade and exports from North-East India.
5. The security personnel should be sensitized about the importance of border trade and should be trained to ensure unrestricted trade so as to encourage traders to take part in border trade in a greater extent.
6. The border trade between India and Myanmar has also suffered due to social conflicts and insurgent activities. There are frequent *bandhs* and clashes in the state, which obstruct the flow of trade activities. At the same time, the rent-seeking activity of extremism leads to high transaction costs. Hence, there is a need to curb anti-social activities to promote trade and development in the region.

Conclusion

The study shows that the NER of India has a huge potential to achieve economic prosperity through cross-border trade with its neighbouring countries. The region could facilitate India's economic integration with Southeast Asian countries as envisaged under the Act East Policy. Among the neighbouring countries, Myanmar is important as India shares both land and maritime borders with it. Presently, the formal cross-border trade between India and Myanmar takes place through two LCSs located at Moreh in Manipur and Zakhawthar in Mizoram. Informal border trade takes place through Nampong in Arunachal Pradesh and Avangkhu in Nagaland and other border points. The Moreh–Tamu sector accounts for the bulk of the cross-border trade between the two countries. Analysis of the data showed that, after an initial spurt during the period 1995 to 1997–98, the volume of border trade between the two countries declined substantially. However, in recent years, there has been substantial growth in the volume of trade between the two countries due to a change in policy regime. The trade between India and Myanmar is observed to be fluctuating in nature and sensitive to socio-political disturbance.

The Nampong–Pangsau corridor, located on the historic Stilwell Road, could connect Nampong in Arunachal Pradesh to the important towns of Myanmar and Far East. The corridor could serve as a gateway for connecting North-East India with Southeast and East Asian countries for trade through Myanmar. The present status of border trade is mainly informal in nature. Nampong LCS is non-functional, but informal border trade in a list of permitted items takes place between the people living alongside the border. The flow of informal cross-border trade is regulated by the state government machinery, and trade is allowed only in a list of permitted items. The volume of trade is found to be low and fluctuating due to restrictions on trade and the movement of people for security reasons. Recent initiatives include construction of a border *haat* at Pangsau. However, there is a huge potential for cross-border trade between North-East India and Myanmar through the Nampong–Pangsau corridor as the export potentials of the two sides are found to be complementary in nature. Trade could be expanded to other Southeast Asian countries provided proper trade-facilitating infrastructure was developed and the road network from Pangsau to Myitkyina (Myanmar) was renovated and developed to facilitate trade. This would drastically reduce transportation cost, accelerate trade, and promote economic development in Arunachal Pradesh as well as in other states of North-East India. The policy should focus on infrastructure development, develop a strong value-chain system, set up manufacturing plants for producing value-added products, build up diplomatic ties with Myanmar, and rein in insurgent activities to realize the goals of the Act East Policy.

Notes

1. ASEAN comprises ten countries: Indonesia, Malaysia, Philippines, Singapore, Thailand, Brunei, Laos, Myanmar, Cambodia, and Vietnam.
2. The twenty-two items notified for trade are bamboo, betel nuts and leaves, chillies, coriander seeds, food items, local vegetables, fruits, garlic, ginger, *katha*, minor forest products (excluding teak), mustard/rape seeds, onions, pulses and beans, reed broom, resin, roasted sunflower seeds, sesame, soyabeans, spices (excluding nutmeg, mace, cloves, cassia, and cinnamon), tobacco, and tomatoes.

References

Arunachal Times (2019), "Border Haat in Pangsau Pass to Be Commissioned Soon", 4 September (https://arunachaltimes.in/index.php/2019/09/04/border-haat-in-pangsau-pass-set-to-be-commissioned/#google_vignette).

Aung, Winston Set (2009), "Role of Informal Cross-Border Trade in Myanmar", *Asian Paper*, 1 September, 43, mimeo, Institute for Security and National Policy, Sweden.

Bezbaruah, M.P. (2007), "Indo-Myanmar Border Trade: The Stakes for the North-East India", *Dialogue*, 9 (1), pp. 83–104.

Commissionerate of Customs (n.d.), "Shillong Custom House" (https://shillongcustoms.gov.in).

CUTS (Consumer Unity & Trust Society) and FICCI (Federation of Indian Chambers of Commerce and Industry) (2017), "Harnessing the Potential for Cross-Border Trade between Northeast India and Its Neighbouring Countries", Jaipur (https://www.cuts-citee.org/pdf/Harnessing_the_Potential_for_Cross-border_Trade_between_North_East_India_and_its_Neighbouring_Countries.pdf).

Das, Ram Upendra (2016), "Enhancing India–Myanmar Border Trade: Policy and Implementation Measures", Department of Commerce, Ministry of Commerce, Government of India (https://www.commerce.gov.in/wp-content/uploads/2020/02/MOC_636045268163813180_Final-Enhancing_India_Myanmar_Border_Trade_Report.pdf).

Das, Rishi Bhargav and Anjan Kumar Bordoloi (2015), "Opportunities of Border Trade in North-East India: With Special Reference to Indo-Myanmar Border Trade", *World Journal of Research and Review*, 1 (1), pp. 4–11.

Das, Samir Kumar (2014), "Border Economy and the Production of Collective Subjects in India's East and the Northeast", *India Quarterly: A Journal of International Affairs*, 70 (4), pp. 299–311.

Dutta, Gautam (2015), "Northeast India–Bangladesh Border Trade Practices", *Foreign Trade Review*, 50 (1), pp. 53–68.

Ge, Y., Y. He, Y. Jiang, and X. Yin (2014), "Border Trade and Regional Integration", *Review of Development Economics*, 18 (2), pp. 300–12.

GoAP (Government of Andhra Pradesh) (n.d.), "Indo-Myanmar Border Trade", Department of Trade and Commerce (https://aruntrade.gov.in/ind_my.html).

GoAP (2011), "Export Potentials in Arunachal Pradesh", Department of Trade and Commerce.

Kshetrimayum, R. (2010), "Border Trade between India and Myanmar through *Moreh*: Its Trends and Problems", October (https://www.researchgate.net/publication/281291101).

Kudo, Toshihiro (2013), "Myanmar's Border Trade with China: Roads, Gates and Peace", in M. Ishida (ed.), *Border Economies in the Greater Mekong Sub-region*, New York, Palgrave Macmillan, pp. 279–95.

Ministry of DoNER (Ministry of Development of North Eastern Region) (n.d.), Government of India (http://mdoner.gov.in).

Ministry of DONER (2025), "NEC Yearbook 2025", Government of India, March (https://www.mdoner.gov.in/static/uploads/2025/08/4ee337cea2a08143726ab363a3ceae91.pdf @ https://lpai.gov.in/sites/default/files/2022-07/LPAI_LCS_Evaluation_Report_Vol1.pdf).

Patnaik, Jajati K. (2016), "Should Stilwell Road Be Reopened?", *Economic and Political Weekly*, 51 (15), 9 April (https://www.epw.in/journal/2016/15/reports-states/should-stilwell-road-be-reopened.html).

Patnaik, Jajati K. (2017), "Stilwell Road: A Game Changer for Arunachal Pradesh", *Arunachal Times*, 16 October (https://arunachaltimes.in/index.php/2017/10/16/stilwell-road-a-game-changer-for-arunachal-pradesh).

Reimeingam, M. (2016), "Moreh–Namphalong Borders Trade", Institute for Social and Economic Change (ISEC), Bangalore, Working Paper No. 346 (https://www.isec.ac.in/wp-content/uploads/2023/07/WP-346-Marchang-Reimeingam-Final.pdf).

Shahriar, Saleh (2020), "India's Economic Relations with Myanmar: A Study of Border Trade", *Journal of Borderlands Studies*, 37 (3), pp. 599–621 (https://www.researchgate.net/publication/344394661).

Singh, T.B. (2007), "India's Border Trade with Its Neighbouring Countries with Special Reference to Myanmar", *Margin: The Journal of Applied Economic Research*, 1 (4), pp. 359–82.

Sohn, Christophe (2014), "Modeling Cross-Border Integration: The Role of Borders as a Resource", *Geopolitics*, 19 (3), pp. 587–608.

Taneja, Nisha and Sanjib Pohit (2001), "India's Informal Trade with Nepal", *Economic and Political Weekly*, 36 (25), pp. 23–29.

Taneja, Nisha, Tin Htoo Naing, Sanjana Joshi, Thiyam Bharat Singh, Samridhi Bimal, Sakshi Garg, Riya Roy, and Manali Sharma (2019), "India's Act East Policy: Facilitating India–Myanmar Border Trade", Indian Council for Research on International Economic Relations, New Delhi, July (https://icrier.org/pdf/India_Myanmar_Border_Trade.pdf).

3

Informal Cross-Border Trade in the Tirap, Changlong, and Longding Region of Arunachal Pradesh

Issues and Prospects

Manngam Wangpan and Sailajananda Saikia

Introduction

Cross-border trade refers to the activity of selling goods between residents of different countries in border areas based on mutual agreement. It involves economic exchanges that can significantly impact local communities (Nuban et al., 2024). Cross-border trade is defined as trade whose commercial transactions take place on both sides of an international border both formal or informal and licit or illicit (Brown et al., 2023). Cross-border trade takes advantage of proximity and enables traders to benefit from supply–demand discrepancies at the border (Das, 2016). Border trade is officially defined as the exchange of commodities from a bilaterally agreed list by persons residing on both sides of an international border. In other words, it is a trade-in of low-value local products carried by residents of border communities (Das, 2014).

Cross-border trade is divided into formal and informal trade. The term "informal cross-border trade" refers to undocumented flows that are not taxed, whereas "formal cross-border trade" refers to taxable flows that are documented (Ogalo, 2010). The term "informal" captures different parameters such as motivations, or actors involved, or the type or way of trading, making it difficult to design policy interventions

Manngam Wangpan and Sailajananda Saikia, *Informal Cross-Border Trade in the Tirap, Changlong, and Longding Region of Arunachal Pradesh* In: *Sub-Regional Cooperation for Trade, Investment, and Employment in North-East India*. Edited by: Ashish Nath, Oxford University Press. © Oxford University Press 2026.
DOI: 10.1093/9780197908938.003.0003

(Karkare et al., 2021). The relevance of the cross-border movement of products and people is crucial to the economies of border states and provinces and the economies of the two countries.

Informal cross-border trade is prevalent across the world and is a common phenomenon in many countries, including developed ones. Generally, the reasons for informal cross-border trade are multifaceted, resulting from a confluence of economic, social, and institutional factors. Also, poor living conditions and a lack of economic prospects in border regions often give significant incentives for the populace to operate and trade illegally. Border trade between India and its neighbours, particularly Myanmar, is strongly influenced by ethnic relations; affinity; long, porous borders; and cheap transaction costs.

Arunachal Pradesh, a state in India, is known for its unique geographical location. It shares borders with three different countries on three sides while its southern boundary is connected to Assam, which serves as the only link to mainland India. Given its extensive international boundary, the state has naturally fostered and historically significant cultural and economic ties with its neighbouring border communities.

The Department of Trade and Commerce of the Government of Arunachal Pradesh highlights the traditional trade relationship that existed between the local people of Arunachal Pradesh and Tibet (China), Bhutan, and Myanmar. Trade connection with Tibet-China was disrupted after the Sino-India conflict in 1962. Despite the Union Government of India actively pursuing the re-establishment of previous trade points in the Indo-China sector, no land customs stations (LCS) could be approved due to lack of bilateral clearance. The Department of Trade and Commerce also provides an example of the Memba tribe to illustrate the impact of the trade discontinuation with Tibet. The Memba tribe of Shi-Yomi district, once known for its business acumen, has now been reduced to small-scale farmers due to trade disruption after the war.

In the context of trade with Bhutan, the interconnection of cultures and historical trade connections between the native communities of Arunachal Pradesh and Bhutan have played a mutually beneficial role in fostering cross-border cooperation within the wider scope of India's "Neighbourhood First Policy". It is worth noting that there are no officially designated trade routes between the state and Bhutan. However, the residents of Trashigang in Bhutan engage in informal trade activities across the border in Lumla and Tawang, located in Arunachal Pradesh (Panda et al., 2023).

A key feature of the trade with Bhutan and China is the existence of numerous informal local routes and active cross-border movements along the India–Myanmar border. Also, the historical context and political complexities of the region make the trade aspect more vulnerable, yet there are prospects of the rejuvenation of the Stilwell Road, the establishment of border *haats*, and LCSs.

India and Myanmar have a 1,643-km border that runs across four states: Arunachal Pradesh, Nagaland, Manipur, and Mizoram. The state of Arunachal Pradesh shares the longest border of 520 km. Therefore, Arunachal Pradesh, by virtue of sharing the longest international border with Myanmar, naturally occupies a crucial position in fostering cultural and economic linkages between the two nations. Throughout recorded history, the state has consistently adhered to the central government's directives concerning border policy. However, the historical connections between Arunachal Pradesh and Myanmar trace back to time immemorial, reflecting deep-rooted ties across both cultural and geographical lines.

Myanmar's historical trade connections with Arunachal Pradesh are rooted in cultural and economic interdependencies, with communities such as the Nagas and Kachins relying on markets such as Nampong, fostering enduring relationships despite post-colonial disruptions and contemporary geopolitical challenges (Singh, 2023). The Pangsau Pass has historically served as a vital trade route between Arunachal Pradesh and Myanmar, facilitating cultural exchange and economic interactions, particularly before and after British colonial interventions, which significantly influenced regional trade dynamics and socio-cultural landscapes (Paduk, 2024).

Tirap, Changlang, and Longding, collectively known as "TCL", are the southeastern districts of the state of Arunachal Pradesh. Before 1987, TCL was once a united district under the umbrella name of Tirap. The districts lie between 95°19' E to 97°11' E longitudes and 26°53' N to 27°40' N latitude. These are the eastern-most border districts of the state of Arunachal Pradesh. The districts share their long international border of approximately 435 km with Myanmar in the east. These three districts also have a common domestic state border with Assam to their west.

Longding district shares a state boundary with Nagaland to its south, and Changlang district shares district boundaries with Lohit, Anjaw, and Namsai in the north.

The TCL region is primarily an agriculture-based economy. The indigenous tribes are mostly engaged in shifting cultivation. The region is regarded as comparatively poor in terms of socio-economic development, despite being one of the earliest regions to be recognized as a district.

The region also lacks the necessary infrastructure for establishing higher education such as colleges. Many areas of the region still lack good-quality roads, and there are still a few settlements that are not linked to the road network; there are also villages where the roads are non-motorable. This might be one of the reasons that informal and primary sectors remain so dominant in the region. In this backdrop, this chapter examines the nature of informal trade in the TCL region of Arunachal Pradesh.

The Economy of the TCL Region

TCL districts are mainly hilly regions with moderate-to-steep slopes. This region is geographically, historically, and culturally closer to its eastern neighbours like Myanmar (erstwhile, Burma) and other Southeast Asian nations than the other mainland states. Also, this border region lacks proper infrastructure and effective administration, and these have intensified the problems in the region over the years. The establishment of fixed boundary delimitation between India and Myanmar has been a complex issue, marked by a series of agreements and boundary demarcation efforts. The post-1967 Boundary Agreement stands out as a significant milestone in this process. This agreement facilitated the erection of border pillars, which played a crucial role in defining the boundary and introducing a degree of flexibility in border dynamism during the delimitation of the entire India–Myanmar boundary.

TCL is inhabited by many indigenous tribes. Among all inhabited tribes, the Nocte, Tangsa, Wancho, Tutsa, Ollo, and Singpho form the majority in terms of population. In addition to the above-mentioned tribes, the region is also home to other communities, including *Deori*, *Lisu* (*Yobin*), *Chakma*, *Nepali*, and *Adivasi*. TCL being a border region identifies with its fellow communities across the borders too. Significant numbers of Ollo, Tutsa, Tangsa, Nocte, and Wancho villages are located on the Myanmar side as well. This has, in a way, kept the TCL region in a very close-knit relationship with the people across international borders.

The communities on both sides of the border share the same languages, follow the same traditions, and live similar lifestyles. These societies existed without boundaries and travelled freely between settlements of their kind for a variety of socio-cultural goals. But the delineation of borders after 1947 became a matter of concern for border dwellers. The border communities believed the newly established boundary to be incompatible with the region's customary boundaries. They also felt a strong feeling of fear as they were consigned to the status of ethnic minorities on both sides of the border.

In order to deal with these issues and promote better cooperation, the Indian and Myanmarese governments established the free movement regime (FMR), which permitted the border settlers to cross the border on either side up to 16 km without a visa. With time, these open borders have helped backward settlements on both sides to procure necessary items and render the needful services on either side. And also, for many other reasons, the international border with Myanmar is very porous.

Methodology

The study is based on a mixed-method approach, incorporating both primary and secondary data. The selection of the study area is based on representation of three districts, where the selection of the villages was purposive, focusing on communities actively engaged in informal cross-border trade with Myanmar and showing significant ethnic and cultural ties across the border.

The study is based on field observation through pilot study. The direct observation was conducted in three border villages—one each from Tirap, Longding, and Changlang district—to document the trade practices, goods exchanged, and the role of local communities in informal trade activities. The brief pilot study of the border villages helped to obtain empirical insights into the socio-economic impact of cross-border trade, and moreover, the interaction with the traders, residents, and concerned local authorities provided qualitative information on trade processes and livelihood implications.

Meanwhile, secondary data were drawn from academic literature, policy reports, government documents, and historical context from relevant archival material. These sources provided theoretical context and supported the interpretation of primary data. Qualitative data, which includes narrative data from observations and interactions, has been thematically categorized to identify the items of trade and also to study the issues and prospects of informal cross-border trade in the study area. The border villages for study (a border village from each district) are

1. Noglo (Tirap)
2. Konsa (Longding)
3. Nampong (Changlang).

The TCL region is lagging behind in socio-economic indicators of development but the other districts in the central and western parts of the state have achieved substantial improvement in terms of social and economic development.

Cross-Border Trade in the TCL Region

Historically, the idea of trade began with the salt trade. People in Assam, the Patkai hills, and even Myanmar relied on the supply of salt collected from East Arunachal Pradesh's salt wells. Salt trade flourished since it was a precious and scarce product in the then North-East region. The Noctes, Tutes, Tutsa, Ahoms, Muttocks, and others made a fortune from the salt trade. The Tutsas and Nocte tribal rulers held approximately eighty-five salt wells in Tirap (Roy, 2006). Apart from the salt trade, interactions with knowledgeable persons ascertained the exchange of gemstones and other ornamental precious items with countries in Southeast Asia such as Myanmar, Thailand, and China.

For centuries, trade relations between this district and upper Burma thrived. Merchants from this district frequently visited Bhamo, a bustling trade hub on the Irrawaddy river, using the passes across the Patkai ranges as trade routes. They exchanged handloom products, tea leaves, salt, and beads for Burmese goods like the *dao* (a traditional machet), iron implements, and garments. Opium was a significant trade commodity, particularly between the Singphos of this district and the Kachins of upper Burma. Despite the international border, illicit trade in items like opium persisted, with smugglers sometimes endangering their lives by using elephant tracks to avoid detection (Choudhury, 1980).

The trade history between Myanmar and the Patkai hills region is also intertwined with the cultural and historical ties that exist between the Naga people, who inhabit both sides of the border. The Naga people have a long history of trade and cultural exchange, and their traditional trade routes often traversed the Patkai hills, connecting the Naga-inhabited areas of Myanmar with those in India (Baruah, 2005).

War then saw the importance of this region as the shortcut route for the English to tackle the advancing Japanese troupes in India, Myanmar, and China. Eventually, the inland route to China was constructed by the Allied soldiers led by the United States during the Second World War in this region. This road was formerly known as "Ledo Road" as it connected Ledo (India) to Kunming (China). The road was built for military purposes rather than trade.

Gradually, after the Independence of both India and Myanmar, the international borders were demarcated, which was totally political, keeping aside the demographic composition of the region. As a result, a divergent line has been drawn over a similar population group that remained united until the demarcation process was completed. Notwithstanding the creation of borders, cross-border movements and exchanges were permitted on the grounds that the region recognizes their kind across borders and that limits would instead breed aggressiveness and extremism against the law in the region, the FMR being the legal policy in support.

During the early post-Independence years, the TCL region (the then Tirap district) witnessed internal progress in various sectors, most prominently in the timber sector. It rose to be one of the known timberlands of the country. At the peak of its advancement through its timber venture, the 12 December 1996 blanket ban on timber business by the apex court caused the chaotic downfall of the TCL region, especially in terms of the employment generation, which drastically affected the economic situation. The region was left in a state of confusion. Throughout these uncertain years, the region seemed to have absorbed the armed rebellion, which eventually hampered the region's overall progress.

These three districts (i.e. Tirap, Changlang, and Longding) were further tagged as "disturbed areas" under the provisions of the Armed Forces (Special Powers) Act, 1958 (AFSPA) by the Union Ministry of Home Affairs (MHA, 1976). This designation is periodically extended every six months, and in the case of the TCL region, the tag has been extended continuously ever since. This designation poses challenges to the region's peaceful way of life, hindering its ability to fully benefit from development.

The region's abrupt downfall, coupled with security, developmental, and political–administrative challenges, significantly impacted its trade dynamics. Traditional forms of border exchange (i.e. the informal trade, once integral to the region's commerce) have been marred by illicit activities, posing grave security threats. These challenges have impeded the region's trade prospects, necessitating a re-evaluation of its economic strategies and security measures.

TCL communities are not limited within international boundaries. Many sister villages of the same ethnic groups are also identified across the border. Therefore cross-border movements are a normal phenomenon in the region, be it formal or informal. The Indo-Myanmar border is an open, porous border with an FMR on both sides of the border within 16 km. However, passes and gateways are the major points of cross-border movements in the region. These points are mostly informal passes, with no government regulations on either side of the border.

There are many important historical passes in the region, namely (i) Hpungan Pass, (ii) Mugaphi Pass, (iii) Gphuka Pass (iv) Chaukan Pass, (v) Hukawng Pass, (vi) Siddi Pass, and (vii) Pangsau Pass, which facilitate movement of goods and people between the two sides. Apart from these routes, informal trades are also carried out through the border villages, using many unidentified tracks. A few of many such border villages are Noglo, Chinhan, and Raho villages of Tirap district, and Wakka and Chongkhaw villages of Longding district.

In spite of many routes and points of cross-border activities, only the Pangsau Pass was deemed as a formal trade route for the region. The sole official point for cross-border trade, the Nampong LCS, approved by the Government of India in August 1951, remains non-operational to this day (GoAP, n.d.). The non-functional lone LCS can be attributed to a variety of factors, including developmental constraints, administrative challenges, and security issues. On the other hand, the porous nature of the border has enabled informal cross-border trade, particularly in border villages, while still recognizing the national boundary delineated by the border pillars.

The Government of Arunachal Pradesh has stressed the importance of reopening and reinstating historical border trade routes with Myanmar on several occasions, such as the (Meeting on Look East Policy, 2007). The government realizes that, over the centuries, inhabitants of Arunachal Pradesh residing in border regions have engaged in trade with their counterparts across the borders, and presently, informal trade continues with Myanmar through the Pangsau Pass and many other unidentified routes. Despite decades of promises, the sole designated formal trade station remains non-functional, a result of government neglect, unsuitable operating conditions, and escalating insurgency activity in the region.

The nature of trade across the TCL region and Myanmar is informal and traditional in nature. It is rooted in centuries-old socio-cultural and economic ties among the border communities. This type of traditional or informal trade occurs through local trade points that are not officially recorded. Moreover, the interdependence of people on both sides has fostered informal trade channels for goods and services. Again, such trade holds significance for the economy and livelihoods of the people in the region. Yet, little attention has been paid to understanding the nature and dynamism of cross-border trade, especially informal trade and its role in local regional development.

The trade channels in the TCL region being unofficial, anything from low-cost deals to domestic home goods are traded across borders. Table 3.1 shows the list of items traded informally from the border villages.

The most common type of commodity observed in the three border villages were grocery items, namely, sugar, salt, biscuits, and noodles. According to the items listed, Noglo village dealt more with spices (black pepper, cardamom, chillies, coffee, ginger) and locally grown food grains such as local rice from Myanmar. Apart from these items, gong and traditional artefacts and ornaments were also traded from Myanmar. Groceries and cold drinks are traded to Myanmar. In Konsa village, trade mainly involves household items such as gong, knives, and machetes from Myanmar. It also trades grocery items and personal-use items (soap, batteries, slippers) plus grocery items to Myanmar. On the

Table 3.1 Commodities traded in the TCL region

Village name	Items traded	
	From Myanmar	**To Myanmar**
Noglo (Tirap district)	Cardamom, ginger, coffee, local rice, black pepper, chilli, gong, traditional artefacts and ornaments	Rice (high-yielding variety rice), salt, biscuits, mustard oil, clothes, sugar, cold drinks, noodles
Konsa (Longding district)	Soyabean, gong, knives, machetes, boots, shoes, traditional artefacts and ornaments	Salt, sugar, biscuits, noodles, chicken meat, clothes, soap, batteries, slippers, cosmetics
Nampong (Changlang district)	Local machetes, biscuits, canned curry, canned fish, balm, fermented fish, traditional clothes, coffee, hens, piglets, cardamom, ginger	Salt, sugar, cooking oil, biscuits, cosmetics, petrol, diesel, utensils, notebooks, noodles, eggs, cold drinks, chocolates, chips

Source: Authors' field survey, January 2023.

other hand, Nampong trades a most diverse range of items, including fuel and stationery (petrol, diesel, notebooks) to Myanmar and buys processed tinned foods (canned curry, canned fish), snacks (chips, chocolates), and live animals (hens, piglets) from Myanmar. Trade also features several traditional items (local machetes, traditional clothes, and fermented fish).

The cultural linkage of the communities of the border areas on either side of the border encourages trade in traditional items such as ornaments and local artefacts. However, apart from all these items, the current insecurity of informal trade in this region is the inflow of illegal items such as opium and other drugs from Myanmar. Moreover, the region's proximity to the infamous "Golden Triangle", the Southeast Asian region (Myanmar-Northern Thailand-Laos), which has been one of the largest opium-producing areas of the world, makes it more vulnerable to this threat.

The impact of informal trade between India and Myanmar on the economy of the TCL region can be substantial, although precise quantification is challenging due to the informal nature of the trade. The items identified through observation from the three border villages gives an overview of the goods traded between India and Myanmar through this region. Salt is the most common and most demanded commodity traded into Myanmar. Indian noodles and biscuits are also in high demand; other items most sought by the Myanmar border population are cooking oil, cosmetics, and clothes. Meanwhile, items traded into India from Myanmar are agricultural products, traditional ornaments, and artefacts.

The overall effects of informal cross-border trade in the context of India–Myanmar trade through the TCL region can be both positive and negative. The positive aspects of informal trade in border regions, especially in the TCL region, are significant as it contributes both culturally and economically. Border trade has enabled these areas to procure essential goods from across the border, thereby fulfilling basic needs. Moreover, in contemporary times, cross-border trade has directly or indirectly engaged the local population, particularly youths, in various trade processes, leading to income generation and employment opportunities. For example, many youths operate as drivers, transporting loads from Nampong to a border point and carrying back items from Myanmar from the border point to Nampong. The push-and-pull factors on Indo-Myanmar cross border trade through the TCL region is presented in Figure 3.1 in terms of a strengths, weaknesses, opportunities, and threats (SWOT) analysis.

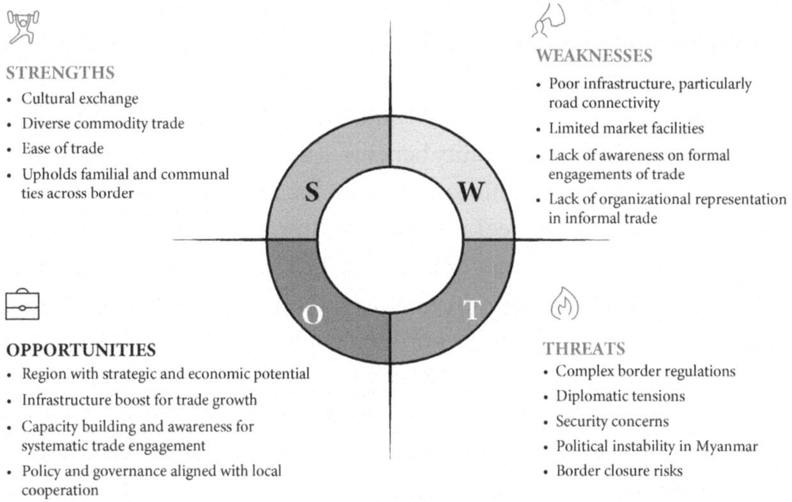

Figure 3.1 A SWOT analysis on Indo-Myanmar cross-border trade through the TCL region
Source: Author.

Culturally, cross-border trade has facilitated the exchange and access to culturally significant items and artefacts, thereby preserving and promoting the rich cultural traditions of border communities. This cultural exchange and interaction has further strengthened the cultural ties between border regions. Moreover, the border residents often cross the border to celebrate annual festivals and other cultural events, and this movement fosters the movement of commodities along with people. This creates awareness on availability of certain goods on both sides which, in turn, stimulates demand and facilitates continued exchange of commodities on either side of the border, channelizing informal cross-border trade.

The informal cross-border trade is also observed to have a negative impact on the economy of the TCL region and state as a whole. The nature of the informal trade is such that it bypasses formal customs procedures and regulations, leading to a loss of potential tax revenue for the state government. This revenue could have been used for infrastructure development and other public services benefiting the local community and the region. The informal nature of deals also involves goods of questionable quality and origin, which can pose both consumer and strategic business concerns.

A common observation based on local knowledge in the study area is that many goods obtained from Myanmar are actually from Thailand and China. One study (Mahadevan, 2020) reported that the Northeastern Region has become a hub for counterfeit Chinese products brought in through informal trade with Myanmar. While this trade has long-standing cultural and community benefits, it also poses a serious threat of dumping. This threat is significant because the influx of low-cost foreign goods could hinder the region's attempts towards industrial development. Likewise, the informal trade in the TCL region could pose a serious risk of potential dumping of banned goods, especially considering that TCL is already a vulnerable border region.

Again, if there is no proper government intervention and formalization of the trade system, then border communities could heavily rely on and become deeply involved in informal trade, exposing themselves to the unpredictable nature of the trade and susceptibility to disruptions. This heavy reliance may also hinder broader economic development by discouraging investment in formal economic activities that could provide more sustainable and diversified income sources.

Issues of Informal Trade in the TCL Region

The informal trade in the TCL region is an issue, given the existence of a number of historical traditional trade routes, the trade profits and benefits it acquires from its eastern neighbours. Moreover, as no attempts are being made to build official trade services in the region, the national ambition of eastern economic cooperation such as the Act East Policy (AEP), particularly through the TCL region, remains a distant dream.

The ambition for the region's economic development through the revival of the Stilwell Road and the establishment of an official post at Nampong in the Pangsau Pass likewise remains dormant. The ambitious national Look East Policy (LEP), now (AEP), which aimed at the expansion and growth of the Northeastern Region's economic potential, has shown no strong implications on the aspects of commerce, connectivity, or security in the region.

Connectivity is one of the major concerns in the region regarding border trade. The road connectivity along the borders is not efficient enough. The degree of connectivity is poor, and also some of the border villages are yet to get a road connection. Rural border roads are likewise poorly maintained and are not all-weather resistant. To measure the degree of road connectivity in the region, the Alpha, Beta, and Gamma indices were calculated (Kasokota et al., 2025). The computed value of the alpha index is 0.10 (10 per cent), while the Beta and Gamma index values are 1.20 and 0.40, respectively for the TCL region.[1] The value of Alpha and Gamma indices ranges from 0 (no circuits) to 1 (maximum circuits) and the Beta index from 0 (no circuits) to 3 (maximum interconnectivity). The higher the index value, the greater is the degree of connectivity in road network. All the calculated values are low, implying that the degree of road connectivity is very poor, with less interconnectivity. Apart from inadequate connectivity and maintenance, cross-border trade necessitates connection on both sides of the border. The lack of connectivity on either side of the border hinders the potential advancement of cross-border trade. This, in turn, contributes to the development of informal trade in the region.

The effort to revive the "Ledo–Kunming Road" or the "Stilwell Road" to its maximum utilization is also lacking. The historic route could serve as a model connection to India's eastern neighbours. Nevertheless, topographical obstacles such as rough terrain, insurgency incidence, and other political issues on both sides of the border have slowed developments on this route.

Geographical limitation such as difficult terrain and isolation also plays a major role in the connectivity aspects of the border villages to the nearest market/towns in the region. As the border villages are situated in hilly, rugged terrain, the geographical isolation and poor connectivity circuit make the region more dependable on the traditional form of business for livelihood through trade among the sister villages. Thus, the porous border and the FMR promote the disadvantaged communities on both sides to use the services from either side. Aside from trading activities, the region's cross-border trade is frequently disturbed by security threats and dealings of illegal substances, and systematic efforts such as talks on border fencing and scrapping of the FMR are underway to manage and regulate the flow of commodities that are a threat to the society. However, due to cultural and ethnic ties, the border cannot be closed, and mobility cannot be restricted. Closing the border would be a tough challenge in terms of both infrastructural construction and communal dealings.

The decision to fence the India–Myanmar border and closing down of the FMR has met with mixed reactions nationwide. According to Choudhury (2024), besides the domestic economic impacts, fencing the India–Myanmar border would harm India's AEP, which aims for stronger economic, physical, and people-to-people ties between India, Myanmar, and Southeast Asia. Currently, formal border trade between India and Myanmar is already very low. Additionally, fencing would hinder progress on developing west-to-east corridors like the India–Myanmar–Thailand Trilateral Highway. This approach goes against the AEP's essence, which was to use North-East India as a gateway to Southeast Asia. Moreover, fencing contradicts the Union government's earlier stance on keeping the border open "to provide connectivity and enhance interaction of the people of Northeastern States of India with the people of Myanmar", as noted in the 2018 Cabinet approval of the India–Myanmar FMR agreement.

Overall, the government's negligence and poor execution of policies and developmental initiatives in TCL's periphery have worsened the problem of backwardness and other geopolitical issues. This has led to the region being devoid of proper awareness and opportunities. And when a region lacks a basic understanding of legal concerns, along with limited chances and poor livelihood conditions, then informal cross-border commerce breeds unlawful activities along the peripheries and deals with illicit items, posing a direct threat to society and the region as a whole. Furthermore, because of its proximity to the "Golden Triangle" and the "Naga Self-Administered Zone", the territory is in a sensitive and vulnerable position. As a result, inadequate governance and a lack of community understanding of the spectrum of commerce and security may intensify the region's risks and current difficulties.

The TCL region holds great significance and position in terms of economic and geostrategic ventures towards the Southeast and East Asian nations. The region, which is currently regarded as backward and unexplored, is viewed with optimism for the exploration of new channels of economic ventures and as a gateway to transnational trade. All of these could be realized with the collective efforts of the border communities and appropriate government policies on both sides of the border. The factors that could push the development of the region are listed below.

1. **The Nampong–Pangsau Pass corridor**: according to the Land Customs Station Evaluation Report (2021), the Arunachal Pradesh state government stated its eagerness to advance the development of border trade with Myanmar via Pangsau Pass (Nampong). It stressed that the re-establishment of trade through the Pangsau Pass (Nampong) has the potential to significantly enhance trade relations between India and Myanmar, while also benefiting the local populations of both countries. Furthermore, the state government opined that the re-opening could potentially serve as a gateway to Southeast Asian countries in the future. The report also stated that the state government has committed to allocate sufficient land for the establishment of an integrated check post at Pangsau Pass (Nampong).

2. **The Stilwell Road**: in today's world, no form of progress can take place in the absence of infrastructure. And concerning the cross-border trade development in the TCL region, infrastructure is a huge bottleneck. The basic infrastructure is road connectivity, which is the sole form of connectivity in the rough terrain of TCL. The core line of the transnational highway in the region (i.e. the Stilwell Road) could emerge as one of the important lifelines of cross-border trade in India. The proactive steps of central and regional government through viable investment in this step could not only provide socio-economic stability but also maintain political stability and good governance over the region. With the proper renewal and mobilization through the "Stilwell Road", many more avenues of border trade and development could sprout.
   (a) It could provide opportunities to the country and the region, in particular, to connect to the economically developed parts of Yunnan and other Southeast Asia via Myanmar, which would establish links for emerging economies.
   (b) transborder communities could be restored through border trade—it could promote both economic and cultural cooperation between India, China, and other Southeast Asian nations.
   (c) It would help not only the TCL region but also the entire Northeastern Region through Assam as it is closely connected by the aforementioned route. Assam, which connects both inland markets, might serve as an intermediary zone for both mainland India and eastern countries.
   (d) With the functioning of this route, the close ethnic ties and historical affinity of the border communities with the Southeast Asian nation could help in the acceptance of the local products and thus create markets over the borders. This would hugely benefit the local traders and boost the regional economy.
   (e) Moreover, with the aforementioned development opportunities, the legality and official operation of cross-border trade can be developed. This would ensure a calm, safe, and stable atmosphere throughout the region, hence establishing stability.
3. **The AEP**: the AEP's consistent and strong efforts on transnational initiatives and regional infrastructure upgradation would greatly improve both cross-border commerce and the region's economic position. With this regulation, the importance and market values

of common items and local articles would likewise be legally listed for trade. This would inspire more local communities to engage in transnational business, therefore increasing regional cooperation for greater objectives through cross-border trade. If the AEP and its rules are effectively developed and executed, cross-border trade will experience fewer conflicts due to illegal dealings from informal activities.

4. **Sub-regional cooperation for border trade—Arunachal Pradesh and its neighbours**: Arunachal Pradesh holds immense geostrategic significance, and the expected trade opportunities, supported by collaboration with neighbouring regions, add to this strategic value. With its borders with Tibet (China), Bhutan, and Myanmar, the state holds the promises of being an international corridor for trade and other socio-eco-political aspects.

The historical and cultural connections with Tibet (China), Bhutan, and Myanmar are deeply ingrained. Particularly with Myanmar, unlike the tightly guarded border with Tibet (China), the border maintains a policy of free movement, remaining porous and loosely guarded. This has facilitated the unrestricted flow of goods, services, and people across the borders, primarily enabling informal trade.

As a border state with international borders on three sides, Arunachal Pradesh's economic dimensions and planning are inherently tied to border trade. The state's geographical location, ethnic connections, and historical significance emphasize the importance of exploring its trade potential. Formalizing and mutually managing border trades could unlock significant potential for economic benefits, highlighting the need for strategic and diplomatic approaches to border-trade policies.

The Nampong–Pangsau Pass, in Arunachal Pradesh's Changlang district, represents a promising geo-economic corridor that could advance India's economic interests with the Association of Southeast Asian Nations (ASEAN). Upgraded highways on the Indian and Chinese sides could connect Nampong to Myanmar and China. Completion of the Myanmar segment would link Nampong to Myanmar and China via Asian Highways AH14 and AH3. Asian Highway AH2 would connect Nampong to Thailand, Malaysia, and Singapore, and AH1 to Cambodia and Vietnam. Developing Nampong LCS would enhance sub-regional cooperation, benefiting Arunachal Pradesh's engagement with ASEAN, the Mekong–Ganga Cooperation (MGC), and the Bangladesh–China–India–Myanmar (BCIM) Forum (Pattanaik, 2021). Collaborative initiatives encompassing infrastructure development, policy harmonization, capacity enhancement, and mutually advantageous geopolitical frameworks would enhance the trade economy and serve as the southeastern gateway of the state.

Arunachal Pradesh holds the potential to serve as a gateway to East Asia. Therefore, it is imperative to consider the development of Special Economic Zones and industrial corridors within the state. Exploring Arunachal Pradesh's potential in the 5H sectors (hydro, herbal, horticulture, handicraft, and handloom) and the 2T sectors (tradition and tourism) through cross-border synergies is essential. On the other hand, it is crucial to address threat perceptions such as drug trafficking, smuggling of small arms, and illegal dumping of Chinese goods. Identifying these challenges and creating a conducive environment for trade is essential for sustainable economic growth in the region (Pattnaik, 2018).

On a cultural prospect, ethnically, the tribal communities of the TCL region share strong ancestral ties. Tribes like Nocte, Wancho, Ollo, and Tangsa identify their own kind across the border and so share a strong affinity with them (Dai, 2001). Similarly, tribes such as the Singpho and Khampti share ancestral ties with the communities of Thailand and Laos. Therefore, the establishment of mutually conscientious policies among these countries that could enhance economic and cultural ties through trade would serve as an exemplary model.

There is anticipation of increased cross-border trade in the border regions with the implementation of proper sub-regional cooperation frameworks and favourable trade policies. This expected rise in border activity may call for an increase in government intervention and presence along the border. Consequently, illegal activities such as insurgency, trafficking of illicit commodities, and foreign threats are expected to decline.

Conclusion

The TCL's emphasis on cross-border trade is essential for the region. The state of informal cross-border commerce and its significance should go hand in hand in order to solve the concerns and challenges it brings to the region. Concerning the issues and prospects of the border region, it may be an abrupt decision of the government to completely close down the FMR and the by-activities such as border trade due to illegal concerns; rather, systematic solutions in policies both politically and economically could be framed with the mutual consent of the border communities. Also, official registration of trade routes, the listing of legal commodities, and proper surveillance of cross-border movements would substantially encourage legitimate trade development in the region.

Furthermore, because the TCL is a significant geostrategic region, appropriate trade growth and socio-economic improvement would significantly safeguard the region both economically and politically. Generally, internal stability is assured if the borders are intact and capable of withstanding external threats; hence, border issues such as border extremism, bilateral trade issues, and unregulated porous border concerns should be prioritized by the government. Effectively, addressing the challenges and seizing the opportunities presented by cross-border trade could pave the way for the TCL region to explore the benefits of trade and foster enhanced regional cooperation. With an optimistic outlook, collaborative efforts and strategic policies could unlock the region's potential as a pivotal hub for trade and connectivity.

Note

1. In the field of transportation geography, several types of connectedness indices have been established, each with its unique set of meanings such as Alpha Index, Beta Index, and Gama Index. Alpha, Beta, and Gamma indices are graph theory-based metrics used to analyse road network connectivity. The edges and vertexes counted into consideration for calculating the following indices are the National Highway, State Highway, and Local (rural roads). The total number of vertex and edges counted 212 and 256, respectively.

Indices	Formula	Vertex	Edges	Value
Alpha (α)	e-v + 1/2v–5	212	256	0.10
Beta (ß)	e/v	212	256	1.20
Gamma (ɣ)	e/3(v–2)	212	256	0.40

Source: Authors' calculation.

References

Baruah, Sanjib (2005), *Durable Disorder: Understanding the Politics of Northeast India*, New Delhi: Oxford University Press.

Brown, Alison, Bhaskar Chakrabarti, Peter Mackie, Crispian Fuller, Rajesh Bhattacharya, Soumyabrato Bagchi, and Debapriya Chakrabarti (2023), "Contested Spaces of Exchange: Informal Cross-Border Trade on the India–Bangladesh Border", *Forum for Development Studies*, 51 (1), pp. 121–143 (https://doi.org/10.1080/08039410.2023.2255211).

Choudhury, Angshuman (2024), "Walls in the Era of Bridges: The Many Costs of Fencing the India–Myanmar Border", Centre of Excellence for Himalayan Studies, Shiv Nadar Institution of Eminence, Issue Brief No. 3, March.

Choudhury, S. Dutta (1980), "Arunachal Pradesh District Gazetteers: Tirap District (Vol. 2)", Government of Arunachal Pradesh (https://archive.org/details/dli.ministry.07322/page/n5/mode/2up).

Dai, Mamang (2001), "Arunachal Pradesh: The Myth of Tranquillity" (https://old.satp.org/satporgtp/publication/faultlines/volume5/Fault5-5mdhai.htm).

Das, Pushpita (2014), "Status of India's Border Trade: Strategic and Economic Significance", Institute for Defence Studies and Analysis, New Delhi, Occasional Paper No. 37.

Das, Ram Upendra (2016), "Enhancing India–Myanmar Border Trade Policy and Implementation Measures", Department of Commerce Ministry of Commerce and Industry, Government of India (https://www.commerce.gov.in/wp-content/uploads/2020/02/MOC_636045268163813180_Final-Enhancing_India_Myanmar_Border_Trade_Report.pdf).

GoAP (Government of Arunachal Pradesh) (n.d.), "Indo-Myanmar Border Trade", Department of Trade and Commerce, Government of Arunachal Pradesh (https://aruntrade.gov.in/ind_my.html).

Karkare, Poorva, Bruce Byiers, Philomena Apiko, and Mounirou Alioune Kane (2021), "A System, Not an Error: Informal Cross-Border Trade in West Africa", European Centre for Development Policy Management, Discussion Paper No. 300, 11 June 2021 (https://policycommons.net/artifacts/3757501/a-system-not-an-error/4562996).

Kasokota L., I. Kafodya, T. Mkandawire, and M. Ndwandwe (2025), "Road Network Analysis of Connectivity and Accessibility Indices in Blantyre, Malawi", in Innocent Musonda, Erastus Mwanaumo, Adetayo Onososen, Retsepile Kalaoane (eds), *Development and Investment in Infrastructure in Developing Countries—A 10-Year Reflection*, Balkema: Taylor & Francis Group, pp. 226–34.

Land Customs Station Evaluation Report (2021), "Land Customs Station Evaluation Report Volume 1 and 2", submitted to Land Ports Authority of India, March (https://lpai.gov.in/sites/default/files/2022-07/LPAI_LCS_Evaluation_Report_Vol1.pdf).

Mahadevan, Prem (2020), "Crossing the Line: Geopolitics and Criminality at the India–Myanmar Border", *Global Initiative against Transnational Organized Crime*, Research Report, Geneva, November (https://globalinitiative.net/wp-content/uploads/2020/11/Crossing-the-line-Geopolitics-and-criminality-at-the-India-Myanmar-border.pdf).

MHA (Ministry of Home Affairs) (1976), "Notices", Government of India (https://www.mha.gov.in/en/notifications/notice?title_1=&field_divisions_of_mha_target_id=All&page_5).

Nuban, Y., F.W. Ballo, and M.I.H. Tiwu (2024), "Dampak Perdagangan Lintas Batas Terhadap Perekonomian Masyarakat Lokal di Wilayah Perbatasan Wini—Timor Leste", *Journal of Business, Finance, and Economics*, 5 (2), pp. 356–69.

Ogalo, V. (2010), "Informal Cross-Border Trade in EAC: Implications for Regional Integration and Development", Consumer Utility and Trust Society, African Resource Centre, Nairobi, research paper (https://www.scirp.org/reference/referencespapers?referenceid=3096162).

Paduk, L. (2024), "The Pangsau Pass: Historical, Cultural, and Geopolitical Dimensions of Border Construction between Arunachal Pradesh and Myanmar", *International Organization of Scientific Research Journal of Humanities and Social Science*, 29 (9), pp. 33–36 (https://doi.org/10.9790/0837-2909063336).

Panda, Bhagirathi, Jajati K. Pattnaik, and Chandan Panda (2023), "The Geo-economic and Geo-cultural Significance of the Tawang–Trashigang Corridor: A Perspective on Indo-Bhutan Border Connectivity", *Journal of Land Ports and Border Economy*, 1 (2), pp. 90–102.

Pattnaik, Jajati K. (2018), "Arunachal Pradesh: India's Tri-junction to the East", *Arunachal Times*, 27 November (https://arunachaltimes.in/index.php/2018/11/27/arunachal-pradesh-indias-tri-junction-to-the-east).

Pattnaik, Jajati K. (2021), "Geo-strategic Importance of Arunachal Pradesh in the 21st Century", *Arunachal Times*, 20 February (https://arunachaltimes.in/index.php/2021/02/20/geo-strategic-importance-of-arunachal-pradesh-in-the-21st-century).

Roy, Y. P., and Roy, Y. P. (2006). "Medieval Rajmahal: An Economic Profile", *Proceedings of the Indian History Congress*, 67, pp. 1068–1070. http://www.jstor.org/stable/44148036

Singh, Khwairakpam Goutam (2023), "Borderland Realities: Decoding the Socioeconomic and Political Complexities of the Indo-Myanmar Border", *Journal of Psychology and Political Science*, 3 (50), pp. 8–18 (https://doi.org/10.55529/jpps.35.8.18).

4

Cross-Border Boundaries and Corridors of Connectedness

Assam in Sub-regional Development

Saswati Choudhury

Introduction

India's Northeastern Region (NER), with an area of 265,000 sq. km, is a land bridge between South Asia and Southeast Asia. It is the only region in India to share borders with five countries, namely, Bangladesh, the People's Republic of China (PRC), Myanmar, Bhutan, and Nepal. Until the partition of India, the region was at the forefront of global trade over road, rail, inland waterways, and seaways. The Dibrugarh–Chittagong railways by Assam Bengal railway was one of the earliest projects implemented by the British in India in the late nineteenth century, which laid the foundation for physical and trade connectivity of the region with the rest of the world. The partition of India in 1947 and the Independence of Burma (now Myanmar) made the NER landlocked, severing its transport routes and market access. The push to revive the old connectivity resurfaced with India's Look East Policy by placing it as a gateway to the dynamic East and Southeast Asian economies (Choudhury, 2017). Recognizing the continental access, India built the Friendship Road to Myanmar in 1996, and the inauguration of the road was followed by the Association of Southeast Asian Nations (ASEAN) car rally. India's engagement with Southeast Asia and the Asia Pacific region from 2014 also created a space for North-East India to be at the focal point of regional and sub-regional cooperation, dealing with such bodies as the South

Saswati Choudhury, *Cross-Border Boundaries and Corridors of Connectedness* In: *Sub-Regional Cooperation for Trade, Investment, and Employment in North-East India*. Edited by: Ashish Nath, Oxford University Press.
 DOI: 10.1093/9780197908938.003.0004

Asia Sub-regional Economic Cooperation (SASEC), the Bay of Bengal Initiative for Multi-Sectoral Economic Cooperation (BIMSTEC), Bangladesh–China–India–Myanmar (BCIM) and ASEAN.

This continental linkage can be augmented with development and access to infrastructure. Studies have shown that access and availability of infrastructures within and across borders, particularly connecting areas within a country or countries across a region, have significantly shaped the path of development and growth of the region and countries therein. Infrastructural endowment, together with geographical location and agglomerative sectoral structure, determine a region's development potential. Within such regional agglomerations, growth corridors, which cut across a geographical space, generate economic agglomeration. In recent years, corridor-based development, together with value-chain networks, have emerged as a new feature of networked growth paths for the regional development of a particular area through reducing the time and cost of a transaction. Economic corridors are seen as a "catalyst for regional integration" that generates the necessary push for inclusive growth in lagging regions (Yhome and Chaturvedy, 2017). The creation of economic corridors ensures that within a contiguous area, there is potential to attract investments and generate economic activity.

The emphasis on developing economic corridors is especially helpful for regions where the potential for industrial development exists but is underutilized. The primary prerequisites for developing economic corridors are strategizing and integrating infrastructural development in particular areas and then connecting these areas to adjoining ones. Transportation systems, which link the regions along such corridors, are capable of connecting and integrating the processes of infrastructural development to key sectors such as trade, investments, and other economic agencies. While development of economic corridors has advantages, there are also challenges associated, which include displacement and social conflict. Social impacts arising from displacement of people, political pressure groups, factor market rigidities, and conservatism often outweigh the economic gains and impede such corridor developments. One crucial issue that evades serious consideration in such corridor development under the garb of "social resistance" is the fact that corridor-linked developments involve large-scale environmental impact by the expansion of the transport network and industrial activities. Ecological and environmental concerns remain unaddressed in these projects developed in areas with ecological and environmental resources because the initial depletion is weighted to be negligible, given the overall economic gains flowing from such developments.

Corridor developments mostly cover regions, which are peripheral and somewhat removed from mainstream processes; the case of North-East India is perhaps one of the best examples. The region has often been derided for its slow pace of industrial development. Corridor development moves beyond setting up industries. The "corridors" shape cooperation in several areas, which include not only the industrial value-chain production system but also corridors in respect of tourism network, energy cooperation (both oil and power), and corridors for social connectedness as well. The opening of the 130-km "Friendship" pipeline connecting Siliguri in West Bengal and Parbatipur in the Dinajpur district of Bangladesh on 18 March 2023 seeks to integrate the energy cooperation between India and Bangladesh. This pipeline supplies refined diesel to Parbatipur depot from Numaligarh in Assam. Of the total stretch, 6 km of pipeline lies on the Indian side and the remaining 124 km is in Bangladesh. The pipeline has the capacity to transport 1 million metric tonnes per annum; initially, India will supply Bangladesh 2.5 lakh tonnes of diesel every year, and gradually it will be increased to 4 lakh tonnes. The project will replace the existing practice of sending diesel by rail covering a distance of 510 km, which will reduce cost and time in transportation and has less environmental impact. Hence, connectivity corridors function in different ways to integrate the social and economic spaces of two regions to create agglomeration of development outcomes, which primarily have both forwards and backwards linkages.

While connectivity may have started with roads and waterways, it also includes power grids and data corridors, education and tourism, energy flows, and cultural contacts. India's prospects of regional connectivity with the littoral countries in the Bay of Bengal (BoB) region (i.e. Bangladesh, Indonesia, Myanmar, Sri Lanka and Thailand, and the larger Indo-Pacific) have become a robust market for economic and non-economic partnerships. The region, after all, is home to approximately 60 per cent of the world population and some of the world's fastest-growing emerging market economies. While self-sufficiency within the domestic economy may be a distant goal, strengthening regional connectedness through corridor developments could contribute to self-reliance among clusters within a globalized framework.

Within the framework of regional development and cooperation in the NER, Assam stands as the connecting node. By improving connectivity and addressing the challenges for smooth commerce and investment, Assam's geostrategic location has made the state a launching pad for economic cooperation. It is uniquely positioned as a central hub in India's Act East Policy, strengthening its role in regional connectivity and economic integration due to its closeness to ASEAN, Bangladesh, Bhutan, India, and Nepal (BBIN), and BIMSTEC nations. Assam serves as the main link between the rest of India and the other Northeastern states and therefore plays a pivotal role in the region for enhancing connectivity, with Southeast Asian countries focusing on transport and communication, socio-cultural, and economic factors.

A Brief Outline of the Economy and Physiography of Assam

Assam is the largest state in the NER in terms of both physiographic diversity and the size of the economy. The physiography of the state comprises a mix of hills, plains, and large tracts of sand bars known as *chars*. The state can be broadly classified into three physiographic divisions, namely, the Brahmaputra valley; the Central Assam hills, comprising Mikir hill in Karbi Anglong and North Cachar hill districts; and the Barak valley, covering the southern part of the state. The Brahmaputra and the Barak are the two major river systems of the state, with a number of tributaries. The Brahmaputra valley is further divided into two banks—southern and northern. Also, the valley is divided into "upper" and "lower" sections with respect to the course of the River Brahmaputra. Based on the physiographic situatedness, Assam is divided into six agro-climatic zones comprising the North Bank Plain Zone, the Upper Brahmaputra Valley Zone, the Central Brahmaputra Valley Zone, the Lower Brahmaputra Valley Zone, the Barak Valley Zone, and the Hill Zone.

The climate of Assam is typically "tropical monsoon rainforest climate", with high levels of humidity and heavy rainfall. The state is prone to multiple hazards and experiences perennial floods, river-bank erosion, landslides, and other environmental catastrophes. The effects of these disasters result in tragic disturbances in the social and environmental sphere together with socio-economic impacts of extreme severity, such as high levels of material damage and the loss of life and means of subsistence for affected communities (OKDISCD, 2019). Just as floods are a perennial problem to the state, similarly the physical remoteness of the border areas limits the connectivity and economic opportunities of the people living in these areas. Besides, there are landmasses surrounded by the courses of the River Brahmaputra and its tributaries, known as the *chars*. These *chars* are, in fact, mid-channel bars, which are an integral part of the fluvial process of the River Brahmaputra and its tributaries in Assam (Assam Human Development Report, 2014). Since these formations are built under a flood environment, they are extremely unstable and, at times, are wiped out by erosion during recurrent floods. An intriguing feature of these *chars* is the in-migration and out-migration of people from these locations. As erosion is a perennial problem along the upstream of the Brahmaputra river, followed by deposition of sand and other particles at the downstream, often flooding and washing away the settlements during floods, the people living in these formations *(chars)* migrate downstream to newer areas.

The physiographic diversities, along with population diversities, create multiple challenges, and often these diversities—both spatial and demographic—overlap each other and create distinct effects on the lives, livelihood, and well-being of the people. Administratively, the state is divided into 31 districts and 219 blocks with 214 towns and 26,395 villages, 2,202 Gaon Panchayats (GPs) (village-level tier of the Panchayati Raj system), and 87 urban local bodies. As per the Ministry of Minority Affairs, 118 blocks across 17 districts in the state have been categorized as minority concentrated blocks. Apart from these demographic and spatial diversities, Assam is also characterized by diverse institutional arrangements of governance. The two hill districts of the state have autonomous district councils (ADCs) formed under the provisions of the Sixth Schedule to the Indian Constitution. Further, four districts (Kokrajhar,

Baksa, Chirang, and Udalguri) were grouped into Bodoland territorial autonomous districts (BTAD) and brought under the Bodoland Territorial Council (BTC) created through an amendment to the Sixth Schedule in 2003. Besides, there are six autonomous councils related to six communities, namely, Rabha-Hasong, Mising, Tiwa, Deori, Thengal Kachari, and Sonowal Kachari. These councils have been formed through state legislations. There are eighteen community-specific development councils created by the Government of Assam, whose primary objective is to work for the development of the specific communities. The diverse spatial, demographic, and institutional arrangements in the state have an important bearing upon the economy and livelihood of the people.

The state shares borders with six states of the region and two neighbouring countries, namely, Bangladesh and Bhutan. Given its geostrategic location, Assam is well poised to meet the import demand of neighbouring countries and the region with the development of its manufacturing capabilities, human resources, and infrastructure including logistics. The strategic regional corridors, such as the East–West corridor, Asian Highway 1, the South Asian Association for Regional Cooperation (SAARC) Rail Corridor 1, and the SAARC Rail Corridor 5, could be the connecting nodes for the state to integrate Assam as India's gateway to ASEAN and connect the Asian Development Bank into the regional networks of development and growth. Given the constraints of physical terrains, a decentralized approach to development for Assam holds the prospect for unleashing economic advantage to the state through three kinds of activity nodes: economic centres, manufacturing centres, and border centres (ADB, 2021). The approach exhibits a historical linkage, and the process creates the potential for supporting manufacturing and services activities coupled with urban development. The current pace of infrastructure and connectivity development in Assam, focusing on transport corridors (roads, waterways, railways, air) and energy corridors (petroleum and power) with its neighbouring states and bordering countries, places it at the perfect juncture to create the required impetus for corridor development. This, in turn, is expected to induce production activities in different sectors such as agro-processing and value addition; basic manufacturing; and service sectors such as tourism, health, and education. The unique diversities of the NER of India have always been projected as its biggest disadvantage. However, this could be augmented as the best strategic leverage for the region's development process with the launching of the Act East Policy based on the five Cs—Corridors for Culture, Commerce, Connectivity, and Capacity building—under the aegis of the "Act East Policy" launched in 2014, which replaced the old "Look East Policy".

The seven states of North-East India have been classified as Himalayan states while Assam is classified as a landlocked state of India along with Chattisgarh, Jharkhand, and Telengana. Over the period 2018–19 to 2021–22, Assam experienced an average annual growth rate of 6.17 per cent in its gross state domestic product (GSDP) at constant 2011–12 prices. This came about at a time when the economy was in the grip of the COVID-19 pandemic. During the same period, agriculture grew at a rate of 13.04 per cent, while the growth rates in the industry and service sector were 2.43 per cent and 4.48 per cent, respectively (DES, 2021–22). Assam's sectoral growth rate in terms of gross value added (GVA) during the period 2011–12 to 2021–22 (i.e. during the past decade) shows that the primary sector grew by nearly 9 per cent, while the secondary sector grew by 11.19 per cent (the highest among the three sectors). On the other hand, the tertiary sector recorded the lowest growth rate during the decade (5.44 per cent). For the primary sector, the leading subsector was mining and quarrying, while for the secondary sector it was electricity, gas, and water supply. The subsector of other services showed the highest growth during the decade. The overall growth of GVA in the state was 7.81 per cent (DES, 2022–23).

A comparison of Assam's sectoral contribution to GVA with that of India at constant prices during the period 2020–21 shows that while the share of the agricultural sector to India's GVA was about 16 per cent, for Assam it was 21.48 per cent. Manufacturing, electricity, gas, and construction had more or less similar figures for both India and Assam. However, when it came to financial services and real estate, in the case of India the share was a huge 23 per cent, while for Assam it was a mere 8 per cent. This low share also gets reflected in the low growth of the service (tertiary) sector of Assam during the past decade. The state therefore continues to lag behind in respect of the required finance capital for investments in the industry and manufacturing sector which, in turn, induces investment in the services sector.

Convergence for Mutual Gains: Assam, North-East India, and South and Southeast Asia

Given the existing macroeconomic scenario of the state, an attempt at convergence of activities with market potential and export potential can break through the sluggishness of growth in the state. A study on the export preparedness of Indian states by the Institute for Competitiveness[1] shows that Assam ranks twenty-first among the states in India. The report shows that Assam ranks fifteenth in respect of policy support for export and twenty-sixth in respect of export ecosystem. In terms of actual performance (i.e. export performance index), Assam stands twenty-fourth among the states of India, which indicates that there is need for strong policy back-up and the availability of a supportive export environment, and the state is yet to tap the potential for export opportunities existing in the state. This lag in performance is largely due to challenges faced in respect of infrastructure and services, namely, industrial corridors, industrial parks, industrial land and industrial clusters, access to finance, research and development support for innovation and regional agglomeration, and entrepreneurship within the region.

Assam currently exports tea to forty-four countries, automotive diesel to two countries, and coke and semi-coke to three countries. These three sectors have a historical past dating from the colonial times. Tea (plantation for export), jute (cash crop), petroleum, and coal were the major sectors set up by the British Colonial Administration in Assam, and except for jute, the other three sectors continue to be the major industries in the state. The horticulture is an emerging sector with great potential for meeting demand both domestically and in neighbouring countries in the region. Horticultural crops occupy about 15 per cent of the gross cultivated area of the state, with an annual production of more than 67 lakhs metric tonnes of various horticultural produce, which has huge export potential. Commercialization of the sector on a priority basis has been initiated by the state. Assam exported wicker works and agrarian products to the tune of Rupees (Rs) 4,000 crore during the fiscal year 2022–23, despite the absence of adequate export infrastructure in the state. According to the Federation of Indian Export Organizations (FIEO), an initiative undertaken by the Government of India, 70 per cent of the total exports in this sector from Assam are from five districts, namely, Karbi Anglong, Dima Hasao, Dhemaji, Sonitpur, and Udalguri. As per the data from the Agricultural and Processed Food Products Export Development Authority (APEDA), during last six years (2017–18 to 2022–23), exports from Assam have registered an 85 per cent growth. The export items of the state are bhoot jalakia (hot chilli pepper), pumpkin, jackfruit, litchi, pineapple, ginger, turmeric, joha rice, black rice, red rice, etc. There has also been a significant increase in demand for honey, spices, and pork from Assam from the Middle East, the United Kingdom, South East Asian countries, and Bangladesh. As observed in the APEDA report (APEDA, 2023), increase in organic farming industry in the state has created opportunities for Assam to meet the increased demand for such items abroad and emerge as a major supplier. A major issue that continues to impede the progress of organic cultivation of horticulture in Assam is the transport bottleneck as the state or the NER has no direct flights to the export destination countries. The items sent for export from Assam and the NER are air-lifted either to Kolkata or New Delhi, where they are attached with the label of the exporting agency. Apart from this, the region has no facility for certification of organic products. Such products have to be sent to Kolkata for testing and certification, which causes a delay in the process. There is a shortage of adequate vehicles with refrigeration facilities in the state, and this leads to the damage of perishable items. The structural bottlenecks of facility services stand as the biggest challenge to promoting these kinds of value-addition units, which otherwise have potential for growth.

Keeping the vision for expanding the export potential of goods and services, the Export and Logistic Policy of Assam, 2019, announced for a period of five years by the World Economic Forum on 1 November 2019, aims to boost exports where Assam has competitive advantage through increased market penetration besides exploring new markets for the products of Assam. The policy aims to enhance the ease of doing exports through the creation of simple, effective, and efficient institutional mechanisms, simplified processes, and efficient organization and coordination with stakeholders. Towards this end, investments for strengthening the export infrastructures of the state (such as inland container depots (ICDs), border trade centres, common facility centres, integrated cold chain, logistics parks, river ports and material handling facilities, air cargo facilities, quality testing labs, connectivity to ports, etc.) have been taken up. The state has also started investment in product-specific parks, for instance, tea parks, bamboo parks, food parks, pharmaceutical parks, plastic parks, etc. To facilitate the ease of export and ease of doing business, a slew of measures has been introduced to ensure supply and availability of quality power, high-speed internet facility, etc. at land customs stations (LCSs) and at other infrastructures being created for export and related logistical support. While logistic and infrastructure support is a necessary requirement, market demand for products and the economic viability of production is another aspect that needs to be identified in order to create convergence with the logistic and infrastructure support created.

The states of the NER are blessed with diverse energy resources; Assam and Tripura are rich in petroleum resources, Arunachal Pradesh has substantial hydro-power potential, Meghalaya has coal and uranium resources, Mizoram has rich biomass, and Sikkim also has hydro-power potential. Besides, these states also have solar power potential. The NER has opportunities to develop its available energy resources and trade with adjoining countries. Moreover, the advantages of economic integration among NER states and with neighbouring countries and regions stem from political and historical linkages, geographical proximity, socio-cultural commonalities, and economic complementarities. The main opportunities for cross-border trade of energy/electricity lie in hydropower and gas pipelines, in addition to pooling and the interconnection of electric power grids. Assam is poised to expand its market for energy cooperation with countries in the Asian sub-region. In the NER, there are two sedimentary basins, namely, the Upper Assam Shelf and the Assam-Arakan Basin. The Upper Assam Shelf basin covers the plains of Upper Assam and parts of Arunachal Pradesh, whereas the Assam-Arakan fold belt basin covers the hilly terrains of Assam, Arunachal Pradesh, Nagaland, Manipur, Mizoram, and Tripura. The Upper Assam shelf covers an approximate area of 56,000 sq. km, whereas the Assam-Arakan fold belt covers an area of 60,000 sq. km. The basin is well explored (to the tune of 90 per cent), and current production of oil and gas is mainly from here. The Assam-Arakan fold belt is a well-established gas province. Only about 10 per cent of the total area of the Assam-Arakan fold belt has been explored. The major part of the Assam-Arakan fold belt falls between the prolific hydrocarbon-producing regions of Bangladesh and Myanmar. There are sizable economic, environmental, and social benefits to be gained from greater energy connectivity between the NER, its South Asian neighbours, and Myanmar. India's electricity grid is already connected to Bangladesh's grid, and Bangladesh is planning to link its grid with that of Myanmar. As countries recognize the multiple benefits of interconnectivity, significant discussions have arisen over potential energy-sector development needs and electricity potential in North-East India, with a Myanmar–Bangladesh–India natural gas pipeline. These agreements form important milestones in the Union government's Hydrocarbon Vision 2030 for North-East India, which seeks to leverage the region's hydrocarbon potential for enhancing access to clean fuel in line with the NER's growing demand for petroleum products and also to underline Numaligarh Refinery Limited's (NRL) key role in ushering in the socio-economic development of the region.

Although Assam remains the major connecting hub in the NER, with Guwahati as the entry point, there are other centres across the state (such as Nagaon, Jorhat, Dibrugarh, Guwahati, Tinsukia, and Dhubri) that are fast emerging as economic nodes for secondary (manufacturing), tertiary (services), or quaternary (management, research, education) functions of economic significance (De et al., 2018). Traditional exports from Assam such as tea and petroleum products have been historically located in the districts of Upper Assam. Corridor developments within the ambit of sub-regional cooperation could augment export markets for value chain in goods production besides energy and power supply networks. The development of corridors like the Trilateral Highway and BCIM Economic Corridor (BCIM-EC) would provide gains to the economy of the states of North-East India (De et al., 2018). It is well known that gross domestic product (GDP) and road density are the two important determinants of freight flow, and for every 1 per cent increase in GDP, total freight in the region is expected to increase by 0.5 per cent over time (De et al., 2018). The positive relationship between road density and freight implies that the higher the road density, the higher would be the flow of freight between and within the states. The benefits of such advantage could be augmented in two ways: (i) through cheaper imports and (ii) by expanding the basket of export items in so far as trade in goods and services are concerned.

To cite an example, agriculture engages almost 70 per cent of the workforce of Assam, yet the state has a deficit in the production of pulses and depends on imports from North-West India, which have high transport costs. At the same time that Myanmar is traditionally an exporter of pulses and rice, the freight movement through corridors would have less transaction cost and would be cost effective to import these items from Myanmar. Besides, the state could import at a much cheaper rate other essential vegetables (such as onions and potatoes from Myanmar) rather than procuring the same from elsewhere in North-West India. Coal, tea, limestone, and other minerals form the key export-based commodities from Assam. Most of the exports (with tea as an exception) are to countries such as Bangladesh, Myanmar, Bhutan, and Nepal. A study by the Federation of Indian Chambers of Commerce and Industry (FICCI) on the "Gateway to the ASEAN: India's North-East Frontier" (FICCI 2014) identified that there are strong prospects for developing the export potential of the state in edible fruits and nuts, apparels, beverages, lime and cement, fish and aquatic products, salt, and stone. There is high potential as the primary demand for such products exists in the neighbouring countries, which at present are met by other states from India (Choudhury, 2018). The industries for these items, if located in the industrial parks being developed in the state, would have a high logistic cost advantage in boosting trans-regional export. Besides, the value-chain network between the states of North-East India can be developed by exporting semi-finished and finished products rather than exporting raw materials (Choudhury, 2018).

Assam has a strategically advantageous position, given its proximity to BBIN and ASEAN countries, which account for approximately 10 per cent of the total plastic exports of India. Currently, thirty-one industrial units are engaged in the manufacturing of plastic products, with annual installed capacity of 320,000 metric tonnes (Mt). The necessary feed stock for the plastic industry is available from Brahmaputra Crackers and Polymers Limited (BCPL), located near Dibrugarh. A plastic park at Tinsukia, with present allocable area of 4,80,000 sq. m, provides a key zone for investments into the plastics manufacturing sector. The state, with large proportion of educated youths, provides a reservoir of workforce but with low skill and employability. The Indo-Japan collaboration has focused on skill training in the state by dovetailing with the current programme of the National Skill Development Mission. This skill enhancement through requisite training could provide the necessary manpower requirement of the sector and leverage its export potential.

The automotive industry is one of the fastest-growing markets in Southeast Asian countries, with diversified production plants across India. Skill augmenting, together with the relocation of some of the production units to Assam, is poised to bring dividends across the region, with low labour cost and lower logistics cost of transportation, etc. due to the geographical proximity of the production market and demand market. As connectivity and infrastructure remains the major thrust and has seen rapid progress, with a focus on multi-modal transportation, the relocation of production units in automotive industries and their export to Southeast Asia will have lower transaction cost in years to come and would address the problem of employment opportunities in the state and the region at large. Another key area emerging for the expansion of regional connectivity for Assam is the service sector in respect of higher education, health care, and tourism. The demand for accessing higher education at institutions in India from students of South and Southeast Asia is fairly high. State-owned higher educational institutions and opening up of private investments in higher education could leverage the strategic location of the state to develop it into a strong educational hub in the sub-region. The institutions of higher education could create both forwards and backwards linkages. The establishment of a higher education institution not only creates jobs but also promotes economic activities, directly as well as indirectly. Many towns in the southern states of India have grown as educational hubs, creating demand for various goods and services, including basic food, housing, transport facilities, financial services, medical services, etc. Some of the higher education institutions that have global reach have been successful in creating a competitive environment that has produced some of the best contributors in science and technology, finance and businesses, entertainment, and politics, who have furthered the developmental agenda of these states. Assam, which has some of the best state-funded institutions, could emulate the southern states in creating the necessary environment for investment in higher education, focused on growing demands for the same in the sub-region. Medical tourism is an upcoming area of focus wherein the government in the state of Assam has been investing in its tertiary health-care services. The sector is expected to address the demand for health-care services not only among the states of the region but also across the neighbouring countries. Integrated cultural and religious circuitous tourism is being promoted by the state government as an effort to bridge the cultural connectivity of the state with neighbouring countries.

The Natural Allies in Development and Interdependence (NADI)[2] is a step towards people-to-people connectivity (focusing on the importance of ease of living) and ease of doing business (focusing on local strengths), which also allies with the priority of the Government of India. As emphasized by external affairs minister of India, S. Jaishankar, that coming together of the "Act East Policy" and the "Neighbourhood First Policy" has an enormous reinforcing impact, extending beyond South Asia. Important initiatives such as (i) the restoration of historical cross-border rail links;[3] (ii) movement of goods through twenty-eight notified LCSs and three integrated check posts (ICPs) along the border; (iii) negotiations to operationalize the BBIN Motor Vehicle Agreement to ensure seamless vehicular movement; (iv) Indian road projects in Bangladesh, namely, Ashuganj River Port–Akhaura Land Port Road; and (v) agreements on movement of goods from Indian ports through Chittagong and Mongla ports in Bangladesh and from there overland to Tripura and other parts of the North-East are steps to create corridors of development across the sub-region.

The Indo-Pacific cooperation is yet another step to boost regional cooperation and has seen rising Japanese investment in India, with special focus on the NER. One cannot deny the deep-rooted historical connections between Japan and the NER and its engagement with the Indian National Army (INA) during the Second World War. Several recent developments in Indo-Japan[4] relations have underlined the increasing convergence of interests between the two.[5] It was during the first summit-level meeting in 2014 between India's Prime Minister Narendra Modi and Japanese Prime Minister late Shinzo Abe that emphasis was placed on the importance of the NER. The Tokyo Declaration, which they released after that meeting, underscored Japan's commitment to enhancing connectivity and development in the NER. Towards this end, India and Japan established the Act East Forum (AEF) in 2017 (i) for the development of the NER and (ii) to promote connectivity within the region and between this region and Southeast Asia. The AEF is the convergence point between India's Act East Policy and Japan's vision for a free and open

Indo-Pacific. The NER, which stands as the major land bridge of India to Southeast Asia has received a major thrust for the economic advancement of the region, with focus on connectivity projects, disaster management, and environment and people-to-people contacts through tourism and culture. Japan's deepening involvement—not only in networked corridors of connectivity but also in many other spheres, including energy, water supply, health, irrigation, environment, and people-to-people exchanges—has leveraged the Indian government because the investment for infrastructure in the NER has lagged behind and Japanese loan assistance, at negligible rates of interest, is expected to bridge the North-East gap at a much lesser cost to the Indian government vis-a-vis the government's own investment or assistance from other development agencies. There are also strategic dimensions to Japan's engagement in infrastructure and soft-power diplomacy in the NER. Both India and Japan have kept away from the China-led Belt and Road Initiative (BRI), which is a major Chinese initiative in funding infrastructure development in the countries of Southeast Asia. Japan's Free and Open Indo-Pacific Vision aims to ensure that all countries work together to keep the trade routes in the Indo-Pacific free for all, and in this respect, Japan has made substantial investments in Myanmar and Bangladesh. India's North-East provides the missing link to reconnect the old corridors in the region and expand the network in the Pacific region. While development of infrastructure corridors is a major part of Japan's investment in the NER, strengthening local resource-based production such as the bamboo value chain, food processing (including tea industries), organic farming, and horticulture are other areas covered under Japan's support to the region. The cherry blossom festival, a regular autumn festival held now in Meghalaya, is a major soft-power engagement by Japan, which has seen increasing Japanese presence through cultural programmes and cuisines with an eye on promoting tourism.

In lieu of a Conclusion

Regional cooperation and corridor developments have long-term dividends, though gestation periods for such investments are a little longer as most of the corridor developments are focused on regions that are peripheral from the mainland production hubs and export and import nodes of the participating countries. The NER is one of the "earth's greatest highland zones, nourishing its own complexities of race and culture, and exhibiting its own internal environmental contrasts" (Kangjam and Katoch, 2021). India's Northeastern frontier forms part of a larger "Inner Asia" or "Asian space" defined by mountains, slopes, and valleys (Ludden, 2004; Kirk, 1962). India inherited the imperial boundaries along with its territorial administrative rules. Since the 1960s, the China and Pakistan aggression on western borders and boundary disputes at the Northeastern border, coupled with "insurgent movements", left India obsessed with security interests to ensure the anachronistic survival of its internal territorial boundaries fashioned by colonial concerns. Colonial cartography has left its indelible imprint on the traditional channels of human movement and cross-border connections along Asian borderlands (Ludden, 2004). In the current globalized space, it is imperative that these natural corridors be opened beyond national geographies. The states in North-East India need an integrated cooperative model of regional cooperation, developing a unified common market and an integrated complementary production hub. As individual units, the states of the NER are economically weak to wrest their bargaining power in the large cauldron of regional cooperation. Cross-border connectivity initiatives often tend to be undermined by the importance of territorial integrity, particularly when there are border disputes between neighbouring nations. Further, within nations, these efforts are also not always appreciated as engagement of local people in these processes remains limited and the initiatives are mostly top down and largely shaped by the corporate and political gains of participating nations. Nevertheless, a unified common structure addressing the institutional and political arrangements in the region over resource use and the ecological setting of the region could be one step towards augmenting the region's growth potential, based on its own complementarity, allowing it to move beyond the borders of the region.

Notes

1. The Export Preparedness Index (EPI) 2022 is prepared by the National Institute for Transforming India (NITI Ayog) and the Institute for Competitiveness. The

report shows that there has been a decrease in the number of exporters from Assam during the period from 2021 to 2022 from 890 to 335. The trade support system in Assam is yet to kick start with trader exporter interaction, and this remains the biggest challenge.

2. NADI is an initiative under Asian Confluence (https://www.asianconfluence.org) to integrate, converge, and connect ideas, experts, practitioners, and relevant stakeholders from various disciplines dealing with the ecosystem of water, agriculture, livelihood, inland waterways, trade, connectivity, and tourism for a better understanding of the region and to influence policy changes and factor in the sustainability aspect.
3. The Shahabazpur (Bangladesh)–Mahishasan (Assam) rail link, Agartala (India)–Akhaura (Bangladcsh) rail link, Chilahati (Bangladeh)–Haldibari (India) once provided connectivity to Assam to access the Chittagong sea port of East Bengal in the pre Partition days.
4. Japan's investment in promoting global quality infrastructure is embedded in five principles: (i) effective mobilization of financial resources through public–private partnerships; (ii) alignment with development strategies of emerging economies; (iii) maintaining high-quality rules for environmental and social standards; (iv) ensuring quality infrastructure by way of economic efficiency, low life-cycle cost, inclusiveness, resilience, and sustainability; and (v) contribution to the local economy (Ministry of Foreign Affairs, 2015).
5. Japan's policy of infrastructure export aligns perfectly with the Government of India's "Make in India" policy. Japanese Official Development Assistance (ODA) has been providing assistance in enhancing quality infrastructure and modernizing connectivity within India and beyond.

References

APEDA (Agricultural and Processed Food Products Export Development Authority) (2023), "Report, 2023", (https://agriexchange.apeda.gov.in/news/Newssearch.aspx?newsid=48599&Date_28Feb2023).

ADB (Asian Development Bank) (2021), "Assam as India's Gateway to ASEAN", March (https://www.adb.org/sites/default/files/publication/684951/assam-india-gateway-asean.pdf).

Assam Human Development Report (2014), "Assam", 9 March (https://www.undp.org/india/publications/assam).

Choudhury, Saswati (2017), "Northeast India and the Act East Policy: Opportunities and Challenges", *Dialogue* 18 (3) (January–March).

Choudhury, Saswati (2018), "Locating Northeast India in the Look (Act) East Policy of India", in Atul Sarma and Saswati Choudhury (eds), *Mainstreaming the Northeast India in India's Look and Act East Policy*, Singapore: Springer Nature, pp. 301–22.

David, Vumlallian Zou and M. Satish Kumar (2011), "Mapping a Colonial Borderland: Objectifying the Geo-body of India's Northeast", *Journal of Asian Studies*, 70 (1), pp. 141–70.

De, Prabir, Sunetra Ghatak, and Durairaj Kumarasamy (2018), "Assessing Economic Impacts of Connectivity Corridors: An Empirical Investigation", Research and Information System for Developing Countries (RIS) and the Association of Southeast Asian Nations (ASEAN)–India Centre, New Delhi (https://aseanindiacentre.org.in/sites/default/files/Publication/Assessing%20Economic%20Impacts%20of%20Connectivity%20Corridors_Report-5%20July-min_0.pdf).

DES (Directorate of Economics and Statistics) (2021–22), "Economic Survey of Assam, 2021–22", Government of Assam.

DES (Directorate of Economics and Statistics) (2022–23), "Economic Survey of Assam, 2022–23", Government of Assam.

FICCI (Federation of Indian Chambers of Commerce and Industry) and PwC (PricewaterhouseCoopers) (2014), "Gateway to the ASEAN: India's North East Frontier", 27 November (https://www.pwc.in/assets/pdfs/publications/2014/gateway-to-the-asean.pdf).

Government of Assam (2019), "The Export and Logistic Policy of Assam" (https://eodb.assam.gov.in/storage/documents/export_and_logistic_policy_of_assam_2019.pdf).

Kangjam, Yaiphaba Meetei and Hemant Singh Katoch (2021), "Northeast India, World War II and Japan: Past, Present and Future", in Mayumi Murayama, Sanjoy Hazarika, and Preeti Gill (eds), *Northeast India and Japan: Engagement through Connectivity*, Abingdon and New York: Routledge, pp. 238–54.

Kirk, W. (1962), "The Inner Asian Frontier of India", *Wiley on Behalf of the Royal Geographical Society (with the Institute of British Geographers)*, 13 (December), pp. 131–68.

Ludden, David (2004), "Where Is Assam? Using Geographical History to Locate Current Social Realities", Omeo Kumar Das (OKD) Institute of Social Change and Development, Guwahati, Centre for Northeast India, South and Southeast Asia Studies Paper No. 1.

Ministry of Foreign Affairs (2015), "Quality Infrastructure Investment Case Book", Government of Japan, September.

OKDISC (Omeo Kumar Das Institute of Social Change and Development) (2019), "Work and Well-Being in Rural Assam", Guwahati, mimeo.

Yhome, K. and R.R. Chaturvedy (2017), "Emerging Trans-Regional Corridors: South and Southeast Asia", London: Global Policy and Observer Research Foundation.

5

Trade-Led Development for North-East India

Lessons from Manipur

Ch. Priyoranjan Singh

Introduction

There has been an air of unmistakable vibrancy and expectation in the growth and development of India's Northeastern Region (Guha, 2016).[1] During the past few decades, political stability had emerged in most of the states, and the people of the region had also begun to share in India's recent economic resurgence, however tiny a measure. Slowly but unmistakably, the people of the region were steadily emerging out of their self-imposed isolationist and identity-conscious mindsets and participating in the vast economic and non-economic opportunities that the new India of the post-1990s was offering, within the region and across the country (Verghese, 2004).[2] In the first two decades, few job opportunities within the region led to a massive migration of educated and skilled youths into the metropolis of mainland India, mainly in the lower-paid service sector but also, significantly, into engineering, management, health, tourism, and academia. On the other hand, in the past two decades or so, there has also been some perceptible return migration into the region or their own states, establishing enterprises in various professions, mainly in cities and small townships (Krishna, 2016). The new generation had begun to realize that entrepreneurship in their region could be more remunerative than elsewhere, and in fact, it could be more welfare-maximizing. More importantly, back in the farm sector, neo-ideologies had also begun to

Ch. Priyoranjan Singh, *Trade-Led Development for North-East India* In: *Sub-Regional Cooperation for Trade, Investment, and Employment in North-East India*. Edited by: Ashish Nath, Oxford University Press.
 DOI: 10.1093/9780197908938.003.0005

take a grip in the North-East, veritably starting a new green revolution in the region (Singh and Sharma, 2013).[3] The bubble, however, seems to be bursting, as often happens, when efficiency and competitive spirits are least nurtured, when the facilitating hands and programmes of the state are directed more towards political ends, when institutions are not built or misused, and when a vent for surpluses is not found through trade.

At Land's End and of Serious Intent

The Northeastern Region (NER) of India has a unique history of formations, peopling, economic geography, and colonial heritage, which have given rise to peculiar social and political development. The original settlers of the pre-colonial period were of Tibeto-Burman and Southeast Asia origins, who had fled from the state in search of autonomy and escaped from the identity-crushing projects of state-building processes in Southeast Asia. James Scot wrote about the "*Zomia*", spread across Vietnam to North-East India and Yunnan. His view was that the "*Zomia* is the largest remaining region of the world where peoples have not yet been fully incorporated into nation states. Its days are numbered" (Scott, 2009).

In the colonial era, the British Empire took over the monarchies of the Ahoms of Assam, the Manipuries in Manipur, and the Tripuris of Tripura. Lucrative colonial extraction of tea, oil, and timber trade from the great Brahmaputra valley of Assam and the concomitant development of waterways and railways to Calcutta and Chittagong in the Bay of Bengal led to the wide opening of the North-East. Massive sub-planting of tea garden labour from Eastern India and agriculturists from Bengal led to demographic upheavals in the Cachar and Assam valleys. The hill regions around the Barrak and Brahmaputra valleys were the abodes of myriad tribes, classified by the British as "excluded" and "partially excluded" tribes, mainly to keep them at arm's length and prevent parasitic raids on the colonial flow of extractive trade and commerce enterprises and because administering these areas would be of no pecuniary benefit to the Empire (Das, 2013). The British officialized umbrella names for large groups of cognate tribes such as Nagas, Kukis, and Lushais in the Naga and Lushai range of mountains for administrative purposes.

All these political machinations of the colonial administration in the North-East ultimately led to deep-seated identity politics and the dismemberment of Assam into the new states of Nagaland, Mizoram, and Meghalaya (Baruah, 2005).[4] Identity politics still festers and threatens the enabling strides the North-East has made in recent decades in economic development and growth. The first serious enabling strides for the development of the North-East were taken after the visit of the then prime minister, H.D. Devi Gowda to Gauhati on 27 October 1996 (Gowda, 1996).

The Prime Minister endorsed the feeling of stepmotherly treatment of the region and foreign migrants impinging on the identity of the people of the North-East. He also announced a sizeable economic package for the region. However, he emphasized how inward-looking, militant, and terrorism-inflicted states were shunned by investors and openly called for dialogue without any precondition. However, the landmark announcement of the visit was the appointment of a high-level commission to submit a report on infrastructure gaps and basic minimum services backlogs in the region. Thus, what was popularly called the Shukla Commission Report on "Transforming the Northeast: Tackling Backlogs in Basic Minimum Services and Infrastructural Needs" was born.

The Shukla Commission writes that the report is "seen as indicative of serious intent to bring the North-East on par with the rest of the country, within the next five to ten years, in a process of poverty alleviation and infrastructural upgradation" (Government of India, 1997). The structural context of the regional economy was defined as low-productivity agriculture with primitive industries, with little revenue and heavy budgetary deficits, resulting in low entrepreneurial skills and low agricultural surplus and capital accumulation. These structural weaknesses are mainly blamed on the trauma of Partition and its impact on transport, connectivity, and trade, which has "not been appreciated or compensated". In some way, the report also highlights the reorganization of non-viable ethnic states with high establishment costs and incomplete transitions from traditional to modern institutions. On the other hand, the report emphasizes the region's rich resources, which could be gainfully turned into exports on the "historical land bridge" to Southeast Asia. Giving hints into the nascent Look East Policy (LEP) and the Indo-Myanmar

Border Trade Agreement, the Report gave a clarion call to the North-East to take the national responsibility of opening traditional trade and transit routes and markets into Southeast Asia. Therefore, trade-led growth and development have been a core strategy for transforming the North-East since "serious intents" were shown in the Government of India policy documents.

The widely popular and often quoted report ends with a "FINALE" with the terse ending, "The youths of the Northeast need an alternative to the gun" (Government of India 1997). A plea was also made that the Planning Commission might make a special effort to prepare and project a perspective plan that offers a future vision. Thus, the "Northeast Vision 20–20" (Government of India, 1997) was born.

The Northeast Vision document was a more detailed strategic and implementation flow chart for development, based on the Shukla Commission Report and its brief but starkly situational analysis, an endearing critique of the national neglect and regional self-inflicted developmental regression. Top-down planning and non-local, resource-based development were pointed out as a factor of underdevelopment. The political economy of insurgency and central government funds dependency cultures and the emergence of rent-seeking and free-riding social and political value systems, arising out of perverse incentives, were also more explicitly mentioned as factors of underdevelopment (National Institute of Public Finance and Policy, 2007). The positive note was the assessment that the people were tired of identity politics and insurgency and yearned for peace, development, and globalization. The new strategy was brief and stressed (i) participatory planning, (ii) capacity building, (iii) adequate infrastructures and connectivity, (iv) adequate resources for development, and (v) administrative reforms.

This strategy represented a double-edged sword: the North-East could grow at its own pace, for better or worse, by planning independently while the centre took care of funds, infrastructures, and administrative reforms. In some way washing its hands off the development software, the centre was centralizing development and taking the developmental hardware into its own hands. The massive injection of funds and rapid expansion of infrastructures and connectivity have led to fast-paced social and economic transformations in insurgency-prone states such as Assam, Tripura, Meghalaya, and Sikkim. At the same time, the rest of the states are either growing much below potential or stagnating.

Pulled up by growth and development in the critical state of Assam, the industrial and agricultural growth for the region is higher than the national average. In the pre-COVID-19 pandemic period (pre-2020), agriculture grew at a healthy 4.1 per cent and manufacturing at 3 per cent against negative growth in agriculture and 1 per cent growth in manufacturing for India. Across the region, capital accumulation is taking place in the hands of the locals, legitimate or illegitimate, and private investments are rising; in fact, multinational Indian and offshore companies are now roosting in Assam, Meghalaya, and Sikkim. Large-scale industries such as "minerals, cement, pharmaceuticals, brewery, cosmetics, electrical, steel, building materials, and consumer goods" have set foot in these progressive states (Singh, 2019). However, the region is stuck in a low-level equilibrium trap, despite massive agricultural surpluses and nascent manufacturing and service-sector growth. The reason partly lies in the failure of the stated export-led growth strategy so brashly publicized under the LEP and the present Act East Policy (AEP) and the resigned strategy of the "growing at its own pace" paradigm of Vision 20–20.

State governments of the region, still unable to shed the dependency syndrome of the past, have not been able to generate the required ecosystems of higher-order cross-border trading cultures and cultures of producing for and trading with external markets. On the other hand, with the strategy of hand-holding only, and not aggressive leadership in land-based trade for the North-East in Southeast Asia, whatever was gained through the Indo-Myanmar Border Trade Agreement (BTA) has recently been allowed to crumble at the gates in Manipur and Mizoram. Bangladesh is the only focus of India's and North-East India's economic integration with Southeast Asia on the land route under the AEP, and this is turning out to be a great embarrassment to the Indian government. Paradigms of trade-led growth and development for the North-East, and how they are made to fail, are lessons that can be learnt from Manipur.

The Beginning and End of Land Route Trade with Myanmar

India has a chequered history of economic and cultural relations with the Southeast Asian region. Historically, a secondary Silk Route originating in Sichuan in the Yunnan province of China passed through the Irrawaddy and Brahmaputra plains and into the Gangetic plains of India and beyond. Another secondary route passed through Tamu in Myanmar (formerly Burma) and Moreh in Manipur, through which trade in the much-in-demand Manipuri silk and other products found markets in China and Indo-China. The first accurate economic and cultural exchange between the two regions occurred in the third century BC when Emperor Ashoka sent two Buddhist monks to Burma (Singh, 2011). By the fifth century AD, mutual engagements had encompassed a wide field of trade, commerce, religion, law, political philosophy, and culture. A brisk trade was firmly established in the Bengal–Arakan region during the Mughal era, compelling Aurangzeb to extend the empire to Chittagong and take control of the rising opportunities. Britain saw the trade opportunity early, and trade negotiations had started with Ava as early as 1618. Britain's desire for trade sparked a series of wars with Myanmar throughout the 1800s. These conflicts ultimately led to Burma and North-East India coming under British control by the late 1800s.

Complete control of the Burmese economy and financial and commercial business was achieved by the organized migration of Indian bankers, money lenders, merchants, and agriculturists. Some 80 per cent of Burma's rice product was estimated to have been exported to India and Yunnan. Burmese nationalists saw the mainland Indian migrants as partners to the British in colonial extraction activities, and the communal riots of 1931 and 1938 were clear signs of deep-rooted anti-Indian feelings among the Burmese population. The immediate post-Independence civilian government of U Nu made some drastic socio-economic and political decisions for economic reconstruction and minority integration into the Burmese mainstream (Singh, 2011). Cultural assimilation of minorities through conversion into Buddhism, nationalization of land, and forbidding land sale to non-Burmese led to minority uprisings and the exodus of Indians from Burma. Consequent rising internal political problems and an exodus of Indian traders led to the collapse of the Burmese economy and military rule in 1962.

Nationalization of the economy hit the Indians the hardest as they held a significant share in the trade flow in Mandalay, Rangoon, and the Bay of Bengal. It also suited the Burmese government as anti-Indian sentiments had been greatly nurtured during the colonial days. There was a second exodus of Indians in 1983, reducing their population to merely four lakhs from over a million in the pre-war period. Despite the strained relations, in the aftermath of the *Burmanization*[5] (Htoo and Waters, 2024) and nationalization, policies in Burma, and post-Cold War global realignments, India and Burma entered into dialogues because of the compulsion of insurgency in North-East India and Northern Burma, which impinged on the vital strategic national interests of security, trade, economic welfare, and political stability.

India's LEP and enacting the Indo-Myanmar BTA in 1994 was a strategic and national security policy that both countries badly needed. Killing two birds with one stone, as it were, was the textbook dream strategy of the two countries in addressing their twin vexing problems of insurgency and economic development in their most backward and long-neglected regions. In a classic case of "the spirit is willing, but the body is weak"—lack of political will, policy paralysis, institutional failures, and weak people's response on both sides of the border—India's LEP and AEP on the land route came a cropper after initial spurts of visible growth momentum.

The Indo-Myanmar BTA failed mainly because of its structural flaws and the lack of sincere and sustained commitments of the Governments of India and Myanmar to the spirit and letter of the Agreement (Singh, 2011). The BTA allowed traders on both sides of the border to trade at the land customs stations (LCS) at Moreh (India) and Tamu (Myanmar). The three trading regimes were traditional exchange, barter trade, and regular trade.

Traditional exchanges of up to USD 1,000 were headload trades without guaranteed remittance (GR)[6] formalities between people living within 40 km on both sides of the border. Barter trade was trade up to USD 20,000, with GR formalities on the agreed-upon list of tradable goods. Normal trade was regular under the letter of credit system as per EXIM Policy guidelines. The agreed list of tradable items started with twenty-two and was raised to sixty-two. A concessional duty of 5 per cent was charged, but a trader had to balance imports and exports within six months for barter trade and within a day or two for traditional exchange. The traders were penalized if the trade balance was not achieved within the stipulated time.

In the first two decades of barter trade (from 1995–96 to 2014–15), the defining feature of Indo-Myanmar border trade at the Moreh–Tamu LCS corridor was the unpredictable and erratic volumes of formal trade. Formal trade at the Moreh LCS was below USD 10 million in eight years, exceeding USD 40 million in only five years and for the rest of the seven years between USD 10 and USD 40 million. The lowest trade was USD 2.36 million in 2008–09, and the highest was USD 63.91 million in 2006–07. In the twenty years of barter trade, India had a favourable trade balance in twelve years, compared to eight years for Myanmar. India's total exports to Myanmar were USD 221.57 million, and its imports were USD 217.75 million.

The commodities of formal exports from India consisted mainly of cumin seeds, soybean meals, wheat flour, cotton yarn, auto parts, and pharmaceuticals. Imports mainly consisted of betel nut, dry ginger, beans, turmeric roots, resin, and medicinal herbs.

There was, however, a parallel flow of informal trade under the traditional exchange/headload trade mechanism, without formal documentation, at what is known as Gate No. 2. Beyond Gate No. 2 lies the Namphalong Market on the Myanmar side, and streams of headloads of commodities from the market are ferried by Indian casual labour throughout the day during permitted hours. The LCS does not account for these trade inflows from Myanmar, does not collect duties, and only checks for contraband items. Whatever informal duties are collected are mainly pocketed by unscrupulous officials. A survey report of the Government of Manipur, 2011, estimated the informal imports alone at rupees (Rs) 865.14 crore, roughly double the LCS's highest total trade records.

Traded goods under informal trade were varied and diverse. Of the total Indian imports from Myanmar, clothes and footwear accounted for 56 per cent, agricultural products 14 per cent, groceries 13 per cent, electronics and utensils 10 per cent, wood and furniture 5.19 per cent, and plastics 1.59 per cent. "Imports included cereals, fruits, vegetables, aqua products, spices, packaged agro-horticulture products, timber and furniture, clothes and footwear, electronics and utensils" (RIS, 2021).

Indian exports into Myanmar included "processed and unprocessed agricultural commodities, household groceries, textiles, cosmetic and toiletries, pharmaceuticals, construction materials, hardware, transport vehicles and spares" (RIS, 2021). These commodities did not flow through Gate No. 2; they flowed through the unfenced border, mainly at night, bypassing the formal LCS and evading customs duty. These clandestine after-dark informal export transactions could not be captured from Imphal to Moreh or Moreh to Tamu in Myanmar.

The booming informal trade, in contrast to the overall decline in formal barter trade, were all clear indicators of the failure of Indo-Myanmar border trade to take off at the formal level due to a complex of structural, institutional, and trade-related impediments that were either inherent in the Indo-Myanmar Trade Agreement itself or created by various stakeholders of border trade at the Moreh–Tamu land route. That the Government of India unilaterally withdrew the 1995 agreement in 2015 speaks for itself (Singh, 2020).

Regular trade regimes were implemented at the Moreh–Tamu LCS, and trade data from the Myanmar customs revealed how the composition and volume of trade had drastically changed according to Myanmar records, in stark contrast to the Indian customs records on the other side. After introducing normal trade at Moreh in 2015, Indian exports had fallen from a mere USD 2.91 million in 2015–16 to USD 0.43 million in 2018–19. Imports had fallen from USD 15.85 million to zero during the same period. Total trade had thus plummeted from USD 18.76 million to USD 0.43 million during 2015–16 and the pre-pandemic year of 2018–19, after which the borders were closed.

On the other hand, Myanmar customs data show an overall trade volume rise of 70 per cent during 2015–16 and 2018–19 (seven months of data only). Exports had doubled from USD 49.65 million to USD 100.49 million, but imports had decreased by 27 per cent, from USD 16.35 million to USD 11.94 million. Myanmar's positive trade balance rose from 33.29 per cent to 88.55 per cent during the same period.

Trade data available at Moreh LCS and Tamu LCS show that total trade was recorded at USD 41.09 million in 2015–16 at Tamu against USD 18.76 million at Moreh. In 2018–19, Tamu recorded USD 89.92 million against USD 0.43 million at Moreh. Thus, Indian trade records were only 46 per cent and 0.47 per cent of those recorded at Tamu in Myanmar in the two years. These huge accounting differences are indicators of how Myanmar's understanding of the complexity of international trade, its management, and rule-based transactions and required institutions are still primitive and that India and cross-border trading stations like

Manipur are burdened by frustrating impediments to trade development that will take some time to turn into better facilitating environments. Under these circumstances, informal trade will likely rule the roost in Indo-Myanmar trade transactions for quite some time.

Myanmar customs record every commodity that passes through the Indo-Myanmar borders as exports and imports, irrespective of whether it is in the agreed lists of tradable commodities, of whether it is of foreign origin or their own, or whether it meets sanitary and phytosanitary standards, leaving the Indian counterparts at Moreh exasperated or traders bypassing the LCS for good and avoiding duties that should have accrued to the Government of India. Undoubtedly, it is understandable that the Government of India threw up its arms at the failed BTA, threw it away, and imposed normal trade. The tragedy is that, as the Indian side is not imposing or enforcing its own trade rules, Myanmar goes on merrily, importing and exporting commodities at the borders at high growth rates, serving the purpose of all vested interests in the vast illegal cross-border trade. For the North-East, Mizoram, and Manipur, the question is what possible roles they can play in removing hurdles to formalizing Indo-Myanmar trade and what are the central government's responsibilities for pro-active interventions in the region, as well as in Myanmar and the Association of Southeast Asian Nations (ASEAN), to ensure that the North-East is the pivot in India's AEP.

India's foreign trade policy on the land route to Southeast Asia under the Indo-Myanmar BTA failed because of (i) structural flaws in the agreement, (ii) failure to provide the necessary infrastructures on both sides of the border for formal trade facilitation, (iii) traders' preference for informal trade in demanded commodities in the face of high transaction costs of trading in the few listed goods under the BTA, and (iv) lack of political will in both countries for timely course correction in any aberration impacting the desired outcomes of the BTA.

In the first place, traders had to be both exporters and importers and balance their trade quickly, failing which severe penalties had to be faced. Second, banks' failure to provide and institutionalize letters of credit and other financial and currency trading mechanisms on both sides of the border was the most significant disincentive to formal barter trade. Small-time and petty traders, who formed the bulk of the traders, resorted to traditional headload trade, where transaction costs were much lower and no tradable list practically existed. The first two tradable items lists were mainly agricultural commodities and were mismatched with the demand on both sides of the border. The third list included the most traded goods, but the list came out too late because of bureaucratic logjams and needed to be made functional at the LCS. By the time the fourth list had reached the trading posts, the Government of India had abrogated the BTA and introduced normal trade.

Until 2017, normal trade was not enforced at the border, and there was a hue and cry when the Indian authorities enforced it. By 2015, when India unilaterally withdrew the BTA, informal trade had become powerfully entrenched on both sides of the border, and there was a need for more information about the new trade regime by 2017. The Chambers of Commerce at Tamu and Moreh did not know that the Duty-Free Tariff Preference Scheme for Myanmar, an underdeveloped country, enjoyed zero tariffs on 98 per cent of all tariff lines. Nor did they know that under the Tariff Rate Quota World Trade Organization (WTO) provisions, North-East India could import maize at low prices through the land route for the vast feed demands for the livestock and poultry industry if Moreh LCS became designated for the same. Great opportunities were lost because of a lack of political will and a sense of purpose in the governments on both sides of the border. Thus, before the COVID-19 pandemic in 2019, formal trade at the Moreh LCS hit rock bottom at USD 0.43 million.

The Shifting Sands of India's Trade Policy and the North-East on the Trilateral Highway

With the initiation of its New Economic Policy in 1991, in the post-Cold War years, India had firmly embarked on wide-ranging economic reforms, restructuring, and liberalization programmes. Soon, India and ASEAN were no longer "awkward strangers", as in the Cold War phase, and rapidly realized the significant mutual gains that could be achieved through strategic and economic cooperation. Since becoming a mere dialogue partner in 1992, India joined the ASEAN regional forum as a dialogue partner, dealing with multilateral security deliberations outside the United Nations (UN) forum. In 2009, the India–ASEAN Free Trade

Agreement (FTA) was signed, covering 4,000 items on which duties would be reduced to zero or near-zero levels by 2016. In 2012, the FTA on services and investment was signed. In between, FTAs emerged with Singapore, Thailand, and Malaysia. Regional institutional networks such as the Bay of Bengal Initiative for Multi-Sectoral Technical and Economic Cooperation (BIMSTEC), the Mekong–Ganga Cooperation (MGC), and Bangladesh–China–India–Myanmar (BCIM) were initiated to seek a larger context of trade, investment, and economic cooperation in South and Southeast Asia. All these rapid changes in India's trade and foreign policy were envisioned in the significant policy initiative known as the LEP, introduced by Prime Minister P.V. Narasimha Rao in Singapore in 1994. Immediately after, the Indo-Myanmar BTA also came into being in 1995. After a decade and a half, India launched its AEP in 2014. Prime Minister Narendra Modi announced the transition at Nay Pyi Taw, Myanmar, drastically impacting border trade in North-East India.

The AEP has moved beyond Southeast Asia, with a strategic vision of the greater Asia-Pacific, unlike the LEP, which was Southeast Asia-centric. The AEP foresees India to be more closely integrated with global supply chains and production networks by combining "Act East" and "Link West". The AEP has three strategic pillars. First, India's future economic architecture in the Asia-Pacific is to be built with ASEAN as the fulcrum. Second, Cambodia, Lao, Myanmar, and Vietnam (CLMV) are to be the top priority. Third, all other countries are to be engaged bilaterally.

India's trade and foreign policy change was dictated by the recent rise in protectionism and realignments in global geopolitics, geo-economics, and global security. The immediate drivers of the AEP were

1. China's belligerent postures in the South China Seas and the Indian Ocean, with security and strategic concerns in India and Southeast Asia;
2. China interfering in India's neighbourhood and India losing ground;
3. India being intensely felt in the region as a balancing factor in the Asia-Pacific;
4. India strongly needing bilateral trade agreements in Southeast and East Asia;

5. most crucially, the concern that the NER was vital in India's engagement with Southeast Asia and the Far East.

India needed to carry along the NER's neighbouring countries of Bhutan, Nepal, Bangladesh, and Myanmar in its strategic engagement with ASEAN on the land route.[7] The AEP is the only major policy initiative available to the region for the development of trade and commerce (Chaturvedy, 2018). In the very next year, 2015, India unilaterally abrogated the Indo-Myanmar BTA and introduced normal trade. Trade took a nosedive to the bottom, as the COVID-19 pandemic and then the ethnic violence in Myanmar and Manipur led to the closing of the border and LCSs, throwing India's trade-linked development push for the NER on the land route into the doldrums.

India's current position on trade and the AEP has been defined by the Delhi Declaration of 2018 and its withdrawal from the Regional Comprehensive Economic Partnership (RCEP) in 2019 (Singh, 2019). This was spurred by the findings of a study commissioned by the National Institution for Transforming India (NITI Aayog), the government's think tank, on the patterns of India's international trade and its implications. India's exports were more income sensitive than price sensitive; exports to FTA countries performed no better than non-FTA countries; India's exports were getting more diversified into high-value manufactures; and traders were utilizing the regional trade agreements (RTAs) the least in their conduct of trade (only 5–25 per cent). All this led to the decision to take a complex review of all FTAs and ensure fair and equitable trade, ensuring trade growth in the long run with reasonable trade balances and that trade was fair for various sections of the Indian populous.

First, a protectionist trade policy was declared in Delhi, where commerce received the least mention of the three Cs: Commerce, Connectivity, and Culture. The strategic shift meant that India sought long-term relations with ASEAN, favouring manufacturing and balanced trade growth. Second, India would renegotiate all FTAs so that comparative advantages were well considered rather than mindlessly going for free trade. The "India First" ideology was clearly in place. India had withdrawn from the RCEP as its trade deficit with member countries was USD 105 billion, of which USD 54 billion was with China. Thus, India is soft paddling trade with ASEAN, envisioning seamless connectivity first with Southeast Asia and harping upon rebuilding cultural relations with the CLMV countries. The unilateral abrogation of the Indo-Myanmar BTA and reducing NER trade relations with Myanmar and ASEAN to normal trade relations highlights how regional short-term interest can be quickly sidelined in the national interest and "serious intent" severely diluted. All this had given birth to the idea of converting the Trilateral Highway from a mere transport corridor to an economic corridor.

India's withdrawal from the RCEP was but a corollary of its larger foreign policy shift towards maintaining strategic autonomy and protectionist tilt, just as the unilateral abrogation of the Indo-Myanmar BTA and imposition of regular trade, a double whammy for the nascent growth in land-based trade and value chains with Myanmar and beyond, formal and informal. Whether the NER can recover from these setbacks in the lost and to be lost trade and value chain and in regional economic integration with Southeast Asia and beyond will much depend on how the region first reshapes its regional economy in terms of generating tradable goods and services, utilizing existing trade facilitations regimes, measures, and policies. Unless the regional traders and governments more seriously fast-track formal trading cultures and efficient tradable goods production and exports, any given FTA, economic corridors, or border trade facilitations will not deliver the desired results.

In 2019, the Government of India commissioned the Economic Research Institute for ASEAN (ERI–ASEAN)) study on the "feasibility of establishing a seamless, efficient, and end-to-end transportation corridor along the existing Trilateral Highway and its extension toward Cambodia, Lao and Vietnam" (RIS, 2021). The India national study came out as a report entitled "Trilateral Highway and Its Extension to Cambodia, Lao PDR and Vietnam: Development Implications for North East India". When the Trilateral Highway (TLH) is completed, it will speed up the flow of goods and people, lower costs involved in trade, and significantly boost how well the economies of ASEAN and India work together. North-East India and Myanmar will be in the middle of this imagined future economic boom and corridor.

The NER is rapidly growing in agriculture, horticulture, forestry, and non-agricultural production. However, limited infrastructures cannot handle the emerging surpluses, leading to repeated supply gluts and growth stunting. Sharma and Choudhury (2018) observe,

> Supply constraints in the North-East consist of both inabilities to reach excess supplies to the markets and inadequacy in enhancing supplies of tradable goods in excess demand. . .The region is yet to integrate into a common market and economy that efficiently distributes its surplus production regionally or globally and pave the way to capital accumulation, productive investments and export-led growth.[8]

Similarly, the 2021 RIS report (RIS, 2021) notes,

> Linking India's AEP to the productive base of the region and creation of value chains on the TLH to Southeast Asia can take off only when the NER itself has efficient value chains and industrial cultures that can take advantage of the TLH as an economic corridor. The Ministry of DoNER [Ministry of Development of the Northeast Region] of the Government of India and the North Eastern Council is yet to take the lead role in bringing together the individual aspirations and visions of the Sates of the NER in an overarching regional framework and master plan that foresees a sustainable, efficient and competitive utilisation of resources cutting across States.

Moreover, it reasons that

> the building of intra-regional value chains would require inter-state planning and coordination inflows of agricultural and non-agricultural surpluses to the most efficient markets as well as industrial centres. These regional markets and industrial hubs when linked to the TLH by feeder roads and other logistics, can transform the TLH into an economic corridor serving the entire region.

Over and above this, the report asserts,

> The TLH becoming an economic corridor will have its immediate impact on NER and Northern Myanmar, the two most backward regions of the two countries. These are the two vital missing links in the grand design of the TLH. The Mae Sot-Myawaddy region on the Myanmar-Thailand borders is already reaping the gains of value chains and economic integration. As the TLH reaches Lao PDR [People's Democratic

> Republic], Vietnam and Cambodia, the gains from trade are likely to multiply manifold for ASEAN. Progress is likely to come to a halt at the Indo-Myanmar borders if trade through the Moreh-Tamu LCSs on the TLH becomes non-functional and the visualised TLH economic corridor does not extend into the Northeast of India and Northern Myanmar.

Moreover, trade had come to a grinding halt in India's land route trade, bridgehead into Southeast Asia, at the Moreh–Tamu border gates of the TLH in the India–Myanmar borders. The reasons are not far to seek.

A well-planned, coordinated economic hub is emerging on the TLH at Myanmar and Thailand's Myawaddy–Mae Sot trading posts. Value- and production-chain integration and large-scale daily cross-border labour mobility from Myanmar to Thailand are fast growing in and around these trading posts. In the grand scheme of the TLH economic corridor, when such hubs emerge on the border of India, Myanmar, Cambodia, Lao, and Thailand, the economic transformations across the countries could be immense. The TLH as an economic corridor could "well turn out to be a model of economic integration of ASEAN and its' neighbours, given their many complementarities and strategic requirements of bringing in India into the architecture of land based RCEP" (RIS, 2021).

The border town of Tamu is fast developing as income and population have risen and trade has rapidly grown. The Myanmar government sees this town as a critical trade, tourism, industrial, and production hub for Northern Myanmar and North-East India on the TLH. The town has a master plan that includes land for a trade zone of 150 acres and a business zone of 50 acres for the Sagaing division of Myanmar and North-East India. Land for an integrated check post (ICP) at Tamu, across the river and opposite the Indian side of the ICP, has been earmarked and the ICP is to be built by India, including the bridge across the river. While all these are in the pipeline, Tamu town is being shaped into a tourist spot with the rapid rise of new pagodas, gardens, and wide roads. Existing trading infrastructures are primitive and unprepared for higher-order, border international trade. The LCS has a rudimentary weighbridge, makeshift warehouse, food testing lab, plant and animal quarantine labs. Lab samples are mostly sent to faraway Rangoon or Mandalay for actual testing instead of being done at Tamu itself. Three Myanmar banks function in the town, but none offer letter of credit facilities as telecom services are poor, and most currency transactions occur outside the banks at the informal, private level. At best, the trade infrastructures at Tamu are suited to the existing informal trade transactions and the deficient volume of formal trade through the Indian LCS. The container truck parked at the customs premises was clear evidence of all formal or informal trade being recorded by the Myanmar authorities as actual border trade for their purposes.

On the Indian side, the swanky ICP has modern facilities with all necessary services and equipment for international goods and people's transit that can be "activated" on demand. Mostly migration works were handled at the ICP as formal trade had come down to three consignments in a year before the borders were sealed during the COVID-19 pandemic. As such, the food testing lab, plant and animal quarantine facility, telecom with Electronic Data Interchange facility, banks, and medical stations were yet to be manned. Infrastructures such as a warehouse, a weighbridge, cold storage, a parking bay, and a bus bay are all in place, with adequate land for further expansion. The tragedy, therefore, is that after over two decades of border trade, when the formal infrastructures for trade are ready, there are few takers on both sides of the border.

Unlike the clean, planned, and spacious township of Tamu across the border, Moreh on the Indian side gives the look of a comatose shanty town with a collective "temporal mindset" that permeates through the entire haphazard settlement, which seems to have no civic authority to look after. The one-street town was chock a block in the daytime with local tourists, thousands of petty traders, and their carriers. The only liveable three-star hotel in town is mostly booked, and by dusk, as most of the private and public vehicles have left, the town is more or less locked up. Moreh remains a transit town with almost no agricultural activities and a few wood-based activities, traders, petty hoteliers, etc. Though land prices are incredibly high, based on the speculation of better times, few invest in trade-related or residential structures, and local participation in trade is also limited. The result has been that beyond the ICP, the private sector has yet to invest in the growing demands of international business and trade, such as corporate housing and office accommodation, banking and finance, and passenger and cargo transport. The town also needs a municipality or corporation to take care of the commercial and trading town's needs, resulting in physical and infrastructural development chaos. The main historical reason for the state of affairs regarding the development of Moreh is that the town was born out of conflict, and its fate continues to be dictated by non-state actors or the configuration of actors dictates terms on the town's welfare. Insurgency on both sides of the border, drastic demographic engineering, and ethnic configuration have been the bane of the organic growth of the township, which is conducive to the grand designs of India's economic corridor on the TLH.

However, India's AEP for the NER has permanently been anchored on the premise that development is the answer to most of the region's problems, that opening a trade route on land to Southeast Asia and economic integration and value chains would be a strategic necessity, and that the issues of national security and addressing the vexing problem of insurgency in the NER would much fall in line as economic and security cooperations are multilaterally addressed in the South Asia and Southeast Asia neighbourhood. As India's relations with the South and Southeast Asia neighbourhood of the NER in the past decade or so turned in India's favour, dividends had begun to accrue as insurgency began to ultimately end or wane in most states of the region, with peace negotiations coming to the table in the past two decades or so. The recent political upheavals in Myanmar put a complete halt to land-based trade for the North-East. However, this now gives India and the NER the breathing space to give a serious rethink to evolving a new outlook and vision in India's AEP for the North-East. This time, the North-East states cannot afford to be practically mere spectators to what have so far been top-down, trade-led development policies, especially by reflecting on the Manipur experience in India's "North-East Centrality" strategy for its "Look East" and AEP so far. This also gives the states of the North-East the best opportunity to act as one and give their own actionable vision and strategic plans for regional economic integration and value-chain thrusts that could lead to trade-led development and growth. For this to happen, the North-East has to pragmatically examine the levels of "Seamless Connectivity", one of the three pillars of India's current position on the AEP, that the NER has achieved so far.

Road density in the North-East, at 190.14 km per 100 sq. km, is higher than the all-India average of 143.08 km. This is mainly because the state of Assam has a far higher road density of 420.10 km, Tripura 375.41 km, and Nagaland 217.83 km; the rest of the states have much less than the national average. In the hill states outside of Assam, isolated and expansively spread villages must be connected by arterial roads rather than attempting single roads connecting each village, thereby giving a wrong picture of high connectivity deficits in the North-East. Villages are self-relocating nearer to state highways or main roads for survival. However, this has become unsustainable as the roads alone cannot provide sustainable production or livelihoods. The idea of economic integration and value-chain production in the hill states can only be best served if road connectivity is ensured as far as feasible. The region has 2,672 km of rail tracks, constituting 4 per cent of India's total. However, almost all tracks serve Assam, where the railway density is 3.13 per sq. km against the national average of 1.96 km. Except for Tripura, which is 151 km, the rest of the states are barely touched by the railways. Once the railway network in the Brahmaputra and Barak valleys is linked to the hilly states, the region with rich natural resources will likely be substantially transformed as its productive bases are harnessed for economic activities and industries. The railways have reached Noney in the Tamenglong Hill district of Manipur. When it reaches Moreh on the TLH to Southeast Asia, economic corridors on the TLH and India's AEP will become much more real.

The India–Myanmar TLH was conceived in 2003; by 2023, 70 per cent of the construction work had been completed. This project, which links Moreh in Manipur to Mae Sot in Thailand, has been visualized to give a much-needed nudge to trade, business, health education, and tourism growth in India, Myanmar, Thailand, and beyond. The completion of the highway has been hindered by the internal political instability and strife in Myanmar, according to India's external affairs minister, S Jaishankar. In an "Advantage Assam Submit" at Guwahati on 25 February 2025, the minister suggested that "The situation in Myanmar has paused the India–Myanmar–Thailand highway project. . .We cannot allow this Myanmar project to block something so momentous. Practical solutions will have to be found to ensure the advancement of this initiative" (NDTV News Desk, 2025). Somehow or other, India's LEP and AEP seem to have been perpetually jinxed on its tracks. However, one can see some flicker of hope and potential that the TLH can offer towards regional economic integration in the nascent development of visible value chains between Myanmar and Manipur, against formidable odds.

Developing Value Chains on the TLH at the Moreh–Tamu Corridor in Manipur

Manipur's contacts and historical relations are unique, even in the NER of India. The Meities and the Nagas are the original inhabitants of Manipur, and the Meitei kings who ruled Manipur were in continuous conflict with the kingdoms of Burma, interspersed with peace times when trade, technology, and social and cultural exchanges flourished. The Kukis migrated to the kingdom later. The Naga and Kuki tribes are also substantially settled across the border in the neighbouring provinces of Sagaing and Chin. Meities, whose armies had reached Ava, have village settlements in Mandalay and the Sagaing divisions.

On the other hand, Tamils, Marwaris, and Indian Nepalis who chose to settle in Moreh after the Indian exodus in the post-colonial period also have wide networks with the Indian diasporas across Myanmar, especially in Mandalay and Rangoon. The Meitei entrepreneurs started a trade base camp at Tamu to supply essential commodities to war-ravaged Burma and later permanently settled at Moreh on the Indian side. When the Tamil and other Indian traders joined the trade boom in the late 1960s and early 1970s, the products of the Asian Tigers were flooding the markets in Manipur. The informal booming trade at the Moreh-Tamu markets had become the natural Neo-Silk Route from Southeast Asia and Yunnan through Myanmar. Moreh thus became the natural choice of the land route for the Indo-Myanmar BTA and India's LEP, and later for the TLH. Rudimentary value chains had, therefore, emerged quite early, and these primary value chains need to be formalized or lead to higher-level economic integration and product fragmentation, which are only pointers to significant opportunity losses.

The most developed value chains and product fragmentation enterprises through the Moreh–Tamu corridor are the timber-related trade, services, and industries. As the forests of Manipur progressively dwindled and construction materials prices rose, the illegal flow of cheap timber from Myanmar became lucrative. On the other hand, as Tamu developed as a trading hub, the Indian trading diaspora on both sides of the border fuelled the imports of Burmese hardwood and teak wood trade in log and sawn pieces for housing, construction material, and furniture. Later, the Burmese got wiser, and furniture, doors, and windows soon began to reach Manipur in rough breakdown conditions. In the next phase, while better-quality products were sourced from Mandalay and other places, production began in units located in Tamu. Along with this value chain developed transport and other supply-side chains deep into Myanmar. On the Indian side, sawmills were fed by Burmese timber, especially after the Supreme Court banned timber harvesting in the North-East with conditionalities.

On the other hand, there was a spurt in the carpentry and niche furniture industry as finishing works on rough Burmese products were in high demand. Today, house-building hardwood timber in the state's valley regions is almost entirely from Myanmar. Thus, the timber value chains have diversified in various ways, creating income and employment across Manipur, even though the transactions are informal and illegal. In fact, the timber-based industry is almost the only industry functioning at Moreh. This trade has encouraged labour mobility across borders as expert carvers make customer-specific modifications at Moreh. Some are known to be employed by larger firms in the valley in Manipur, and following their trail, skilled Burmese workers are known to be employed in the construction industry in Manipur. The lucrative teak furniture market in India is yet to be tapped.

The second formal trade and value chain is in place in the health sector. Over a thousand patients annually are finding cheaper and better medical treatment in Imphal city because of costs and the availability of state-of-the-art infrastructures and expertise. Patients from Thailand have also started to arrive. The Myanmar government offered land and various concessions for establishing hospitals and providing support. However, the language barriers, the uncertainty of income repatriation, and various other factors prevent entrepreneurs from venturing into Myanmar. Establishing a hospital at Moreh itself is on the agenda of a frontier health entrepreneur. In the meantime, medical personnel's training in Myanmar and Manipur is also happening.

Nascent value chains in the logistics and transport sectors started in the warehousing and goods transit in the Guangzhou, Mae Sot, and

Tamu/Moreh triangle of China, Thailand, and Manipur. Myanmar allows all imports from neighbouring countries such as Thailand and China with a flat duty of 3 per cent and transit of the same goods into India with another 3 per cent "income" tax (rules of origins managed) (Singh, 2020) without much formality or rule-based trade. Entrepreneurs on both sides of the Indo-Myanmar border have organized smooth flows of machinery and even sophisticated medical and surgical goods besides precious stones and gold, feeding the numerous jewellery works in the Imphal valley. Flows into Myanmar informally also include many intermediate inputs, including pharmaceuticals, motor-vehicle parts, and wheat flours, feeding Myanmar's rising pharma, confectionery, and motor repair industries.

A value chain in livestock and fisheries has high prospects. The livestock industry is vibrant, but consumers mostly face a seller's market due to the high feed costs imported from mainland India. In fact, the largest poultry farmers had even had cheap maize imported for feeds from Myanmar but withdrew from the clandestine trade because of the risks involved. If the WTO-mandated quota of maize imports from Myanmar could be utilized, the livestock, poultry, and fishery sectors would gain a lot and drastically reduce fish and livestock deficits in Manipur as well as North-East India. There is a heavy demand for cheap Myanmar fish in the state, competing with imports from the faraway mainland southern state of Andhra Pradesh. Myanmar's main "*Ruhu*" fish variety does not compete with the local variety for size, taste, and cultural reasons.

Food- and fruit-processing industries are fast emerging in Manipur. The largest firm in the state imports orange pulp from Nagpur in Maharashtra, on the Arabian Sea, and is severely stressed by raw fruit input shortages for its industry. The firm still needs to explore the prospects of a value chain with the rich fruit-producing states of Myanmar, such as the Shan State, Yunnan, or Thailand, which will have little impact on mainland horticulture sectors.

The most talked-about possible product fragmentation and value-chain prospects with Myanmar are in the mineral sector. As in the case of Bangladesh, the rich limestone deposits of Manipur could quickly start cement factories in the neighbouring Sagaing division of Myanmar, just as gems and semi-precious stones from Myanmar could easily create another value chain between Myanmar and Manipur.

Epilogue

Value chains, economic corridors, and economic integration on the TLH are faraway dreams for Manipur and the NER of India. However, the prospects are vast, and informal value chains and economic integration are already afoot, being only held back as India and Myanmar are yet to seriously engage with each other on behalf of the NER of India and the Northern Region of Myanmar, in concrete terms rather than empty announcements. Why not renegotiate a new BTA II with Myanmar, just as India renegotiates all FTAs?

During the negotiations for the signing of a Memorandum of Understanding (MoU) between Manipur University and Monywa University (Manipur University and Monywa University, 2022), the author as an expert member representing Manipur University in 2022 had observed, "Sustainable value chains and economic integration in the hinterland of the Moreh–Tamu bridgehead on the TLH can only happen with high-level Trade Body dialogues, and Joint Academic Research outputs of Universities and Academia, work together and evolve grounded and implementable pathways acceptable to both countries."[9]

Put differently, North-East India and Northern Myanmar governments need collaboration structures to plan and develop trade and economic zones along the TLH. Ultimately, however, unless broader but critical issues of trade facilitation across South Asia and Southeast Asia (such as the Motor Vehicle Agreement, Rules of Origin, transit trade parameters, and non-tariff barriers) are renegotiated and settled on a fast track, economic integration of South and Southeast Asia will remain incomplete. It is here that India and ASEAN must negotiate with political will and mutually beneficial outcomes that facilitate the creation of an economic corridor on the TLH. Political hiccups in Myanmar or the North-East of India should be no reason for abandoning midstream an idea waiting to happen.

Notes

1. Guha (2016: 1–22) opines that India's Northeastern Region emerged as a distinct region in the medieval period, and the British Empire shaped its regional character and political form during the nineteenth century.

2. Insular mindsets, protectionist developmental outlooks, fear of exogenous capital and agencies carting away gains from resource exploitation, and undue fear of mainstream industrialization are psychic features of the political economy of North-East India. Since the liberalization of the 1990s, a fast change in mindsets has fuelled recent accelerated growth in North-East India.
3. The social dimension of the peasantry adjusting to state failures in agricultural development through crop diversification into high-value agriculture is evident in the peasantry's progressive search for survival autonomy in a progressive agriculture sector.
4. The post-colonial reorganization of North-East India into states, mainly based on ethnic lines, is at the root of insurgency and the politics of development. Barua provides an insightful narrative on this issue.
5. Burmanization, Htoo and Waters (2024: 15–29) state, is an ideology initiated by General Ne Win after the *coup d'état* in 1962. The ideology seeks to homogenize the country linguistically, racially, and culturally. It promotes the vested interests of the Burmans at the expense of the minorities instead of recognizing and respecting ethno-religious diversity.
6. A Reserve Bank of India (RBI) exchange control document used by exporters to declare that they will realize export proceeds within 180 days of shipment. These formalities help the RBI to monitor and manage foreign transactions.
7. The AEP centralizes North-East India in the new policy. Chaturvedy (2018: 4) asserts that "the Act East Policy is the only major policy initiative available to the region for the development of tangible trade and commerce with neighbouring countries".
8. Integrating the regional economy and building a common market has long been talked about but has yet to be given serious regional attention.
9. Manipur University has signed an MoU with Monywa University of Economics, Sagaing Division Myanmar for Joint Research and Academic Exchange. Preliminary trade body meetings have also taken place on various occasions.

References

Baruah, Sanjib (2005), *Durable Disorder: Understanding the Politics of Northeast India*, India: Oxford University Press.

Chaturvedy, Rajeev Ranjan (2018), "Interpreting India's Act East", National University of Singapore, Institute of South Asian Studies (ISAS) Working Paper No. 284, 29 January.

Das, Samir Kumar (2013), *Governing India's Northeast: Essays on Insurgency, Development, and the Culture of Peace*, New Delhi: Springer.

Government of India (1997), "Transforming the Northeast, Tackling Backlogs in Basic Minimum Services and Infrastructural Needs", Planning Commission, New Delhi (https://archive.org/details/dli.csl.1258).

Gowda, H.D. Deve (1997), "New Initiatives for the Northeast Region", Statement by the Prime Minister, Gauhati (https://eparlib.sansad.in/bitstream/123456789/50226/1/11_IV_26021997_p54_p60_t53.pdf).

Guha, Amalendu (2016), *Planter's Raj to Swaraj*, Gauhati: Anwesha Publications.

Htoo, Saw Eh and Tony Waters (2024), *General NE Win's Legacy of Burmanization in Myanmar: The Challenges to Peace in the Twenty-First Century*, Singapore: Palgrave Macmillan.

Krishna, Geetanjali (2016), "Manipur's Young Moving Ahead in This Isle of Turbulence", *Business Standard*, September 05, 2016 (http://www.business standard.com/article/economy-policy/Manipur-s-young-moving ahead-in-this-isle-of-turbulance-116090400719_1.html).

Manipur University and Monywa University (2022), "Memorandum of Understanding", 19 April (https://www.manipuruniv.ac.in/p/collaboration-2).

NIPFP (National Institute of Public Finance and Policy) (2007), "Peace, Progress, and Prosperity in the Northeastern Region: Vision 20–20", New Delhi: NIPFP.

NDTV News Desk (2025), "World News", 25 February.

RIS (Research and Information System for Developing Countries) (2021), "Trilateral Highway and Its Extension to Cambodia, Lao PDR and Vietnam: Development Implications for Northeast India", RIS and Association for Southeast Asian Nations (ASEAN)–India Centre at RIS, New Delhi, October (https://aseanindiacentre.org.in/sites/default/files/Publication/TH%20Report-19%20October.pdf).

Scott, James C. (2009), *The Art of Not Being Governed: An Anarchic History of Upland Southeast Asia*, New Haven, CT and London: Yale University Press.

Sharma, Atul and Saswati Choudhury (eds) (2018), *Mainstreaming the Northeast in India's Look and Act East Policy*, Singapore: Springer Nature.

Singh, Ch. Priyoranjan (2011), "Border Trade in Manipur: Ground Level Survey and Status Report", Department of Commerce and Industries, Government of Manipur.

Singh, Ch. Priyoranjan (2019), "Development Dreams: The Act East Policy Context in the North East", Jayashree Roy Memorial Lecture, Special Centre for the Study of North East India, Jawaharlal Nehru University, New Delhi, 6 December.

Singh, Ch. Priyoranjan (2020), "India–ASEAN Free Trade Agreement and Act East Policy for Northeast India", New Delhi: Northeastern Council, Ministry of Development of the Northeast Region (DoNER), Government of India.

Singh, Ch. Priyoranjan and H. Ishworchandra Sharma (2013), "Peasants of Manipur: Agrarian Change, Land Tenure and Emerging Patterns of Repeasantization in India", *Agrarian South: Journal of Political Economy*, 2 (3), pp. 291–314.

Verghese, B.G (2004), *India's Northeast Resurgent: Ethnicity, Insurgency, Governance, Development* (Rev. edn), New Delhi: Konark Publishers.

6

The Border between Meghalaya and Bangladesh

Economic and Social Space

Saswati Choudhury

Introduction to the Meghalaya Bangladesh Border: A Colonial Frontier

The integration of the Khasi polities into the British colonial framework was part of a broader process of constructing an imperial frontier geography. This integration was driven by cartographic production, legal boundary-making, and the establishment of communication networks, alongside treaties and commercial agreements. The Khasi hills, while not fully incorporated into the British colonial revenue system, became increasingly entangled in the expanding imperial political economy. The formation of the modern boundary between present-day Sylhet (now in Bangladesh) and Meghalaya (in India) has its roots in the events of the 1780s, particularly two distinct yet interconnected conflicts on Sylhet's northern frontiers. As David Ludden (2003, 2019) highlights, these conflicts were escalated by the famine of 1787, creating instability that lasted until 1790. Despite their common connection to the broader process of boundary-making, the conflicts had different origins and implications, setting the stage for the eventual separation of the Sylhet plains from the Khasi and Jaintia hills.

In 1774, a penal expedition under Captain ElZiker was sent to Jaintiapur by the East India Company, but the struggle was localized in

Saswati Choudhury, *The Border between Meghalaya and Bangladesh* In: *Sub-Regional Cooperation for Trade, Investment, and Employment in North-East India*. Edited by: Ashish Nath, Oxford University Press.
 DOI: 10.1093/9780197908938.003.0006

Jaintiapur. The expedition is attributed to some aggressions against the inhabitants of the adjacent plains of Sylhet (Giri, 1998). The lime quarries at Pandua near Bhologanj attracted European traders towards the end of the eighteenth century.[1] The East India Company formalized a boundary below Pandua, a critical point marking the outcome of these conflicts.[2] This new boundary separated British Bengal from the mountainous regions that would later form part of Meghalaya. The demarcation followed the base of the Khasi hills and split the route from Sunamganj to Pandua, institutionalizing the territorial division between the plains and the hills. It symbolized the consolidation of British control over the Sylhet plains while acknowledging the autonomy of the Khasi polities in the mountains. This political boundary became a social boundary on both sides. The East India Company used every strategy at its disposal to subjugate the Khasi hills to English rule. The company gained the friendship of the Khasis for a number of reasons. First, the English deemed it necessary to have a mail service across the hills from Sylhet to Assam. In order to facilitate trade and commerce, they also saw the necessity of connecting the two valleys via the hills (Giri, 1998).

The significance of this boundary lay in the balance of power that shaped it: while the British secured victories in the plains, the Khasis maintained dominance in the mountains. The boundary marked a limit to British expansion in this frontier region, establishing a clear distinction between the revenue-generating territories of Sylhet and the politically distinct Khasi and Jaintia hills. This territorial line not only divided the region geographically but also laid the groundwork for the divergent political and historical trajectories of Sylhet and Meghalaya. The demarcation of this boundary was a pivotal moment in the colonial transformation of Northeastern India as it reflected both the military realities of the time and the legal processes of British boundary-making. The events surrounding its creation underscored the complex nature of frontier governance, where sovereignty was negotiated through war, treaties, and commercial agreements, and the colonial state had to navigate the distinct political landscapes of the plains and the hills. As Gunnel Cederlöf (2009) emphasizes, the British sought to extend their revenue collection beyond traditional agricultural land, incorporating resources such as forests, minerals, and animals into their taxation and extraction systems. Additionally, they established tribute relationships with local authorities, positioning themselves as protectors in exchange for economic contributions. However, the Khasi hills posed a challenge to the straightforward application of this framework. The terrain, the political organization of the Khasi polities, and the socio-economic systems in place made full integration difficult.

Nevertheless, the British administration affected the Khasi hills. While revenue collection in the traditional sense—through agriculture or direct taxation—was limited, the region's natural resources (particularly limestone and coal) became integral to British commercial interests. The leasing of mines and plantations, combined with labour migration, connected the Khasi hills to broader imperial networks of trade and production. The British established agreements with local chiefs to secure access to these resources, thus embedding the Khasi polities within the colonial economic system even as they remained outside the conventional revenue-collection framework.

This partial integration of the Khasi hills illustrates how colonial expansion operated on multiple levels. Even where direct control through taxation and land appropriation was limited, the British were able to exert influence through commercial interests in resource extraction. The British tied the Khasi hills to the larger structures of the imperial economy through extraction of key economic (mineral) resources and yet maintained the region's distinct status as a frontier space governed by exceptional legal and political measures. The British colonial engagement with the Khasi, Jaintia, and Garo hills offers a distinct perspective on the imposition of sovereignty and legal frameworks in the Northeastern frontier of India, which was inhabited by people of different racial stock than the rest of British India. From the mid-eighteenth century, this region, part of the larger Himalayan border lands, gradually transformed into a frontier of the British Empire and highlights the plural and divisible nature of sovereignty in the region. Early British administrators, like Robert Lindsay, identified the Khasi polities as separate from the plains populations, describing the Khasis as "hill tribes" distinct in race, religion, and social structure. Lindsay's (Syiemlieh, 1997; Board of Revenue Papers, 1787) report, based on his experiences as a trader and collector in Sylhet, reinforced the racialized and spatial notions of the "tribal" hill populations and the "civilized" plains. This racialization, however, did not immediately drive boundary-making.

Gunnel Cederlöf (2009) suggests that in the early nineteenth century, commercial interests were prioritized over civilizational or racial hierarchies. The limestone trade, centred on markets like Pandua, was a crucial point of engagement between the Khasi chiefs and the East India Company (Board of Revenue Papers, 1782, 1783). Lindsay himself had personal trading interests and had large investments in trading limestone from the Khasi hills. Through a series of treaties in the 1820s and 1830s, the British secured control over these lucrative resources while gradually eroding the sovereignty of local politics. In 1835, the British formally incorporated the region, which would later become Meghalaya, into the province of Assam. Despite this incorporation, the Khasi, Jaintia, and Garo hills were maintained as distinct entities under a semi-independent status. This was facilitated through a treaty relationship with the British Crown, which allowed these areas to remain relatively autonomous, particularly in terms of local governance and customary laws. The British administration classified the region as a "non-regulation" or "excluded" area,[3] meaning that the laws of British India did not apply in the same way as they did in other parts of the country. The hills became legally distinct areas as a result of agreements, treaties, ordinances, and decrees. One of the most notable of them is Bengal Regulation XII of 1833, which set up the establishment of special administrative and legal areas where the rules and laws of the presidencies would not be applicable. Frontier hills were referred to as "backward" or "truly backward" tracts, planned districts, or non-regulation territory. Relationships between the central administration of the East India Company in Bengal; local administrative officers along the Northeastern border; and the headmen, chiefs, and rajas recognized as possessing indigenous or local power in the Khasi, Jaintia, and Garo hills were governed by treaties. The concepts of sovereignty that colonial agents carried with them, leading to treaties, agreements, and decrees, lacked the necessary terminology to translate or take into account existing land relations and authority.

In the post-Independence period, giving up the strategy of isolating the tribes was one of India's accomplishments after gaining freedom. Assam made some progress towards more inclusive governance in this regard, but not enough, and it had an impact on the state's unity. As a result, throughout the 1950s and 1960s, the hill people called for their independence from Assam. The Assam legislature's decision to designate

Assamese as the official language of the state—within a state that had a number of languages and dialects spoken in any Indian state—was what actually sparked their push to secede from Assam (Syeimlieh, 2022). The new territorial boundary of Meghalaya, created in 1972, opened new space for engagement in the political, social, and economic spheres keeping the interests of the local hill people. The borders drawn along the earlier "homogeneous space" down the foothills up to Sylhet plain during Partition opened newer challenges to negotiate trade and business along the cartographic realities of two nations that continue to be a site of newer experiments even today. New policies and engagements continue to reshape the border relations between Meghalaya and the neighbouring areas across the Bangladesh border. In this context, this chapter presents the evolution of the state of Meghalaya over time and the resources and the advantages of the state that could push the growth prospects with neighbouring countries.

From Colonial Frontier to Becoming the State of an Independent Nation

The imperial law and sovereignty was enforced on the frontier in ways that defied simple classification. The colonial administration navigated a complex legal landscape, where indigenous rights and political autonomy was gradually subverted to establish British control over both land and commerce. This period of history in the Khasi, Jaintia, and Garo hills exemplifies how law and colonialism intersected to transform dynamic border lands into rigid colonial frontiers, framing the indigenous populations in legal and racial terms that justified imperial domination. The East India Company used every strategy at its disposal to subjugate the Khasi hills to colonial rule. The Company realized the necessity of a mail service across the hills from Sylhet to Assam for administrative purpose, and in order to facilitate trade and commerce, they also saw the necessity of connecting the two valleys via the hills (Giri, 1998).

The East India Company quickly realized the great mineral potentialities and other trade goods that the Khasi hills might offer after meeting the Khasis. The quarries they owned provided a cheap supply of lime to deltaic Bengal. Silk, wax, honey, ivory, iron, and other commodities were widely available. The well-known Khasi orange, which seems to be native to these hills, was another significant export. In the southern part of the district, orange cultivation was just as important as potato cultivation in the northern part. Originating from the warm southern slopes of the hills in Khasi and Jaintia districts, the orange was known in Calcutta as the *Chhatak* or Sylhet orange as this was widely grown there. Sir George Bird Wood[4] mentioned that Arab traders took oranges from Garhwal, Sikkim, and Khasia to Syria, and "Crusaders helped to gradually propagate them throughout Southern Europe." The oranges from the Khasi hills were treated as native to these hills. The oranges from Meghalaya continue to be an important item of trade even today.

Meghalaya became a part of the new province of Eastern Bengal and Assam after the partition of Bengal in 1905, and when the partition was revoked in 1911, it became a part of the province of Assam. During the pre-Partition period, most of the local products/minerals of the hills were traded with the neighbouring plains areas of the erstwhile Bengal (present-day Bangladesh). The villages of the southern foothills prospered and developed, mainly because of the existence of trade with other parts of Eastern Bengal. The Partition of India in 1947 profoundly disrupted the lives and livelihoods of the Khasi, Jaintia, and Garo communities, who had long-established economic, social, and cultural ties with Eastern Bengal (present-day Bangladesh). Before Partition, these tribes were economically more integrated with Sylhet and Mymensingh in Eastern Bengal than with the Assam plains, engaging in a thriving border-land trade that supported their livelihoods. However, the creation of the new international border between India and East Pakistan (now Bangladesh) severed these traditional links, creating a boundary that not only bisected their lands but also fractured their communities.

As a result of Partition, approximately 150 miles of borders were drawn across the Khasi–Jaintia hills, dividing the territories historically inhabited by the Khasi, Jaintia, and Garo people. The demarcation of the border split these communities into Indians and Pakistanis, depending on where their residences fell, leading to profound social and economic dislocation. Many of these tribes had members living on both sides of the border, which resulted in the separation of families, communities, and economic networks. The erection of border posts and the closure of the previously fluid border trade severely impacted their livelihoods.

Partition's most significant effect on the border land people was on agricultural work. Many cultivators found themselves separated from their fields, which were now across an international border. This dislocation of agricultural work was compounded by the fact that disputes over the newly drawn border left many of these lands neglected for years. In some cases, the border ran between people's homes and their farmland, forcing them to navigate a complex and restrictive new geopolitical landscape.[5] Despite the challenges, people in these border lands continued to cross the boundary for work, although this became increasingly difficult due to new regulations. The porous nature of the border, with its many minor access roads, made it challenging for authorities to patrol effectively. Smuggling,[6] driven by economic necessity, became a common practice for those living in the region. For many Khasi, Jaintia, and Garo families, smuggling was not only a means of survival but also a way to maintain connections across the border, defying the restrictions imposed by Partition.[7]

Partition was not merely a cartographic reorganization for these communities but a deeply political and social event that redefined their identities and transformed their daily lives. Those who found themselves on the "wrong" side of the border were forced to adapt to new nationalities and political realities, often under conditions of uncertainty and insecurity. The boundary drew artificial lines through regions where cultural, social, and economic ties had historically transcended borders. Even today, the effects of Partition continue to reverberate in the lives of the Khasi, Jaintia, and Garo people. The fluidity of the borders and ongoing disputes over boundary demarcation and negotiations over citizenship have ensured that Partition remains a process rather than a concluded historical episode. These communities continue to grapple with the legacy of separation by a border that reshaped their identity, politics, and livelihoods.

The Border Space Economy and the Trade of Meghalaya

The post-Partition development trajectory of Meghalaya went through sharp turns in the absence of road connections of the frontier villages with the major trading centres within the state.[8] There were no efforts before partition to develop road communication systems, and there was no effort to provide markets for products of border areas within the state. While commenting on the impact of closure of trade and commerce, Donkupar Roy (1987) said, "It was a sudden fall from the period of prosperity to the period of depression." The border *hats* such as Shella, Majai, Phali, Balat, Tyllap, etc. were cut off as trading points, and this affected about 1,500 villages. In the early 1950s, the government implemented provisional and experimental measures to mitigate the economic challenges caused by Partition, particularly in regions like Shella, known for orange production. One such initiative was the airlifting of oranges from Shella to Calcutta. This was intended to help to sustain the trade in oranges, which had been disrupted by the closure of traditional trade routes with Sylhet and other parts of East Pakistan (now Bangladesh). However, the airlifting experiment proved to be temporary and inadequate. It failed to transport even a significant portion of the oranges produced in the region, making it ineffective in addressing the larger economic needs of local farmers. The logistical challenges and high costs of airlifting, combined with the sheer volume of production, meant that this initiative could not serve as a sustainable solution. As a result, the programme was abandoned after only a few years of operation, leaving the region to grapple with the long-term economic consequences of Partition and the disruption of traditional markets.

In the aftermath of Partition, the border areas of Assam, including the Khasi, Jaintia, and Garo hills, faced significant economic challenges. Recognizing the urgency of the situation, the Government of Assam appointed three separate committees for the Garo hills, Khasi hills, Jaintia hills, and Mizo hills to assess the prevailing economic conditions and recommend suitable measures. The reports, submitted in 1958, offered important insights into the causes of the economic crisis in these areas and proposed various remedies (Bhagwati, 2007). The Committee for the Garo Hills attributed the economic crisis in the border areas to the communities' reliance on cash crops, noting that food crop cultivation was challenging due to the distinct soil conditions. It recommended several measures, including the construction of roads to improve connectivity, subsidies for the transportation of foodstuffs, test-relief works, and allocation of funds to enhance agricultural programmes. Importantly, the committee emphasized that the solution did not lie in relocating the border people or changing their cultivation patterns but in providing adequate transport and marketing facilities for local products. The construction of roads, organizing cooperative marketing societies, and ensuring better transport facilities for border products were seen as key measures to improve the economic conditions.

The committees made significant recommendations, including the construction of roads to facilitate the marketing of border products, providing subsidies for food in border areas, and setting up fruit preservation and canning factories. The Committee for the Khasi and Jaintia Hills also focused on improving the administrative measures, such as establishing fair-price shops and supporting border products with subsidies. The report stressed that the problems of the border people could not be solved by mere rehabilitation; instead, fostering self-reliance was crucial. The challenges persisted despite the government's efforts, which became a significant concern for the leadership of the newly formed autonomous state of Meghalaya in 1970. The state leadership sought alternative solutions, including identifying new markets for local products and expanding road communication networks between the border areas and key towns within the state. The committee also proposed setting up small- and medium-scale industries to utilize the minerals from the southern foothills, potentially creating employment opportunities for the local population. In an attempt to revive cross-border trade, in 1971 the Meghalaya government made efforts to allow Pakistani traders from East Pakistan (now Bangladesh) to visit certain designated markets (known as *hats*) on the Indian side of the border. Fourteen such markets were initially opened, with plans to open twelve more. As an experimental measure, Pakistani traders were temporarily permitted to visit the Shella market (*Hat* Shella) four days a week to collect materials such as shingle, boulders, and limestone.

The reopening of a few border *hats* for a limited time highlighted the shared economic suffering of people living on both sides of the international border. However, the number of markets available for trade transactions was limited, and the people living in border areas demanded the opening of more *hats* to facilitate the exchange of perishable goods between India and East Pakistan. While this was seen as a potential way to alleviate the deteriorating economic conditions in the border regions, the complexity of trade relations with East Pakistan, and later Bangladesh, meant that the Union government had to carefully navigate diplomatic efforts. Despite best efforts, convincing the Pakistani government to revive border trade remained a complicated issue, and progress was limited. Overall, while various committees offered recommendations for improving the economic conditions of border areas, the long-term solution lay in enhancing infrastructure, improving market access, and fostering cross-border trade, all of which depended on careful negotiation and policymaking at the national level.

At the time of Indian Independence in 1947, what is now the state of Meghalaya was part of Assam and comprised two districts—the United Khasi and Jaintia hills, and the Garo hills. These areas enjoyed limited autonomy within Assam under the Sixth Schedule of the Indian Constitution, which provided for certain protections and self-governance mechanisms for tribal regions. In 1960, a movement began advocating for a separate hill state, driven by the desire of the Khasi, Jaintia, and Garo people for greater political and cultural autonomy from Assam. After years of agitation, on 11 September 1968, the Government of India proposed a plan to create an autonomous state within Assam, which would include areas outlined in Part A of the Sixth Schedule of the Constitution.[9] In 1971, the Indian Parliament passed the North-Eastern Areas (Reorganization) Act, which granted full statehood to Meghalaya.[10]

Economic Space and Developmental Intervention in the State of Meghalaya

When Meghalaya became a fully fledged state in 1972, the government recognized the urgent need to develop road communication networks to restore and improve the economic conditions of the border areas. Prior to Partition, the roads of the border areas traditionally flowed southwards to Sylhet and Mymensingh (in present-day Bangladesh). After Partition, this trade route was severed, and goods needed to be redirected northwards towards Shillong and onwards to Assam and other parts of India. Despite the importance of these road networks, the development of infrastructure linking the southern border areas to the rest of the state fell short of expectations. In the Meghalaya Legislative Assembly, B.B. Lyngdoh, the then chief minister of Meghalaya, acknowledged the challenges faced by border communities, stating that the state government was fully aware of the suffering caused by the suspension of cross-border trade. He also admitted that the developmental programmes in the region had not matched the area's needs, leading to further economic deterioration.

One of the major measures taken by the state government was the introduction of a crash scheme to facilitate the marketing of border products. The goal was to help local producers sell their goods at reasonable prices both within and outside the state. Additionally, relief measures were introduced to ease the distress faced by border communities. The state government also submitted development plans to the Government of India, which included proposals to set up a corporation for marketing border products and improving communication infrastructure. These efforts were deemed crucial to addressing the unique challenges faced by the border areas and reviving the local economy.

Meghalaya, being a landlocked state with rugged terrain, faces significant challenges related to transportation and agricultural development. With road transport serving as the sole major mode of transportation due to the absence of rail networks and limited air connectivity, the state's infrastructure plays a crucial role in its economy. The total road length is 40,258 km, of which 18,112 km (44.98 per cent) is surfaced road.[11] The road density in Meghalaya is 1,794.91 per 1,000 sq.km and 14 km per 1,000 of the population.[12] The total length of national highways in the state is 1,156 km, which is only 0.9 per cent of the country's total, and this shows the remoteness in connectivity of the state with rest of the country. A total of 1,098 km of national highways in the state is either less than two- or two-lane road, and only 57 km of road length is more than four lanes with a density of 0.39 per 1,000 of the population. One of the major reasons for low coverage of national highways in the state is the low utilization of funds for construction of national highways, as revealed from the data of the Ministry of Road Transport and Highways, 2018–19. The length of state highways is 768 km, which is only 0.43 per cent of the total road length of state highways in the country; and the density of roads per 1,000 of the population is 0.3 km. The low coverage of state highways reflects poor intra-connectivity status within the state, although the rural roads density is one of the highest in the country but the share of surfaced rural roads is only 35.5 per cent. The urban areas in Meghalaya have better surface conditions, with 98.7 per cent of the roads being surfaced, but road density per 1,000 of the population is only 0.19.

Given that 80 per cent of Meghalaya's population resides in rural areas, where agriculture is the main occupation, the state's geography poses additional constraints. The hilly terrain, with steep slopes and deep gorges, limits the land available for agriculture. Only 15 per cent of the total geographical area (343,601 hectares) is under crop cultivation, which includes areas where traditional shifting cultivation (often called "*jhum*" cultivation) is practiced—typically associated with lower productivity. Approximately 42 per cent of Meghalaya's land (946,248 hectares) is covered by forests, further limiting the land available for farming (Meghalaya Socio Economic Review, 2020).[13]

These geographic and infrastructural factors highlight the paucity of connectivity and transportation systems, which has its bearing on developing trade networks across borders. The economic challenges faced by the border areas of Meghalaya were highlighted as far back as 1974 by the then governor, L.P. Singh, in his address to the Meghalaya Legislative Assembly. In his speech, he expressed the government's concern over the difficult economic conditions of people living in the border regions. To address these issues, the government established a separate department dedicated solely to handling the problems of these areas. Besides agriculture, Meghalaya has rich deposits of limestone[14] and coal.[15] Limestone mining in the Khasi hills of Meghalaya has a long history, dating back to at least the eighteenth century. According to the *Assam District Gazetteer* (Allen, 1906), limestone quarrying and trading were well established in the Khasi hills during British rule, serving as a lucrative business for both the local Khasi population and the people of Sylhet (now in Bangladesh). Limestone was primarily quarried along the southern slopes of the Khasi hills and transported to Sylhet, and during the rainy season, it was transported via the Surma river using flat-bottomed canoes. The primary use at the time was for producing lime, which was a valuable commodity for construction and other uses. Europeans were significantly involved in the industry, controlling much of the limestone mining, production, and trade during the British colonial era.

While initially focused on small-scale production, largely for edible lime, the advent of cement manufacturing in the mid-twentieth century shifted the scale of limestone mining. Mawmluh Cherra Cements Ltd (MCCL), established in Cherrapunjee in 1955 (originally Assam Cements Limited), became Meghalaya's first cement manufacturing unit. It was later acquired by the Government of Assam in 1964 and the Government of Meghalaya in 1974. This marked the beginning of large-scale limestone mining for cement production in the region. In more recent times, Lafarge Umiam Mining Pvt. Ltd (LUMPL) began extensive limestone mining in the Shella–Nongtrai area of East Khasi hills in 2005 to supply limestone to Lafarge Surma Cement Ltd (LSC) in Chhatak, Bangladesh.

Bridging the Lost Connection: The Indo-Bangla Border and Meghalaya

From the time of Bangladesh's Independence in 1971, India was seen as a friendly ally, especially due to India's crucial role in supporting Bangladesh during the Liberation War. In February 1972, the prime ministers of both countries, Indira Gandhi and Sheikh Mujibur Rahman, met in New Delhi, pledging "Eternal Friendship" and signing the Treaty of Peace and Friendship on 19 March 1972. This treaty laid the foundation for closer bilateral relations, particularly in areas such as economic cooperation, transport, and communication (Articles 5 and 6). The Indo-Bangladesh Trade Agreement, signed shortly afterwards on 28 March 1972, formalized trade relations, including provisions for both formal and border trade. However, tensions soon arose when Bangladesh raised concerns about large-scale smuggling across the border, leading to the scrapping of the original trade agreement in October 1972. A revised version was signed in September 1973, but relations took a downturn following the 1975 assassination of Sheikh Mujibur Rahman and the subsequent military rule in Bangladesh. Disputes over issues like the sharing of Ganges river waters and illegal migration further strained ties, negatively impacting trade between the two nations.

Bilateral relations saw significant improvement when Sheikh Hasina, leader of the Awami League, became Bangladesh's prime minister in 1996.

A new phase of cooperation began, highlighted by regular exchanges of visits between leaders and government officials. This strengthened the prospects for sub-regional cooperation and mutually beneficial trade, leading to the revival of traditional "border *hats*" (border markets), such as Kalaichar and Balat (now called "border *haats*", Ministry of Commerce and Industry, 2010), aimed at boosting economic growth in border areas. In a joint statement on 7 September 2011, Prime Ministers Sheikh Hasina and Manmohan Singh reaffirmed the importance of friendship, trust, and understanding between their nations. They also emphasized the significance of border *hats*/*haats* in fostering growth, particularly in border regions. The concept of border *haats* was integrated into broader policies such as India's Look East Policy (later renamed the Act East Policy), which sought to enhance economic and strategic ties with Southeast Asia. In this context, traditional border *hats* were viewed as valuable tools for fostering cross-border trade and connectivity, especially between India and Bangladesh.

Historically, border *hats* played a crucial role in the lives of people living in the border areas of Assam, Meghalaya, Tripura, Mizoram, and West Bengal as well as in the bordering regions of Bangladesh. These markets, held at regular intervals, facilitated the exchange of locally produced goods and services. In Meghalaya, for instance, border *hats* have existed for centuries along the foothills of the Khasi–Jaintia and Garo regions, enabling economic and political interactions between the hills and the plains. Key goods traded historically included iron, lime, oranges, honey, ivory, timber, betel nuts, and potatoes from the hills, in exchange for rice, salt, dry fish, and silk from Bengal and Assam.

In modern times, the significance of cross-border trade has extended to include large-scale exports of minerals such as limestone and coal from Meghalaya to Bangladesh. These exports are regulated by the Government of Meghalaya and authorized under the Open General Licence (OGL) framework. Major companies such as Lafarge Umiam Private Limited (LUPL) and Kommorrah Limestone Company Limited (KLCL) export limestone from areas such as Nongtrai and Shella to cement industries in Bangladesh. A 17-km cross-border conveyor belt transports limestone from Meghalaya to Bangladesh, where it is used for cement production. In the Jaintia hills, Jaintia Cement Limited in Sutnga village was established in 1986. Limestone mining in this region significantly expanded after 2004, when Cement Manufacturing Company Limited (Star Cement) set up operations in Lumshnong, followed by other private cement companies. In the Garo hills, limestone mining for cement production began in 1991. More than a dozen cement manufacturing plants are now in operation across Meghalaya, which has emerged as a major supplier of limestone for cement industries. Additionally, coal is exported through land customs stations (LCSs) in border areas, namely, Dawki, Shella Bazaar, and Bholaganj.

The southern borders of the Khasi hills, particularly in the East Khasi hills, are well known for the production of lime, made possible by the availability of limestone, firewood, and coal. Villages like Mawlong and Shella are home to numerous lime kilns, which produce large quantities of lime each year, contributing to the local economy and providing employment for many. In addition to minerals, forest products such as timber and rubber are also significant exports. The revival of border *hats* (in the form of border *haats*) has helped reconnect the economic and cultural links between the people of India and Bangladesh, especially those living in border areas. These markets have provided a platform for the exchange of goods, fostering trade and economic growth while also serving as a lifeline for communities on both sides of the border.

Meghalaya at present has eight LCSs, of which only Dawki in the Jaintia hills and Dalu in the West Garo hills facilitate cross-border passenger movement. Among the eight functional LCSs, Borsora LCS only exports coal and limestone besides import of coal; Bholaganj LCS exports only limestone, quartz, stone, and boulder stone; Shellabazar LCS export only limestone and boulder stone; Baghmara and Ghasupara LCS exports only coal; and Mahendraganj LCS exports–imports coal, boulder stone, crushed stone, bamboo, ginger, tamarind, and dry fish. Besides passenger movement, Dawki LCS also facilitates export–import of coal, limestone, quartz stone, boulder stone, oranges, ginger, and raw hides and skins.

The rapid exploitation of minerals in Meghalaya, boosted by the border trade of these items with Bangladesh (particularly coal and limestone) has resulted in significant growth in traffic intensity, especially with the increased movement of heavy vehicles transporting these resources. This surge in traffic has placed immense pressure on the state's road infrastructure, which was not originally designed to handle the current volume or weight of the vehicles. The roads, many of which traverse hilly and rugged terrain, are vulnerable to damage from frequent use by heavy trucks involved in the mining and transport industries. This deterioration not only impacts the efficiency of transportation but also impinges upon expansion border trade in horticultural products, which suffer largely from a transportation bottleneck and lack of proper storage facilities due to their perishable nature.

The importance of the border and goods traded, which include consumables such as betel leaves, bay leaves, fresh tomatoes, fresh ginger; shoes and slippers, vegetables like cabbage and radish; and citrus fruits such as oranges, meet the supply needs across the Bangladesh border. Besides auto tyres, cricket bats, printed cartons, and raw hides are exported from Meghalaya, which meet the demand requirements of small manufacturing units in Bangladesh. The major items imported from Bangladesh include Pran drinks, Pran edible packaged food, plastic furniture, household articles such as PVC doors/windows, tissue paper, door panels, PVC pipes and tubes, ready-made garment, melamine articles, and wooden furniture. A large proportion of these imported items have a ready market across the North-East region, where comparative prices of products from Bangladesh are sold at rates cheaper than the same items brought in from the rest of India.

Besides the LCS, there are two border *haat* points in Meghalaya, one at Kalaichar (South West Garo hills district), in India connecting with Baliamari (Kurigram district) in Bangladesh, and the other exists between (East Khasi hills district), in India and Lauwaghar (Dalora) (Sunamganj district) in Bangladesh through pillar No. 1213. These *haats* trade in local goods, benefiting communities on both sides by allowing the exchange of locally produced commodities. These include vegetables, fruits, spices, bamboo, bamboo grass, broomsticks, *gamcha* (a small traditional towel), *lungi* (a draper round the waist for men), the *dao* (a traditional cutter made with iron), ploughs, spade, chisel, axes, melamine products, processed food items, fruit juice, toiletries, cosmetics, plastic products, aluminium products, and cookeries.[16]

The market for these items is generated by both local demand and supply and depends on preference, price, and quality difference, including unavailability of the product at the local level. For example, there is a perceptible demand for Indian cosmetics and toiletries in Bangladesh;

women from Bangladesh often buy these items in bulk from the *haat*. They consider Indian cosmetics and toiletries to be of better quality than the same products manufactured in Bangladesh. Even women from distant districts of Bangladesh visit these *haats* to buy these products.[17] Other Indian items for which there is a high demand in Bangladesh are garments, processed foods, nappies and baby foods, and spices. On the other hand, there is considerable demand for live and dry fish from Bangladesh in India due to differences in price and taste and issues of availability on the Indian side, especially in the Northeastern states. Pran, a food and beverage company from Bangladesh, is a common brand name whose products are traded easily across borders in Meghalaya, Assam, and Tripura. Bangladeshi agri-implements, bakery products, melamine, and plastic products are in high demand in India as they are cheaper. The border *haat* committees decide the commodities for trade in the border *haats*.

However, at the Kalaichar–Baliamari border *haat*, the trade is mainly limited to locally produced betel nuts and locally grown vegetables and fruits. The need-based trade between the communities living on the border helps to mitigate the economic imperatives of the border people. First established on 23 July 2011, this border *haat* lies at the zero line, close to sub-pillar 19 of international pillar 1072, along the Meghalaya–Bangladesh border. Such markets provide a venue for local vendors and buyers from both countries to engage in trade, fostering cultural exchange and economic benefits for border communities. The border *haat* at Kalaichar was operational until March 2020, when it was suspended as a preventative measure due to the COVID-19 pandemic. The revival of the Baliamari border *haat*, located along the Bangladesh–India border near Rajibpur upazila in Kurigram district, will once again allow local communities from both sides of the border to trade goods, promoting economic activity and strengthening cross-border relations.

Border *haats* remain an essential tool for grassroots diplomacy, reinforcing the bond between the people of Bangladesh and India. Border *haats*, like the one at Kalaichar (India) and Baliamari (Bangladesh), are a necessity to facilitate trade in basic requirements of the communities living at the border. The cross-border relations at the border between the communities of the two countries serve as feeders to meet the demand-and-supply imperatives at the local level. These border points between

Bangladesh and India along the Meghalaya border are located far from their mainland centres of economic activities. Given its long stretch of international boundary of 443 kms with Bangladesh, which sets a unique advantage for setting up of industries based on local resources, the government of Meghalaya has established industrial estates to encourage growth of small- and medium-scale industries besides setting up the Export Promotion Industrial Park (EPIP) at Byrnihat. The setting up of these industrial estates and the EPIP[18] provides a leverage to augment local production for cross-border trade as transportation cost to the border points are comparatively lower.

However, the recent spurt in industrial activities to foster the manufacturing sector has impinged upon its power scenario. A power surplus state a few decades ago, Meghalaya has an electricity deficit and is unable to meet demand. Although Meghalaya made significant progress in rural electrification, the power supply in electrified villages is extremely unreliable. The state has a base load of 250 megawatts (MW) of power while the state availability is only 140 MW, leaving a deficit of 110 MW.[19] Theoretically, fostering manufacturing activities at the local level based on available resources would have multiplier effect on income and employment generation; however, one cannot wish away the social and cultural norms that shape the economic activities of a region or geographical space. The Khasis, who have been terrace cultivators along mountainous space within a "non-market" space, stand at the cusp of a transformative social space where market and monetized social space define the new order of the day. It needs to be emphasized that border spaces are mediated by a complex set of social and structural components, ethnically embedded social relations, and local state policies, and diplomatic relations between the nations impact the disparate economic complementarities.

Border *Haats*: New Space for Negotiation

It is an undeniable fact that communities living across the border share ethnic affinity and communality, and a border line demarcating two nations artificially divides the people. India's Look East/Act East Policy is perceived to open the linkage between North-East India and the bordering countries. While trade through LCSs can bring dividends to the regional trade, it is the border *haats* that can foster and negotiate peace and stability with the neighbouring countries of Myanmar and Bangladesh along the Northeastern border. These border *haats* are the *lingua franca* of the communities living across borders. However, many venders and vendees in these *haats* also work as transporters of goods (handload/headload) on behalf of the people who do not access the licence of a vendee (Sarma, 2023). This arrangement has led to a precarious situation where people engaged in this activity have been reduced to daily wage earners. While the very purpose of the *haats* was to ensure a secured life to the people in the borders in terms of access to basic amenities and necessities of life, the experience of many living on the borders reflect externally controlled economic transaction where the locals have little say or control. As mentioned earlier, the exposition to market-based transaction for a community hitherto living in communal ownership of resource and its use often fails to negotiate the trading intricacies. This results in impoverishment within their own ethnic communal settings, often building up resistance and retaliation to changes and border engagements. Cross-border engagement in market exchange requires exchangeable commodities within the border space. Often when communities fail to produce the complementarities of demand and supply, business lobbies outside take advantage by appropriating border *haats* to procure goods from across the border (Sarma, 2017). Within the ecology of the border space, there also continues exchange of goods required by people from two sides of the border—items of daily consumption to household uses get exchanged to meet the basic needs of the people living on the border.

Borders typically restrict the free movement of factors (e.g. labour and capital) and limit the trade of goods and services, which can slow the growth of local economies in these areas. However, regions near major trading corridors benefit from their strategic position. These corridors facilitate transportation and trade, boosting economic activity close to border crossings (or international gateways). The "*Circuity* Effect" (Clark, 1994) captures the idea that border regions far from these corridors often lag economically as they lack the infrastructure that concentrates near trade hubs. A common solution is to improve border-crossing efficiency or to establish Special Economic Zones (SEZs) that foster cross-border production and economic activities. However, this focus on trade hubs can inadvertently neglect border regions that do not lie along these corridors. Infrastructure meant to facilitate international trade may not always meet the economic needs of local populations, who might require a different approach to economic development than just facilitating bilateral trade. Clark (1994) differentiates the impacts of international border's on national economies (hinterlands) versus their effects on regions close to the border (border lands), categorizing them into "primary" and "secondary" effects.

- **Primary effects**: these are broad impacts on the national economy, which are linked to national-level trade policies and cross-border connectivity infrastructure. Primary effects influence everyone within a nation by shaping the overall environment for trade and economic exchange with other countries.
- **Secondary effects**: these are specific to border zones, influenced by the physical location of the border and the presence of border-crossing points. Secondary effects influence the microeconomic decisions and day-to-day lives of residents within these border lands. Only those in close proximity to the border experience these secondary effects, which Clark identifies as follows:
  1. **Cross-border market size**: this factor depends on the population density and purchasing power of people on both sides of the border. High population concentrations on either side of a border can create a "paired city" effect, where twin cities (such as San Diego–Tijuana or Mexicali–Calexico along the US–Mexico border) experience significant retail and trade activity due to the demand from people across the border. Similar "paired city" dynamics are seen in South Asia, for instance, between Comilla in Bangladesh and Agartala in India, where historical, social, and economic ties foster cross-border market activity.
  2. **The permeability of borders**: permeability refers to the ease with which people, goods, and services can cross the border. Where borders are "hard" or restrictive, often due to administrative challenges or lack of natural barriers, informal trade can flourish as people seek alternative ways to access resources and opportunities across the border. For example, when formal trade is difficult,

residents might rely on informal channels, particularly if geographical features do not strongly divide the two regions.

3. **Differential pressure across national boundaries**: this refers to the disparities in income levels and retail pricing policies between neighbouring countries, which strongly influence consumer behaviour in border regions. These differences can create incentives for residents to purchase goods on the side of the border where prices are lower or products are more accessible. For instance, if one country has higher per capita income or different taxation policies that make goods cheaper, consumers from the neighbouring country may cross the border to buy these goods. This often happens in border lands where, due to income and price differences, residents selectively source goods based on affordability or availability. However, while these cross-border shopping patterns benefit individual consumers, the infrastructure set up to facilitate bilateral trade often doesn't meet the daily commercial needs of local populations in border lands.

   This is evident, for example, along the India–Bangladesh border, where border *haats* help meet the daily needs of local communities, providing a platform for small-scale, people-to-people trade that serves local consumption more directly than large-scale bilateral trade initiatives.

4. **Transfer costs**: transfer costs refer to the expenses incurred when goods, services, or people move across national boundaries. These costs encompass both direct and indirect expenses associated with cross border activities. The key components include
   - **Formal compliance costs**: these are the direct costs of complying with regulations, such as documentation fees, taxes, duties, and transportation expenses. These costs are typically unavoidable and are imposed by governments to manage and regulate the flow of goods and services across borders.
   - **Informal and indirect costs**: these are less tangible but still significant costs, including the time, effort, and resources needed to navigate cross-border transactions. This might involve searching for appropriate sellers or buyers, marketing products to cross-border customers, or building relationships to facilitate trade across boundaries. These costs can increase if information is

> scarce or if communication barriers exist, making transactions more complex and expensive.

High transfer costs along the border can often discourage trade, limit economic interactions between border communities, and make imported goods more expensive, which may lead to reduced cross-border commerce and economic growth in border lands. Conversely, when transfer costs are minimized—whether through simplified documentation, reduced taxes, or efficient transportation networks—cross-border exchanges become more accessible and beneficial for local economies. The formal trade through border areas across the North-East with its neighbouring countries often require documentation and compliance with rules of the land, which is one of the reasons why volume of trade through LCSs have not registered much growth over the years. On the contrary, informal trade, which brings down the compliance and has lower transaction cost burden, has seen expansion along the borders with both Myanmar and Bangladesh.

Paired urban concentrations (Ford, 1988) near border zones create strong demand for retail solutions tailored to cross-border consumers. These paired cities or towns, positioned close to international boundaries, often develop interconnected economies due to their geographic proximity and the population density on each side. The location of Shillong in Meghalaya is a case in point, which is located in close proximity to Balat, Bholaganj, and Ryngku along the Bangladesh border. In such cases, the large populations in the urban centre drive significant demand for retail infrastructure, which caters to residents from both sides of the border. This leads to the growth of border-specific retail solutions, such as markets, shopping complexes, and service facilities that serve a dual audience. Large urban centres that are within a short travelling distance of the border also have a pull effect, attracting customers across it for a variety of goods and services, even if they are not right next to it. Cross-border economic interdependence is strengthened by these factors, which also push local markets to adjust by offering goods and services that suit the tastes and budgets of a varied, binational clientele.

It is here that state interventions become important in the case of North-East India to help the communities at the border to negotiate the transition through capacity enhancement in organized trade and business such that the communal economic spaces can be integrated within the larger market transaction where the ethnic communities do not lose command and control over their resources. Rather, the resource control and use can be steered to ensure a secured economic and social space for the people at the border space. Communities close to international borders benefit from this trade in a number of ways, including increased access to a greater variety of goods and services, work possibilities, and local economic growth. Given the economic importance of cross-border trade for border zones, local community leaders and local bodies such as the Dorbar Shnong are essential components required within the larger policy framework and implementation architecture for promoting cross-border relations. The efforts of the Meghalaya government in recent years have been one step towards this that needs to be complemented by India's diplomatic engagement with Bangladesh to sustain the border relations between Bangladesh and India along the strategic Northeastern frontier region of India.

Notes

1. In 1783, the Khasis attacked Pandua to avenge an insult by the Havildar of Lindsay, and the servant of Lindsay was killed and his lime kilns destroyed. During his tenure in Sylhet from 1778 to 1790, Scottish colonial official Robert Lindsay held the positions of district collector and magistrate, after initially serving as a supervisor. In addition to overseeing certain magisterial responsibilities, he was in charge of maintaining district authority and protecting it against hill raiders. The lime (*chunam*) industry was one of Lindsay's own commercial endeavours; he later expanded to include betel nuts, rattan, and elephants.
2. For details, one can refer to the letter from Fisher, Surveyor, North Bengal, Sylhet, N.1. Ferguaod Esquire, Magistrate of Sylhet, 10 September 1829 (Assam State Archive).
3. These regions were maintained under a particular administrative structure and have not been impacted in the least by the amendments of the Colonial Laws. Any provincial or federal laws do not cover them, unless the governor or the governor-general specifically requested it. Nearly all of these regions were "scheduled districts" under the India Act XIV of 1874 prior to the reforms of 1919. They were protected by separate laws and administrative processes that were either established by announcements under the All India Statutes or by enactments for specific tracts.

4. See Sir George Birdwood's introduction to the "First Letter Book of the East India Company: 1600–1619", p. xxxvi.
5. Field survey (2023), "Cross Border Interactions along International Borders of North-East India", Omeo Kumar Das Institute of Social Change and Development (OKDISCD, 2023).
6. Smuggling is used here to mean trading in goods not within the trade regulation of the two countries but through personal contacts at the border between two newly created spaces by cartographic division.
7. Field Survey (2023), "Cross Border Interactions along International Borders of North-East India", OKDISCD.
8. Border space economy defines the space where economic activities and transactions take place among the communities living across contiguous areas of the land border across two nations. This may involve trade and exchange among communities living along the border with items of mutual requirements or items traded by local merchants for selling in nearby towns and villages along the territorial borders.
9. This proposal culminated in the passage of the Assam Reorganization (Meghalaya) Act of 1969, which officially created an autonomous state of Meghalaya within Assam. The new autonomous state comprised the United Khasi hills, Jaintia hills, and Garo hills and came into effect on 2 April 1970. Meghalaya was granted a thirty-seven-member legislature, operating under the provisions of the Sixth Schedule.
10. On 21 January 1972, Meghalaya officially became a separate state with its own Legislative Assembly, marking a significant moment in the region's political history. The name "Meghalaya" (meaning "Abode of clouds") was coined by geographer S.P. Chatterjee in 1936 and was accepted for the new state.
11. Basic Road Statistics of India (2018–19), Ministry of Road Transport and Highways, Government of India.
12. The density of National Highways is 51.5 per sq. km; State Highways is 34.2 per 1,000 sq. km, rural roads is 1,450.66 per 1,000 sq. km, urban roads is 25.46 per 1,000 sq. km. (Basic Road Statistics of India (2018–19), Ministry of Road Transport and Highways, Government of India).
13. Meghalaya Socio-Economic Review (2020), Directorate of Economics and Statistics, Government of Meghalaya.
14. Cherrapunjee, Mawlong, Ishamati, Shella, Komorrah, Borsora, and Bagli in the Khasi hills district; Lakadong, Lumshonong, and Nongkhlieh in the Jaintia hills district; Darrang Era-Aning, Siju, and Chokpot in the Garo hills district.
15. Langrin and East Darrangiri in the Khasi hills district, Bapung in the Jaintia hills district, and West Darranggiri in the Garo hills district.
16. See https://megindustry.gov.in/border_haat.html.
17. Field Survey (2023), "Cross Border Interactions along International Borders of North-East India", OKDISCD.

18. The industrial estates are located at Shillong, Tura, Jowai, Williamnagar, Mendipathar, Nongstoin, and Umiam and the EPIP is at Byrnihat.
19. Meghalaya Power Policy (2024), Power Department, Government of Meghalaya.

References

Allen, B.C. (1906), "The Khasi and Jaintia Hills, the Garo Hills and the Lushai Hills", *Assam District Gazetteer*, Volume x.

Bhagawati, Dhiren (2007), *Meghalaya: Issues and Legacies of Its Early Years*, Guwahati: DVS Publication.

Board of Revenue Papers (1782), "Assam State Archive (ASA) File No. 8, Serial No. 3".

Board of Revenue Papers (1783), "ASA File No. 12, Serial No. 2".

Board of Revenue Papers (1787), "ASA File Nos 10 and 13", 29 December.

Cederlöf, Gunnel (2009), "Fixed Boundaries, Fluid Landscapes: British Expansion into the North East Bengal in the 1820s", *Indian Economic and Social History Review*, 46 (4), pp. 579–613.

Clark, T. (1994), "National Boundaries, Border Zones, and Marketing Strategy: A Conceptual Framework and Theoretical Model of Secondary Boundary Effects", *Journal of Marketing*, 58(3), pp. 67–80.

Ford, L. (1988), "Behavioural Implications of Urban Growth along the United States/Mexican Border", *Journal of Architectural and Planning Research*, 5 (3), pp. 208–14.

Giri, Helen (1998), *The Khasis under British Rule 1824–1947*, New Delhi: Regency Publication.

Ludden, David (2003), "The First Boundary of Bangladesh on Sylhet's Northern Frontiers", *Journal* of the *Asiatic Society* of *Bangladesh*, 48 (1), pp. 1–54.

Ludden, David (2019), "India's Spatial History in the Brahmaputra–Meghna River Basin", in Neeladri Bhattacharya Joy L. K. Pachuau (ed.), *Landscape, Culture, and Belonging: Writing the History of Northeast India*, New Delhi: Cambridge University Press, pp. 23–37.

Ministry of Commerce and Industry (2010), "Memorandum of Understanding for 'Establishing Border Haats across the Border between India and Bangladesh", Government of the Republic of India, 23 October (http://commerce.nic.in/trade/MOU_Border_Haats_across_Border_India_and_Bangladesh2010.pdf).

Roy, Donkupar (1987), "A Configuration of Poverty in Border Areas of Meghalaya", PhD thesis, Economics Department, North Eastern Hills University, Shillong.

Sarma, Akshay Jyoti (2017), *Does Informality Matter—Understanding the Interactions along and across the India–Myanmar and India–Bangladesh Borders*, Guwahati: Omeo Kumar Das Institute of Social Change and Development.

Sarma, Akshay Jyoti (2023), "Paradox of Development in India's Northeast: The Act East Policy and Beyond", *Social Change and Development*, XX (1), pp. 26–39.

Syiemlieh, D.R. (ed.) (1997), *Anecdotes of an Indian Life—Robert Lindsay*, Shillong: North East Hill University Publications.

Syiemlieh, D.R. (2022), "Transition in Time: An Overview of the Administrative Structure, Policy and Pattern in the Hills of North East India 1822–1972", N.M. Lahiri Memorial Lecture 2022, State Convention Centre, Shillong, 12 November (https://meghsja.gov.in/sites/default/files/Reading-Materials/RM2.pdf).

7

Mizoram and Its Neighbours

Exploring the Trade Potential and Opportunities

Konthoujam Gyanendra Singh

Introduction

The Look East Policy was launched in 1992 with the objective of strengthening India's economic and political relations with the Association of Southeast Asian Nations (ASEAN) in the post-Cold War era. The policy gradually went on to encompass India's engagement with Japan, the Republic of Korea, and China, and in recent years, it has extended to Australia, New Zealand, and the Pacific Island countries. In 2014, it was upgraded to the Act East Policy underlying the need for a more action-orientated strategy to deepen India's focus on the countries to India's east. At the same time, the policy is increasingly projected as the new economic development strategy for India's Northeastern Region. The major policy objective is the economic integration of the region with Southeast Asia and to achieve this, the emphasis is on the three Cs: Commerce, Connectivity, and Culture (Taneja et al., 2019).

India's current external economic engagement is shaped by the Act East Policy and the Neighbourhood First Policy, both of which emphasize improved connectivity and development partnerships across India's immediate and extended neighbourhood (Taneja et al., 2019).

The Indian government's Foreign Trade Policy 2015–20 underlined the importance of foreign trade in the growth of Indian economy and aimed at doubling India's export of goods and services. Consequently, India ratified the World Trade Organization Agreement on Trade Facilitation in April 2016 and, soon after, unveiled the National Trade

Konthoujam Gyanendra Singh, *Mizoram and Its Neighbours* In: *Sub-Regional Cooperation for Trade, Investment, and Employment in North-East India*. Edited by: Ashish Nath, Oxford University Press.
 DOI: 10.1093/9780197908938.003.0007

Facilitation Action Plan 2017–20, which seeks to transform the trade ecosystem by reducing the time and cost of doing business.

The Northeastern Region accounts for about 8 per cent of India's geographical area and has an international border of around 5,182 km (RIS, 2011). It is connected to the rest of India via the ~22 km-wide Siliguri corridor (the "Chicken's Neck"). The region has strategic importance, diverse natural resources, and tourism potential (India Brand Equity Foundation, 2023).

The eight North-East states of India share international borders with Bangladesh (1,596 km), Bhutan (455 km), Myanmar (1,640 km), Nepal (97 km), and China (1,395 km). Bangladesh and Myanmar are strategic partners and are members of the Bay of Bengal Initiative for Multi-Sectoral Technical and Economic Cooperation (BIMSTEC), while China, along with them, is a part of the Bangladesh–China–India–Myanmar (BCIM) Forum for Regional Cooperation.

Myanmar is vital for the economic development of the Northeastern Region. It is the only ASEAN nation with which India shares both a land and maritime border. Four North-East states of India share a border with Myanmar, namely, Arunachal Pradesh (520 km), Manipur (398 km), Mizoram (510 km), and Nagaland (215 km). Similarly, Bangladesh also shares the border with four North-East states of India, namely, Assam (263 km), Meghalaya (443 km), Mizoram (318 km), and Tripura (856 km).

The land trade of the Northeastern Region of India with the neighbouring countries is carried through the designated land custom stations (LCSs) and integrated check posts (ICPs). The volume of trade of North-East India is rather miniscule, accounting for about 0.13 per cent (rupees (Rs) 30.9 billion) of India's total exports in fiscal year 2019 (DGCI&S, n.d.). The major exports include bulk minerals and ores, coal, coke and briquettes, petroleum products, fresh fruits, natural stones and products, and iron and steel. Imports mainly consist of cement and clinker, marine products, cereal preparation, processed items, and iron and steel. The bulk of trade is with Bangladesh, followed by Bhutan and Myanmar. Against this backdrop, this chapter investigates the historical and policy-driven evolution of border trade between Mizoram and its neighbouring countries—Myanmar and Bangladesh—with a focus on identifying opportunities, challenges, and implications for regional integration under India's Act East Policy.

Mizoram: Economic Overview

Mizoram is a North-East Indian state bordered by Tripura, Assam, and Manipur and internationally by Myanmar and Bangladesh. The state's economy is dominated by agriculture and allied activities, including shifting cultivation (*jhum*) in parts of Mizoram, alongside horticulture and livestock. Handloom/handicrafts and tourism are important supplementary sectors, and state policy documents emphasize connectivity and market access as key constraints and opportunities (Planning and Programme Implementation Department, n.d.; India Brand Equity Foundation, 2023; National Bank for Agriculture and Rural Development, n.d.).

Mizoram's primary activities revolve around agriculture, with the majority of its population engaged in farming and related activities. The state's agrarian economy is characterized by practices such as *jhum* cultivation (slash-and-burn agriculture), and it produces a variety of crops, including rice, maize, and vegetables. Additionally, Mizoram has a growing handloom and handicraft industry, reflecting its rich cultural traditions in textiles and art. In recent years, the state has focused on developing its tourism sector, leveraging its scenic beauty and unique cultural heritage to attract visitors.

Mizoram–Myanmar Border Trade Dynamics

Mizoram shares a 510-km length of international boundary with Myanmar. The border trade point between Mizoram and Myanmar at the Zokharthar–Rih sector was opened on 30 January 2004. Zokharthar is 28 km from district headquarters at Champhai and 228 km from Aizawl, the capital of Mizoram. The nearest rail link is the Bairabi railway station in the Kolasib district of Mizoram, which is about 320.4 km from Zokharthar. The Lengpui Airport of Mizoram is about 242.1 km from Zokharthar. There is only one inland container depot (ICD) in the entire North-East, and it is in Amingaon at Guwahati, Assam and is about 717.2 km from Zokharthar.

The building of Zokharthar Land Customs Station (LCS) was inaugurated on 25 March 2015. A border township comprising twelve Assam-type residential quarters is also constructed in Melbuk village, which is

9 km from Zokharthar LCS in order to accommodate the officials and staff of the LCS. The Zokharthar LCS is managed by the Assam Rifles. The Mizoram Police also remain present for immigration.

The Zokharthar LCS has undergone different types of trade mechanism since its opening. Initially, traditional/free exchange mechanism and barter trade systems were operational. Under traditional/free exchange mechanisms, locally produced commodities by the people living within 40 km on both sides of the border are permitted to exchange, and the value of each transaction should be less than USD 1,000. The export is to be balanced by importing goods of equivalent value within a few days, and vice versa. Customs duty is not chargeable under this mechanism.

Under the barter trade mechanism, the exporter and importer need to have an Importer–Exporter Code (IEC) certificate issued by the director general of foreign trade (DGFT), Ministry of Commerce and Industry, Government of India. They are permitted to trade on notified tradable items, and the value of trade should not exceed USD 20,000 per transaction. Customs duty, cess, and other duties need to be paid on such trade, and exports should be balanced by importing equivalent value within six months. A total of twenty-two tradable items were notified in 2004, and this was increased to forty tradable items in 2008, which was further increased to sixty-two tradable items in 2012. The sixty-two tradable items were mustard/rape seed, pulses and beans, fresh vegetables, fruits, garlic, onions, chillies, spices, minor forest products, betel nuts and leaves, food items for local consumption, tobacco, tomatoes, sesame, coriander seeds, soyabeans, roasted sunflower seeds, katha, ginger, rice, wheat, maize, millets and oats, scented tobacco, edible oil, bamboo, reed broom, resin, paints and varnishes, coal, fabricated steel products, handlooms and handicrafts items, hardware/minor construction materials, lime, semi-precious stones, bicycles and parts, lifesaving drugs, fertilizers, insecticides, cotton fabrics, stainless steel utensils, menthol, agarbatti, cosmetics, plastic items, sewing machines, textile fabrics, three-wheelers/cars below 1,000cc, and motor cycles and motor cycle spare parts.

However, the above trade mechanism ceased to exist after 2015, following the Reserve Bank of India notification (RBI, 2015) whereas trade between India and Myanmar was switched over to the normal/regular trade mechanism with effect from 1 December 2015, and all trade transactions were to be settled in any permitted currency in addition to the

Asian Clearing Union Mechanism. Accordingly, all goods and items are tradable under this mechanism except for the restricted or prohibited items as mentioned in Schedule 1 (Import Policy) and Schedule 2 (Export Policy) of the Indian Foreign Trade Policy as declared by the DGFT, India. The composition and volume of trade through Zokharthar LCS are summarized in Table 7.1 (LCS Zokhawthar and Customs Division, Aizawl, n.d.).

The above table shows that there were almost no exports to Myanmar during the past few years, and imports, too, have declined over the years; moreover, only one item was imported, namely, betel nut (areca nut). One of the main reasons for decline in import, as opined by the officials as well as traders, is the 100 per cent increase of import duty from 4 per cent to 40 per cent and the addition of 5 per cent Goods and Services Tax (GST) and 2 per cent cess. So effectively, an importer has to incur about 50 per cent as duties and taxes for import of betel nut, which has led to its decline over the years. Again, the trade procedures and documents required for export/import are also complicated and time consuming. The documents required are listed below:

1. Sale contract
2. Invoice
3. Swift message
4. Packing list
5. Bill of lading
6. Certificate of origin
7. Phytosanitary certificate
8. IEC/Goods and Services Tax Identification Number (GSTIN)/ Permanent Account Number (PAN)
9. Import manifest
10. Bill of entry
11. Undertaking bond for private/public warehouse
12. TR-6 bank challan (used to deposit cash)
13. Sample result
14. Clearance/out of charge.

The importer and exporter enter into a sales contract, which is usually valid for ninety days. The importer in India deposits the cost of

Table 7.1 Trade pattern at Zokhawthar LCS

Year	Import				Export			
	Commodity	No. of consignment	Quantity (MT)	Assessable value (rupees)	Commodity	No. of consignment	Quantity (MT)	Assessable value (rupees)
2010–11	Betel nut	01	11.68	4,33,548.00	Nil	–	–	–
2011–12	Betel nut	07	60.00	22,27,548.00	Nil	–	–	–
2012–13	Nil	–	–	–	Soyabari	01	6.40	1,85,600.00
2013–14	Betel nut	14	140.00	1,61,56,394.00	Soyabari	02	29.00	18,12,500.00
2014–15	Betel nut	66	584.00	8,15,04,710.00	Nil	–	–	–
2015–16	Betel nut	134	1,132.00	16,74,14,039.00	Nil	–	–	–
2016–17	Betel nut	67	1,500.00	27,24,66,127.00	Nil	–	–	–
2017–18	Betel nut	06	63.60	1,60,83,152.00	Nil	–	–	–
	Black pepper	02	10.00	19,40,590.00	Nil	–	–	–
2018–19	Nil	–	–	–	Nil	–	–	–
Upto April 2019	Betel nut	01	20.00	54,51,825.00	–	–	–	–

Source: LCS Lokhawthar and Customs Division, Aizawl (n.d.), "Trade Statistics for Zakhawthar LCS (Administrative Records)".

goods to the account of the exporter in Myanmar. It is deposited with Housing Development Finance Corporation (HDFC) and Industrial Development Bank of India (IDBI) banks, Champhai as only these two banks have forex facilities. Once the amount is credited to the exporter account, a swift message is provided by the bank to the importer which they then take to the Customs Office at Zokharthar LCS. Customs prepares the duty based on the cost of goods and a bank challan (TR-6) is issued. The importer pays the customs duty as per the TR-6 at the State Bank of India (SBI) Champhai. The SBI Zokharthar does not accept challans; it is mainly an account-handling branch for daily transactions. The importer can bring the goods to the LCS Zokharthar once the duty is paid. Here, the goods are kept in the warehouse, or they are open dumped, or put in a warehouse, in which case a bond is signed between the importer and officials at the LCS. From the consignment, a sample is drawn and sent for testing either at Imphal, Manipur, or Guwahati, Assam. It is usually done in Imphal. This process usually takes ten to fifteen days. Once the test results are obtained, the goods are ready to be moved from the LCS to anywhere in the country. The process is complicated and delays the movement of goods. This not only reduces the value of the products but also increases the transaction costs.

High import duties, lengthy procedures, poor road conditions, and inadequate border infrastructure are among the key factors behind the decline in formal trade along the Zokhawthar–Rih route (Das, 2021; Hmar, 2019). Although imports of betel nut have declined and there were no exports in recent years, daily informal transactions continue. Table 7.2 lists commonly observed items imported from Myanmar and items exported from Mizoram (Singh, 2019).

It should be noted that many goods are of third-country origin rather than originating in Myanmar. Similarly, in the case of exports, most items are sourced from other parts of India, except for ginger. In addition to the listed items, there are reports of smuggling of restricted/prohibited goods such as gold, drugs, heroin, and arms and ammunition. Customs authorities seize such items on being informed or their being found, while low-value goods for local consumption often move through informal channels. Informal trade therefore remains prevalent in this corridor, while formal trade has become negligible. Potential drivers include kinship links across the border, a porous frontier, and price differentials for everyday consumer goods (Das, 2021; Hmar, 2019).

Table 7.2 Items traded between Myanmar and Mizoram

Imports from Myanmar	Exports from Mizoram
Food/edible items	Fertilizer
Energy drinks	Hair
Soaps, detergents	Pharmaceuticals
Cigarettes, tobacco	Chemicals
Cosmetics	Ginger
Mosquito repellent	–
Canned beef and fish	–
Blankets	–
Watermelons	–
Petrol, diesel	–
Cement	–
Garlic	–
Building materials	–
Apples	–
Electronics items	–
Juice	–
Garments	–
Shoes	–
Hardware items	–

Source: K.G. Singh (2019), "Field Survey on Border Trade and Commodity Flows in Mizoram" (unpublished primary data).

Mizoram–Bangladesh Border Trade

The Mizoram–Bangladesh border extends approximately 318 km and is primarily associated with the districts of Lunglei, Mamit, and Lawngtlai. Kawrpuichhuah, in Lunglei district, is Mizoram's first notified ICP for trade with Bangladesh (RIS, 2011). The demarcation agreement and subsequent protocol governing the India–Bangladesh land boundary provide an important legal basis for cross-border administration and cooperation (Ministry of External Affairs, 1974, 2011). Mamit district, known for its vibrant tribal culture and exquisite handicrafts, and Lawngtlai district, known for its diverse flora and fauna, are at the forefront of this crucial international juncture.

The Kawrpuichhuah ICP was formerly notified as an LCS in 1994 and later upgraded to an ICP. The ICP is non-functional, and the building of the ICP is yet to be constructed. However, the land, measuring an area of 21.4876 acres for setting up the ICP, has already been earmarked. Kawrpuichhuah is a village along the Bangladesh border alongside the river Karnaphuli, the international boundary line between India and Bangladesh. It is about 7 km away from Tlabung, formerly known as Demagiri. Tlabung is about 97 km from the district headquarters at Lunglei. Lunglei is about 178 km from Aizawl, the capital of Mizoram.

The two–lane national highway road measuring a length of 11.85 km connecting ICP Kawrpuichhuah and Tlabung is under construction. Tlabung and the proposed ICP Kawrpuichhuah are alongside the River Karnaphuli. The Karnaphuli river originates from Saitah village in the Mamit district of Mizoram and is navigable up to Chittagong Hill Tract and Chittagong, Bangladesh before it enters into the Bay of Bengal. It has the potential to be developed as an inland waterway. However, Kawrpuichhuah is prone to flooding and, as such, proper flood control mechanisms and disaster management plans need to be established. Moreover, the river may require dredging so as enable year-round transportation with maximum loading capacity. In the present day, the river has a navigability of maximum of 10 tonnes only.

There is a proposal for the construction of a double-lane bridge over the riverine boundary to connect India and Bangladesh over the Theka river (Thenganallah), a tributary of the Karnaphuli river. The proposed bridge would connect Kawrpuichhuah and Thegamukh, the border town on the Bangladesh side. The officials from India and Bangladesh conducted a joint survey in 2018 and fixed the coordinates of the proposed bridge to be constructed.

A trade facilitation centre under the aegis of the Commerce and Industries Department, Government of Mizoram, was constructed and inaugurated on 9 December 2011 in Tlabung. The building consists of guest rooms, conference hall, office rooms, etc. However, it remains non-functional to date, and no officials are present/stationed in the office except for a caretaker.

This riverine route between India and Bangladesh is an old route and can be traced back to the 1870s. However, post-Independence and the subsequent Partition has reduced the route's significance. It may be

Table 7.3 Items traded between Bangladesh and Mizoram

Imports from Bangladesh	Exports from Mizoram
Plastic items: buckets, water bottles, racks, dustbins, soap cases	Bamboo
Melamine items: dinner sets, cups, plates, spoons, trays, bowls	Teak
Toiletry items: toothpaste, soaps, detergents	Broom
Food items: dry fish, onions, garlic, mustard oil, *dhal* (*masoor*, *matar*—white peas), condensed milk, potato chips, dry cake, fried peas, *bhujia*, juice (*litchi*)	Ginger
Fruits: apples, grapes	Turmeric
Cotton *gamcha* (a small, traditional towel)	–
Water filters	–
Gas cylinders	–
Petrol/diesel	–
Cement	–

Source: K.G. Singh (2019), "Field Survey on Border Trade and Commodity Flows in Mizoram" (unpublished primary data).

mentioned here that communities inhabiting both sides of the border, including Chakma populations, exchange goods for their daily needs and local consumption. The items commonly traded between Bangladesh and Mizoram are presented in Table 7.3 (Singh, 2019).

The export of teak is banned, and there are seizures of logs of teak by the Border Security Force (BSF). Although there is no formal trade, the security forces allow export and import of other items except teak in this riverine route as these are mostly for local consumption. They have also stopped import of *matar dal* (white peas) in large quantities as it is transported to Silchar, Assam beyond Mizoram.

It may also be mentioned here that a crude form of informal border market exists in Tlabung. The market operates for three days a week (Tuesday, Thursday, and Saturday), apart from normal shops and vendors, which are open throughout the week (closed on Sundays). On these market days, especially on Saturday, people from both sides of the border come together and exchange their goods.

The inhabitants of Tlabung as well as Kawrpuichhuah are very much aware of the proposal for setting up the ICP and take a keen interest in establishing a formal trade route along this border. They are of the view that a formal trade route would help immensely in meeting their needs at a cheaper rate and improving their livelihoods. The state capital as well as the district headquarters being far away from this area, and the border being at closer proximity, it would be beneficial for inhabitants of this area to engage in trade.

The BSF personnel posted in Silkore and Tlabung expressed a similar view that opening the border formally for trade would be beneficial for both sides of the border. As of now, no proper notifications are given formally for opening the border, and so the local populations take their own routes for exchange of items. However, considering the socio-economic conditions of the locals, the security personnel in most cases allow the exchange of goods as they are mainly for local consumption, except for teak and *matar dal*.

However, for formal trade to become operational, an enabling infrastructure needs to be completed. Key priorities include construction of the ICP building, improved road connectivity from Aizawl to Tlabung and onwards to Kawrpuichhuah, and progression on the proposed bridge linking Kawrpuichhuah (India) and Thegamukh (Bangladesh). A mutually agreed list of tradable items is also required. The Trade and Commerce Department, Government of Mizoram has prepared a preliminary list of tradable items with Bangladesh, including the following (Trade and Commerce Department, n.d.):

1. Bamboo
2. Sesamum
3. Teak
4. Citrus fruits
5. Sugar
6. Groceries
7. Dry and fresh fish
8. Building materials
9. Ginger
10. Chillies
11. Cotton
12. Rice
13. Cement

14. Electronics items
15. Clothes
16. Others

Thus, cooperation and connectivity are important for improving socio-economic conditions in international border areas. Consequently, a number of regional cooperation initiatives with Myanmar and Bangladesh have been proposed or undertaken, particularly under India's Act East Policy (Sumi, 2025; RIS, 2011).

- **Mizoram State Roads II—Regional Transport Connectivity Project**: this World Bank-supported initiative focuses on improving road links to strengthen regional connectivity and facilitate trade, including with Myanmar and Bangladesh. Improved road infrastructure is expected to reduce transport costs and increase market access for border communities (Sumi, 2025; RIS, 2011).
- **Kaladan Multi-Modal Transit Transport Project (KMTTP)**: jointly conceived by India and Myanmar, the KMTTP aims to link Northeastern states to the port of Sittwe in Myanmar through a multi-modal network, improving access to maritime routes and diversifying logistics corridors for the region (Sumi, 2025).
- **Kolodyne Hydro-Electric Project II (Kolodyne HEP II)**: the proposed projects on the Kolodyne river (which flows from Myanmar into Mizoram) have been discussed in the context of power generation and improved connectivity, including possible links towards the Sittwe corridor (Sumi, 2025).
- **Strategic location for India's Act East Policy**: Mizoram's geographical proximity to Myanmar makes it a crucial element in India's Act East Policy. This policy underscores the importance of economic, strategic, and cultural relations with the Asia-Pacific region. Myanmar serves as a vital land bridge, facilitating interactions between South Asia and Southeast Asia.
- **Security and counter-insurgency cooperation**: India and Myanmar have engaged in joint security operations along the Mizoram–Myanmar border. This cooperation is critical for stabilizing the region, thereby laying the groundwork for successful economic and infrastructure projects.

- **Cultural and people-to-people ties**: the historical and cultural connections between communities in Mizoram and Myanmar are profound. Ongoing efforts to strengthen these ties through cultural exchanges, tourism, and educational initiatives are essential for fostering mutual understanding and cooperation.
- **Trade and economic relations**: both regions actively seek to enhance trade relations, especially in agriculture, energy, and infrastructure sectors. Mizoram's strategic location as a gateway to Southeast Asian markets through Myanmar is significant in this regard.
- **Development of border infrastructure**: initiatives such as ICPs and border markets (*haats*) can reduce transaction costs and support small-scale, cross-border commerce, although governance and security constraints require careful design (Bhaumik, 2020; RIS, 2011).
- **Energy-sector cooperation**: Mizoram's proximity to Myanmar's rich natural resources, especially hydrocarbons, positions it as a key partner in energy cooperation. This collaboration is vital for resource sharing and energy security.
- **Participation in regional organizations**: Mizoram (as part of India) and Myanmar's involvement in organizations like BIMSTEC highlights their commitment to fostering regional cooperation among Bay of Bengal countries.

Thus, the cooperation between Mizoram and Myanmar is vital for bolstering trade. Mizoram's strategic position as a conduit to Southeast Asia is particularly advantageous for trade with Myanmar. This collaboration could lead to a diversified economic base for Mizoram, with potential exports from India including cement, engineering goods, transport equipment, and pharmaceuticals. In return, Mizoram could import commodities like betel nuts, turmeric, and dry ginger from Myanmar, fostering a balanced trade relationship. Projects like the Mizoram State Roads II initiative could play a significant role in improving transport connectivity. This enhanced infrastructure is expected to boost trade, reduce transportation costs, and provide access to larger markets. The cooperation extends to strengthening cultural and social ties. This aspect is fundamental in building a robust cross-border community and reviving historical cultural links. People-to-people relationships, fostered through travel and trade, contribute to an integrated and socially cohesive region. The cooperation aligns with India's Act East Policy, enhancing economic cooperation, cultural ties, and strategic relationships in the region. Myanmar's role as a bridge between South Asia and Southeast Asia supports the foreign policy objectives of both countries, fostering a stable and prosperous region. Increased connectivity could open opportunities in education and health care as well.

Similarly, initiatives have also been taken to strengthen the cooperation between Mizoram and Bangladesh, focusing on trade facilitation, logistics, and border infrastructures.

- **Mizoram State Roads II—Regional Transport Connectivity Project**: this World Bank-funded project, with a USD 107 million credit, aims to enhance transport connectivity for Mizoram, facilitating regional trade with neighbouring countries, including Bangladesh. The project will improve road links between Mizoram and Bangladesh, providing greater bilateral trade opportunities and access to important ports such as the Port of Chittagong. This enhanced connectivity is expected to impact positively trade and employment both within Mizoram and between Mizoram and neighbouring regions.
- **Infrastructure development for border trade**: the governments of Mizoram and Bangladesh are taking steps to build infrastructure, including ICPs and road connectivity, to maximize the potential of border trade. There have been discussions about setting up a border *haat* at Silsury (India)—Sajek (Bangladesh) and developing an ICP at Thegamukh on the Bangladesh side. This infrastructure would synchronize efforts to formalize trade between the two regions.
- **Joint spot verification for border trade**: Mizoram and Bangladesh have held bilateral talks to expedite the construction of the ICP at Kawrpuichhuah in Mizoram's Lunglei district. This initiative includes a joint spot verification visit to streamline and boost border trade. The aim is to operationalize border *haats* along the Indo-Bangladesh border to facilitate trade and commerce.

The cooperation with Bangladesh will boost cross-border trade. Mizoram can export agricultural products, handicrafts, and forest products to Bangladesh, boosting local industries and economies. Similarly, Bangladesh can export textiles, manufactured goods, and other commodities to Mizoram, providing diversity in the market. Enhanced cooperation will lead to better road connectivity, improving trade and movement between the two regions, including opportunities for cultural exchange programmes, which could strengthen the bond between the people of Mizoram and Bangladesh. This would also promote tourism between Mizoram and Bangladesh, which would lead to an increased understanding and appreciation of each other's culture and natural beauty. Given the shared biodiversity and ecological concerns, the two regions could collaborate on conservation projects and sustainable resource management. Effective cooperation will lead to better management of the border, helping in tackling issues such as smuggling and illegal immigration. Finally, for India, cooperation with Bangladesh through Mizoram would support its "Act East Policy", fostering stronger ties with Southeast Asian countries.

References

Bhaumik, Subir (2020), "Border Haats on India–Myanmar Border: Opportunities and Challenges", Consumer Unity & Trust Society (CUTS) International, Jaipur (https://cuts-crc.org/pdf/briefing-papers-border-haats-on-india-myanmar-border-opportunities-and-challenges.pdf).

Das, Pushpita (2021), "Trade through Mizoram: A Study on the Indo-Myanmar Border", *Journal of North East India Studies*, 11 (1), pp. 45–60.

DGCI&S (Directorate General of Commercial Intelligence and Statistics) (n.d.), "Regional Export Statistics for North East India (Fiscal Year 2019)", Kolkata.

Hmar, Ruatdiki (2019), "Globalization and the Look East Policy: Dimensions of Connectivity in Indo-Myanmar Border Trade", *Mizoram University Journal of Humanities & Social Sciences*, 5 (1), pp. 23–35.

India Brand Equity Foundation (2023), "Mizoram" (https://www.ibef.org/states/mizoram).

LCS (Land Customs Station) Zokhawthar and Customs Division, Aizawl (n.d.), "Trade Statistics for Zokhawthar LCS (Administrative Records)".

Ministry of External Affairs (1974), "Agreement between the Government of the Republic of India and the Government of the People's Republic of Bangladesh concerning the Demarcation of the Land Boundary between India and Bangladesh and Related Matters", Government of India (https://www.mea.gov.in/Portal/LegalTreatiesDoc/BG74B2547.pdf).

Ministry of External Affairs (2011), "Protocol to the Agreement between India and Bangladesh concerning the Demarcation of the Land Boundary between India and Bangladesh and Related Matters", Government of India, 6 September (https://www.mea.gov.in/bilateral-documents.htm?dtl/5256/Protocol+to+the+Agreement+between+India+and+Bangladesh+concerning+the+demarcation+of+the+land+boundary+between+India+and+Bangladesh+and+6related+matters).

NABARD (National Bank for Agriculture and Rural Development) (n.d.), "Snapshot of NABARD's Initiatives in Mizoram", NABARD Mizoram Regional Office, Aizawl (https://www.nabard.org/auth/writereaddata/tender/pub_190723070139674.pdf).

Planning and Programme Implementation Department (n.d.),"Government of Mizoram" (https://planning.mizoram.gov.in).

RBI (Reserve Bank of India) (2015), "AP (DIR Series) Circular No. 26", 5 November (https://www.rbi.org.in/Scripts/NotificationUser.aspx?Id=10112&Mode=0).

RIS (Research and Information System for Developing Countries) (2011), "Expansion of North East India's Trade and Iinvestment with Bangladesh and Myanmar: An Assessment of the Opportunities and Constraints", Ministry of Development of the Northeast Region (DoNER), Government of India, New Delhi; RIS; and North Eastern Council, Government of India (https://www.ris.org.in/sites/default/files/Publication/NER_Report-17-9-2012-final.pdf).

Singh, K.G. (2019),"Field Survey on Border Trade and Commodity Flows in Mizoram", unpublished primary data.

Sumi, T.H. (2025), "Connectivity Projects of North-East India under Act East Policy", *Dimapur Government College Journal*, X (1), pp. 120–45 (https://dimapurgovtcollege.in/wp-content/uploads/2025/05/Connectivity-projects-of-North-East-India-under-Act-East-Policy-Tolivi-Sumi.pdf).

Taneja, Nisha, Tin Htoo Naing, Sanjana Joshi, Thiyam Bharat Singh, Samridhi Bimal, Sakshi Garg, Riya Roy, and Manali Sharma (2019), "India's Act East Policy: Facilitating India–Myanmar Border Trade", Indian Council for Research on International Economic Relations, New Delhi, July (https://icrier.org/pdf/India_Myanmar_Border_Trade.pdf).

Trade and Commerce Department (n.d.), "Department Profile", Government of Mizoram (https://tradeandcommerce.mizoram.gov.in/page/trade-and-commerce-department-profile).

8

Exploring the Possibility of Improving Trade between India and Myanmar through Nagaland

T. Zarenthung Ezung

Introduction

Trade is defined as the exchange of goods and services between persons, regions, and countries. The reason why nations trade with each other is basically because of differences in factor endowment. Countries differ in terms of natural resources, climatic conditions, mineral resources and mines, labour and capital resources, technological capabilities, entrepreneurial and managerial skills, and a host of other variables that determine the capacities of countries to produce goods and services (Mannur, 1995). These differences in factor endowment can lead to differences in production process between different countries. Some countries can produce more of one type of goods while others can produce more of other goods. Thus, the need for exchange of goods and services among nations arises because no country can meet the needs of its citizens by itself and has to depend on others.

Now cross-border trade is an alternative term for "international trade" or "external trade". In short, it is trade beyond the boundaries of a nation. This trade is differentiated into formal trade and informal trade. "Informal cross-border trade" refers to undocumented cash flows that are not taxed, while "formal cross-border trade" refers to documented cash flows that are taxed (Ogalo, 2010). In other words, cross-border

T. Zarenthung Ezung, *Exploring the Possibility of Improving Trade between India and Myanmar through Nagaland* In: *Sub-Regional Cooperation for Trade, Investment, and Employment in North-East India*. Edited by: Ashish Nath, Oxford University Press.
DOI: 10.1093/9780197908938.003.0008

trade can be defined as an exchange of goods and services that takes place between two neighbouring countries. The importance of cross-border movement of goods and people are vital to the economies of the border states and provinces as well as for the two national economies. There are a number of industries, which differ from region to region, that rely on cross-border movements either for the provision of raw material or for delivery of goods to the markets. The movements of people either for daily employment or business or, more occasionally, for tourism are also important for the economic and social factors of cross-border trade (EBTC, 2003). Besides, border trade has the potential to increase production and consumption in regions that are often far from the main cities (Aseff et al., 1995).

Cross-border trade has now become vital for any country's economic growth. Poverty can be reduced to a certain extent by way of income generation through the development of cross-border trade. A statement by the International Chamber of Commerce (ICC, 2003) rightly pointed out that countries which have successively integrated themselves into the global trading system are enjoying faster economic growth, higher-paid jobs, and rising prosperity. But, of course, the problems and challenges that are being encountered in the cross-border trade are not to be neglected, the first and foremost being security and prosperity, then the migration problems associated with cross-border trade. Finally, there is the danger of one country dumping its goods upon another country. There is no denying the fact that having good relations with neighbouring countries improves the economies of both the nations. It is here that cross-border trade between neighbouring nations acts as a string that binds the two nations more strongly. In this regard, the nearest countries that India can trade with are its bordering countries, such as Myanmar, Bhutan, Bangladesh, and Nepal, which all lie in the Northeastern part of India.

The state of Nagaland was established in 1962 as a fully fledged state for the Nagas in India after a ceasefire agreement between the Government of India and the Naga people. Nagaland was just a district in the state of Assam until 1957, known as "The Naga hills" (Nagaland Legislative Assembly, n.d.). However, not all the Naga people are under the same administration, and the people and their land have been divided and distributed among different adjoining states of Nagaland for reasons best known to the Indian government. Nagaland is bounded by Assam in the west, Myanmar (Burma) in the east, Arunachal Pradesh and part of Assam in the North, and Manipur in the south.

Though Indo-Myanmar trade has been going on for a long time through a porous border from the Northeastern part of India, it could be much improved if the declared international trade centres in Nagaland, India were well developed. Nagaland being located on the Northeastern part of India bordering Myanmar makes it a crucial strategic area for influencing India's relationship with Southeast Asian countries and overall regional security. The four international trade centres declared by the state government are strategically located at the North-West border of Myanmar (inhabited by the Naga ethic group), which is in the vicinity of China's Yunan province. Thus, improving trade through Nagaland would have a great impetus on India's Act East Policy and its relationship with China. Therefore, some influence from the state on border trade would provide an important tool for the policy planner in framing and implementing it. This chapter tries to highlight the present trade taking place (formal and informal) and the challenges of Indo-Myanmar trade by taking a field survey on the four declared international trade centres in Nagaland, India. The chapter concludes by highlighting some suggestions that would further boost the trade between the two countries.

The Challenges of Indo-Myanmar Trade through Nagaland

India and Myanmar have been connected to each other through trade, though informally, across the Northeastern part of India over along period of time. This can be seen through the inflow of Myanmar goods such as blankets, electronic goods, accessories, household utensils, etc. into the Indian markets, especially into the Northeastern part of the country. The reason for the floating of Indian markets (especially by Myanmarese goods) could be the lenient foreign trade policy of the Indian government towards Myanmar, which is less developed than India, or the borderless boundary that exists between India and Myanmar. The two countries have been connected by the formal border trade through the state of Manipur and Mizoram both before and after India's Independence. The trade route towards India, especially from Manipur, is Moreh

International Trade Centre. In the 1990s, the goods from Moreh used to be marketed at Mao Gate (Manipur) before reaching Kohima and then going on to Dimapur, from where they went out to the rest of India. However, with the passage of time, the goods started to be sent to Dimapur and from there to the rest of the country. Thus, Dimapur is a gateway for Indo-Myanmar trade on the most eastern part of the country.

As a part of its Act East and Neighbourhood First Policies, India has signed the following list of agreements and Memorandum of Understanding with Myanmar (Government of India, n.d.) regarding trade and development: USD 500 million Line of Credit to Myanmar by India, Air Services, Border Area Development, Establishment of Joint Trade and Investment Forum, Cultural Exchange Programme (2012–15), and establishing of border *haats* on the border between Myanmar and India. Even though Myanmar often plunges into political turmoil, India's trade with Myanmar continues. India's export to Myanmar decreased from USD 893.03 million during 2021–22 to USD 614.30 million during 2022–23. On the other hand, imports decreased from USD 1001.87 million to USD 954.74 million during the same period, but it again increased to USD 1533.95 million during 2024–25. However, the trade taking place between the two countries through Nagaland was very insignificant.

The state of Nagaland has a long border with Myanmar. Presently, the state has four declared international trade centres located at Longwa in Mon district, Pangsha in Tuensang district, Mimi in Kiphire district, and Avangkhu in Phek district (Government of Nagaland, 2024). The main objective of setting up these trading centres in the state was to boost the economy. However, the findings showed that these centres are yet to become an international trade centre in the true sense. Table 8.1 highlights some of the hard facts regarding the international trade centres in the state.

The survey conducted at the trade points between Myanmar and Nagaland reveals the following observations:

1. The survey revealed that Longwa is located at Mon district and is 42 km away from the district headquarters, Pangsha is located at Tuensang district and is 35 km away from the district headquarters, Mimi is located at Kiphire district and is 110 km away from the

Table 8.1 Facilities at international trade centres: Nagaland (India)

Trade centre	Distance from district headquarters	Pucca/ Kutcha	Exports from India	Imports of India	Types of trade
Longwa. Mon	42 km	Pucca	Salts, sugar, clothes, chocolates, etc.	Medicines, beer, chainsaws, spices, bikes (two-wheelers), etc.	Barter, or monetized, or both
Pangsha, Tuensang	35 km	Semi pucca	Do	Do	Do
Mimi, Kiphire	110 km	Kutcha	Do	Do	Do
Avangkhu, Phek	226 km	Pucca	Do	Do	Do

Source: Author's field survey, 2022.

district headquarters, and Avangkhu is located at Phek district and is 226 km away from the district headquarters.

2. The road connectivity to these trading centres varies from centre to centre. It was found that Longwa has *pucca* ('solid, high-quality') road connectivity while Pangsha is connected with semi-*pucca* roads. Mimi was found to be connected by *kutcha* ('makeshift') roads. Avangkhu has a *pucca* road. It was also found that road connectivity to these centres from Myanmar side is *kutcha*.
3. There are no available banking services in these trading centres. The nearest banking services available in these centres are their district headquarters or subdivisional headquarters. The nearest banking services for Longwa are at Mon town (i.e. 42 km away), for Pangsha they are at Tuensang town (i.e. 35 km away), for Mimi they are at Kiphire town (i.e. 110 km away), and for Avangkhu they are at Meluri town (i.e. 160 km away).
4. Owing to the limited availability of banking services, trading in these centres takes place both in barter and in monetized form.
5. It was found that exchange in these centres is mostly comprised of local products.
6. It was also found that people from across the border (Myanmar side) come to Nagaland for education.

7. It was also found that the unskilled labour from Myanmar comes across the border in search of work. But from the Indian side, it is only rarely that people cross the border in search of work.
8. Apart from the local commodities that are being marketed in the centres, it was also found that many illegal trading takes place across the border owing to the borderless border with Myanmar, namely, gold, Marijuna, and timber (from the Myanmar side).
9. Being a borderless border, there are no custom offices in these areas. Thus, trade that exists in these area or centres can be termed as informal trade.

Apart from the existing infrastructural bottlenecks at these trade centres, the state also faces a complex ethnic and political landscape, including historical conflicts with India and Myanmar. The continuous conflicts between the Naga freedom fighters for sovereignty in these two countries has become a limiting factor for trade expansion through this region.

Policy Recommendations

With so much hype over India's Look East policy (now the Act East policy) during recent years, it was found that the policy has only been given lip service. From the above discussion, it was found that nothing has been done by the Government of India to boost the economic activities of the Indian border state, especially with regards to Nagaland. The reason why the two governments (Myanmar and India) are not developing these border areas could be that since the Nagas are being divided between the two countries, any development of these areas will bring oneness among the Nagas from Myanmar, which will affect patriotism in India. But this assumption is wrong because many resentments and revolutions in the world happen because some sections of people are left out from the parameters of development. This is the case with the Naga people; on the Indian side of the border, one finds a more developed and polished upcoming generation, while on the Myanmar side of the border, one finds people still trapped in primitive ways of life. The comparison of the Naga people living in these two countries shows a very high inequality in terms of socio-economic conditions.

It is here that cross-border trade between India and Myanmar through Nagaland state could play an important role in developing and raising the standard of living of the people in the border areas. By opening up and maintaining these trade centres, India (being more advanced and developed than Myanmar) would obviously have good trade prospects over Myanmar. Nevertheless, Myanmar too would gain from trading with India, and the standard of living for people in border areas would automatically improve. The bilateral relationship and connectivity through Myanmar is crucial for India's Look East Policy (Subramanian, 2021), and to enhance more bilateral trade between the two neighbouring nation, the following few suggestions are laid down:

1. In order to rectify the historical blunder inflicted on the Naga people and their land, tripartite talks involving the Naga people from the two nations, the Government of India, and the Government of Myanmar would be required in order to find a lasting solution to the protracted Naga political problem. In the absence of any political solution for Naga people, it would be another Jammu and Kashmir-like situation and would create another world militarized zone. This would have an adverse impact on the India's Act East Policy as well as its trading activities with Myanmar and the rest of the eastern countries. Peace being an important factor in trade as well as for any developmental activities, a proper understanding and solution to the problems of the Naga people would contribute immensely to the growth and development of trade not of only Indo-Myanmar but also with China, which is in close proximity to the Naga-inhibited areas of Myanmar.
2. The importance of solving the Naga problem is also related to the existing borderless boundary between the two countries, which can never be fenced because it would be strongly opposed by the Naga people. Thus, if the problems in this region were not solved, it would have an adverse impact on the working of the custom office and the dumping of goods by other countries in India and

also any illegal business carrying on around the borders would go unabated.

3. Physical infrastructure being the main backbone of economic growth, if the Indian Government is serious about its Act East Policy, it is suggested that physical infrastructure should be developed in these centres, especially road infrastructure (to at least two-lane), the reason being that if these centres were developed well, people living across the border would not look to Yangon (which is miles away) for their daily needs but towards India. This, in turn, would increase consumption demand on the Indian side and would automatically lead to an increase in employment and income.
4. Education being important for developing human capital which, in turn, leads to an improvement in the living standard of the people, these centres could be a cradle of education for the people residing at the border in Myanmar who do not have any access to a modern education system. Thus, developing education institutes in these centres would automatically attract people living across the border to the Indian side for education. Moreover, it would lead to dissemination of knowledge and the export of skilled persons across the border to Myanmar as it is less developed than India.
5. Health being important social capital, if the Government of India could establish proper health care in these centres, it would attract more people from Myanmar, and health tourism would increase many-fold.
6. Myanmar being less developed and abundant in labour, the development of these centres would bring cheap labour from the other side of the boundary to India. This would strengthen the labour market of India, which would boost up economic development.
7. Proper establishment and maintenance of these centres would curb the dumping of goods (especially Chinese goods) to Indian markets, which come through Myanmar. Moreover, the existence of illegal marketing could be checked to a certain extent.
8. India being more industrialized and developed than Myanmar, proper maintenance and proper road connectivity to these trade

centres would help India in pulling in all the necessary raw materials from Myanmar at a cheap rate.

9. Moreover, proper infrastructure development in these centres would help in increasing India's exports of final products to Myanmar and other eastern countries and the adverse balance of payment in India may be partially checked.
10. Finance being an engine to any growth and development, the opening of banks in these centres becomes important because it would help to expedite the transaction process. This, in turn, would give a boost to all the business activities going on in these centres.

References

Aseff, J., J. Espejo, and J.A. Morales (1995), "The Importance of Border Trade: The Case of Bolivia", Institute of Socio-economic Investigations (IISEC) Document No. 01/95, April (https://www.iisec.ucb.edu.bo/papers/1991-2000).

EBTC (Eastern Border Transportation Coalition) (2003), "The Importance of Efficient Canada/US Border Crossings", (https://ebtc.info/wp-content/uploads/2014/07/ebtc-whitepaper.pdf).

Government of India (n.d.), "India–Myanmar Relation", 22 November (https://www.mea.gov.in/Portal/ForeignRelation/Myanmar22Nov.pdf).

Government of Nagaland (2024), "Basic Facts of Nagaland", Directorate of Economics and Statistics, Government of Nagaland, Kohima (https://ipr.nagaland.gov.in/sites/default/files/2025-03/Nagaland%20Basic%20Facts%202024.pdf).

ICC (International Chamber of Commerce) (2003), "Business and the Global Economy", Evain Summit, 1–3 June (https://www.iccwbo.org/Data/ Documents/G8-G20/2003-G8-Evian-Summit).

Mannur, H.G. (1995), *International Economics*, 2nd rev. edn, New Delhi: Vikas Publishing House Pvt. Ltd.

Nagaland Legislative Assembly (n.d.), "About Us" (https://webtest.nagaland.gov.in/nla/about-us).

Ogalo, V. (2010), "Informal Cross-Border Trade in EAC: Implications for Regional Integration and Development", research paper, Consumer Unity & Trust Society (CUTS) African Resource Centre, Nairobi, (https://www.scirp.org/reference/referencespapers?referenceid=3096162).

Subramanian, Nirupama (2021), "Connectivity through Myanmar Crucial for India's Look East Policy and Ties with ASEAN", *The Hindu*, 4 December (https://www.thehindu.com/news/international/connectivity-through-Myanmar-crucial-for-indiaslook-east-policy-and-ties-with-asean).

9

Locating Sikkim in the Sub-regional Cooperation

Gadde Omprasad

Introduction

Sub-regional cooperation in South Asia has emerged as a response to the limitations of the South Asian Association for Regional Cooperation (SAARC), particularly due to its institutional stagnation and political deadlocks (Gambhir, 2020; Palit and Islam, 2011). These limitations also include limited local-level participation (Hosen, 2019; Murthy, 2008). The sub-regional frameworks offer local-level participations and functional alternatives grounded in shared geography, cultural affinities, and economic complementarities (Shukla, 2019; Chakma, 2020). They reflect a shift from rigid institutionalism to more flexible, issue-based cooperation that often bypasses formal regional structures. As Brunet-Jailly (2022) argues, the sustainability of cross-border linkages is deeply influenced by the interplay between central governments and local actors, suggesting that sub-national regions are not merely passive spaces but active agents in shaping regional dynamics. In this context, the attention of the regional cooperation must shift from nation state-centric to local state to underline the importance of border states like Sikkim. Even though the border states are far from the centre, they play a key role in improving regional connections and cooperation.

The role of sub-national units, particularly strategically located border states like Sikkim, remains inadequately explored in both policy frameworks and academic literature. Existing analyses of sub-regional

Gadde Omprasad, *Locating Sikkim in the Sub-regional Cooperation* In: *Sub-Regional Cooperation for Trade, Investment, and Employment in North-East India*. Edited by: Ashish Nath, Oxford University Press. © Oxford University Press 2026. DOI: 10.1093/9780197908938.003.0009 cooperation tend to focus predominantly on sovereign actors and macro-level geopolitical dynamics, thereby overlooking the agency and developmental potential of smaller states such as Sikkim in fostering cross-border linkages. Given its geographic proximity to Nepal, Bhutan, and the Tibet Autonomous Region of China and its cultural and historical interconnectedness with the Eastern Himalayan sub-region, Sikkim occupies a unique position that could contribute meaningfully to the architecture of sub-regional integration. However, the absence of systematic inquiry into how Sikkim could be integrated into existing or emerging sub-regional frameworks, such as Bangladesh–Bhutan–India–Nepal (BBIN) or other trans-Himalayan corridors, presents a critical research gap. This chapter, therefore, seeks to examine the potential and limitations of locating Sikkim within the evolving landscape of sub-regional cooperation in South Asia, addressing both structural constraints and opportunities for transformative engagement.

This gap, however, requires a closer look at the intrinsic regional characteristics that make Sikkim central to sub-regional imaginaries. Imagining sub-regional cooperation without Sikkim would be incomprehensible as the state shares historical, socio-cultural, and religious linkages and ethnic similarities with its neighbouring countries, that is, Nepal and Bhutan. Sikkim acts as India's geographical link between Bhutan and Nepal and also shares the Teesta waters with Bangladesh as an upper riparian region. Thus, the sub-regional cooperation in general and BBIN in particular provide strategic, ethnic, economic, and geographic significance to Sikkim.

Sikkim: An Outline of the Economy

In order to understand the significance of Sikkim in the economic sphere in the sub-regional cooperation, it is essential to understand the economic conditions of the state as well as the gross state domestic product (GSDP) composition. Sikkim is one of the fastest-growing states in India, with an average growth rate of 13 per cent in current prices and 6.92 per cent in constant prices over a decade. This growth rate is the result of contributions made by sectors such as manufacturing and

Table 9.1 The GSDP of Sikkim

Year	GSDP (value in rupees crore)	Growth rate (percentage)	GSDP (value in rupees crore)	Growth rate (percentage)
	Current prices		Constant prices (2011–12)	
2023–24	48,937	14.67	24,902	8.52
2022–23	42,677	13.35	22,948	8.04
2021–22	37,650	14.03	21,240	8.61
2020–21	33,018	5.02	19,557	0.33
2019–20	31,441	10.70	19,492	4.66
2018–19	28,402	9.36	18,625	5.38
2017–18	25,971	25.54	17,673	14.78
2016–17	20,687	14.71	15,397	7.15
2015–16	18,034	17.05	14,370	9.93
2014–15	15,407	11.14	13,071	7.9
2013–14	13,862	12.35	12,114	6.07
2012–13	12,338	10.51	11,421	2.29

Source: Ministry of Statistics and Programme Implementation (2024), "Sikkim Economy" (https://statisticstimes.com/economy/india/sikkim-economy.php).

services, providing an immense opportunity for the state to contribute significantly to regional economic relations with neighbouring states.

Sikkim's GSDP data from 2012–13 to 2023–24, as given in Table 9.1, indicates a robust and sustained economic growth trajectory both at current and constant prices, reinforcing its emerging role as a dynamic sub-regional economic actor. The GSDP at current prices has more than tripled from rupees (Rs) 12,338 crore in 2012–13 to Rs 48,937 crore in 2023–24, reflecting strong nominal expansion, largely driven by industrialization, hydropower generation, and increased service-sector contributions. Importantly, the constant price growth, an indicator of real economic performance, also reveals resilience, particularly post-COVID-19 pandemic of 2020, with growth rebounding from a mere 0.33 per cent in 2020–21 to 8.61 per cent in 2021–22 and 8.52 per cent in 2023–24. This sustained real growth underscores the structural stability of Sikkim's economy, with the potential to contribute meaningfully to BBIN and the Bay of Bengal Initiative for Multi-Sectoral Technical and Economic Cooperation (BIMSTEC) and BIMSTEC initiatives. The state's industrial and energy sectors, especially its hydropower surplus, make it a critical player in cross-border electricity trade, particularly with Nepal and Bhutan. Simultaneously, the service sector, anchored in eco-tourism, health tourism, and education, can foster people-to-people linkages and regional circuits, especially if integrated into trans-Himalayan tourism initiatives. The economic momentum also opens opportunities for regional value chains, cross-border investments, and harmonized trade regimes. Sikkim's growth pattern not only signals domestic economic strengthening but also aligns with the imperatives of greater sub-regional economic integration in the Eastern Himalayan neighbourhood.

Table 9.2 provides a glimpse of sector-wise contribution to Sikkim's economy. Sikkim's economic structure, as reflected in the sectoral share of gross state value added (GSVA), offers significant opportunities for sub-regional cooperation, particularly in the context of its strong industrial base and emerging service sector. The dominance of the secondary sector, accounting for over 61 per cent of GSVA at current prices and nearly 64 per cent at constant 2011–12 prices, is driven primarily by manufacturing (notably pharmaceuticals) and electricity, gas, and water supply, positioning Sikkim as a potential hub for cross-border energy trade and industrial collaboration with neighbouring Bhutan and Nepal under BBIN and BIMSTEC frameworks. The relatively modest but stable tertiary sector (30.2 per cent at the current price, 30.11 per cent at constant price) offers further scope for cooperation in tourism, transport services, and trade, particularly as road connectivity improves and cultural circuits across the Himalayan belt are developed. Although the primary sector remains marginal, the state's organic agriculture and eco-sensitive practices open new avenues for niche markets and agro-based partnerships in the region. Moreover, sectors such as public administration, real estate, and trade services demonstrate resilience and can be leveraged for capacity building and institutional linkages across borders. With growing infrastructural investment and a strategic location at the tri-junction of India, Bhutan, and Nepal, Sikkim's economy holds transformative potential for deepening sub-regional economic integration. Given these economic indicators, the state also has major thrust areas where it can play a crucial role in sub-regional trade relations.

Table 9.2 Sector-wise contribution to gross state value added (2023–24): Sikkim

Serial no.	Sector	Percentage share in current prices	Percentage share in 2011–12 prices
1	Primary sector	8.2	6.08
1.1	Agriculture, forestry, and fishing	8.15	6.02
1.11	Crops	6.83	5.18
1.12	Livestock	1.1	0.64
1.13	Forestry and logging	0.17	0.16
1.14	Fishing and aquaculture	0.05	0.05
1.2	Mining and quarrying	0.05	0.05
2	Secondary sector	61.6	63.81
2.1	Manufacturing	33.12	36.17
2.2	Electricity, gas, water supply and other utility services	23.32	22.84
2.3	Construction	5.16	4.8
3	Tertiary sector	30.2	30.11
3.1	Trade, repair, hotels and restaurants	7.85	7.37
3.11	Trade and repair services	7.47	7
3.12	Hotels and restaurants	0.39	0.36
3.2	Transport, storage, communication and services related to broadcasting	2.13	2.64
3.22	Road transport	1.53	2.02
3.23	Communication and services related to broadcasting	0.6	0.63
3.3	Financial services	1.35	1.52
3.4	Real estate, ownership of dwelling and professional services	3.39	3.21
3.5	Public administration	6.8	6.7
3.6	Other services	8.68	8.67

Source: Ministry of Statistics and Programme Implementation (2024), "Sikkim Economy" (https://statisticstimes.com/economy/india/sikkim-economy.php).

Organic Farming: Spices, Floriculture, and Tea

Sikkim has a total land area of about 7,29,900 hectares, out of which agricultural activities are done in about 74,343 hectares, accounting for about 10.20 per cent of the area. The rest of the land is filled with forest coverage and non-agricultural activities. Farming activities are done with the help of a rain-fed integrated farming system and other rural livelihood options, including horticulture, poultry, animal husbandry, and so on. In 2003, the state initiated the Sikkim Organic Mission and undertook measures including the development of required infrastructure, capacity building for the farmers, a certification process, and marketing measures, and in 2016, it was declared as a fully organic state with the coverage of about 75,000 hectares. In the process, it also faced problems of low productivity, shortage of organic manure, lack of effective pesticides, fungicides, price fluctuations, poor marketing, etc. To address these problems, the state government focused on high-value crops such as large cardamom, ginger, turmeric, and buckwheat under the Mission for Value Chain Development for North East Region (MOVCDNER) for export-orientated activities. Fruit and vegetable cultivation is being given emphasis, and the state is also focusing on developing cold-storage chains to address the shortages (Ecotourism & Conservation Society of Sikkim, 2020). Hence, the state can offer the experience and has a potential business opportunity in the supply of organic manure, pesticides, fungicides, cold-storage units, etc.

Sikkim is known as the kingdom of flowers (State Institute of Rural Development and Panchayati Raj, SIRD&PR). The state is the home of over 600 kinds of orchids, over 100 rhododendrons, and a host of primulas. The farmers of Sikkim supply flowers and bulbs to Kalimpong, Kolkata, Delhi, Bihar, and Uttaranchal. Apart from orchids, farmers also grow other varieties of flowers, such as amaryllis, cymbidium, haemanthus, tiger lily, and catalia. The global floriculture market is of more than USD 8.5 billion, and India occupies a share of less than 1 per cent in it, providing a huge opportunity for the sector's development and exports from Sikkim (SIRD&PR). The National Horticulture Board (Government of India, GoI) has developed its branch to provide logistic support in the state; on the other hand, the Indian Council of Agricultural Research (ICAR) established its Orchid Research Centre in the state. The government of Sikkim also signed a Memorandum of Understanding (MoU) with the Netherlands for the development and promotion of floriculture in Sikkim. In 2014–15, about 248.51 thousand hectares of area were under cultivation in floriculture (Sarmah, 2019).

Sikkim has an organic tea plantation (Tea Board of India, n.d.) of about 500 acres, and about 100 tonnes of tea is produced every year (SIMFED, n.d.) Out of this produce, about 25 per cent of tea is consumed domestically and about 75 per cent is exported to other countries, including Germany, the United States, France, Canada, and Japan (Guha, 2018).

The export profile of organic products from Sikkim is not very enthusiastic. Though attempts were made to introduce private-sector participation in export-orientated activities in 2010–11, they were not successful due to the long shipment period, resulting in the spoiling of the products. The large cardamom is marketed to various parts of the country, especially to Delhi and Amritsar markets, from where these are sent to Pakistan, Afghanistan, the Middle East, and other countries as well.

Table 9.3 shows Sikkim's agricultural-related exports to the neighbouring countries valued in USD millions. It reveals a clear asymmetry in export destinations, with Bhutan as the principal market. Exports to Bhutan increased steadily from USD 1.98 million in 2014–15 to a peak of USD 6.78 million in 2021–22. The subsequent decline may be linked to COVID-19 disruptions, changing demand patterns, or policy and logistical constraints. These agro-related products include rice, fresh

Table 9.3 Sikkim's agri-related exports to neighbouring countries (in USD millions)

Year	Export to Bhutan	Export to Nepal	Export to Tibet (Nathu La)
2024–25	2.11	–	–
2023–24	2.64	–	–
2022–23	5.80	–	–
2021–22	6.78	–	–
2020–21	3.88	–	–
2019–20	0.72	–	–
2018–19	1.16	–	1.61
2017–18	0.95	0.09	0.21
2016–17	2.21	–	3.24
2015–16	2.16	–	2.52
2014–15	1.98	–	0.79

Source: APEDA (Agricultural and Processed Food Products Export Development Authority) (n.d.), *Agri Exchange Portal* (https://agriexchange.apeda.gov.in/India/port/Index).

vegetables, maize, dairy products, honey, etc. There is no data on the formal trade between Sikkim and Nepal except during 2017–18, and this highlights limited border trade infrastructure and weak market linkages. It can also be assumed that there exists local-level, informal trade between Sikkim and Nepal, which is absent in the case of Bhutan as the topography and geography do not allow for it. Agri-related exports to Tibet via the Nathu La corridor display a highly fluctuating pattern. While exports were relatively significant in 2015–16 (USD 2.52 million) and 2016–17 (USD 3.24 million), it declined sharply to USD 0.21 million in 2017–18 and remained absent in subsequent years in the post Dokhlam stand-off between India and China.

The Tourism Sector

Sikkim has a variety of tourism activities, including ecological, adventure, wildlife, pilgrimage, cultural, and Himalayan mountain tourism. Eco-tourism caters to the needs of travelling to nature and staying and mixing with local people in rural areas. The concept of home-stays provides accommodation and experience to tourists. Most of the foreign tourists visit Sikkim to engage in adventure tourism. A large number of bikers from within and outside the state are also involved in this type of tourism. The flora and fauna, forest coverage, rare species of animals, and Kanchenjunga National Park provide and offer opportunities for wildlife tourism. Sikkim also hosts a large number of Buddhist gompas. There are more than 200 monasteries, and among them, the monasteries like Pemayangtse, Rumtek, Enchey, Phensang, Tashiding, Ralong, Namchi, etc. are historical as well as attractive to tourists. The ethnic composition of Sikkim (namely, Bhutias, Nepalis, and Lepchas) and their language, dress, culture, way of life, festivals, songs, dance, etc. provides the cultural aspect and attracts tourists who are interested in it. Sikkim is located in the Eastern Himalayas, which has much biodiversity and cultural heterogeneity with distinctive ethnic groups, mountain peaks, and ecology. Himalayan tourism is the most prevalent type of tourism in Sikkim.

Tourism is the most important economic activity in Sikkim. Each district has attractive tourist places, and these places play an important role in driving the state economy.

Table 9.4 The tourist places of Sikkim

Districts/places	Tourist spots/places
East Sikkim	Enchey Monastery, Tsonmgo lake, Sikkim Research Institute of Tibetology (SRIT), Banjakri water falls, Tashi and Ganesh viewpoints, Saramsa Garden, Rumtek Dharma Chakra Centre, and Nathu La
West Sikkim	Pemayangtse Monastery, Rabdentse Palace ruins, Sanga Choling Monastery, Darap, Khangchendzonga waterfalls, Dubdi Monastery, Phamrong waterfalls, Limboo Cultural Centre, Dentam valley (4,800 ft), Singshore Bridge (6,500 ft), Uttarey (7,600 ft), Chewabhanjyang Pass (10,300 ft), Singalila Peak (12,980 ft), Pelling, Soreng, Yuksam, and Sang-Choling Monastery
North Sikkim	Phensang Monastery, Phodong Monastery, Labrang Monastery, Chunthang, Lachung, Yumthang valley, Seven Sister waterfalls, Lachen, Gurudongmar lake, and Yumthang
South Sikkim	Namchi, Temi Tea Garden, Rabongla, Menam hills, Siddhesvara Dhaam, Samdruptse, Rock Garden, and Indian Himalayan Centre of Adventure and Eco-Tourism (IHCAE)

Source: Tourism and Civil Aviation Department (n.d.) (https://www.sikkim.gov.in/departments/tourism-civil-aviation-department).

The tourists places shown in Table 9.4 are only indicative and could place Sikkim in a better position for cooperation not only within India but also with the neighbouring countries. There are many other tourist attractions as well.

Pharmaceutical Production

Sikkim hosts about forty-five pharmaceutical companies (Ministry of Chemicals and Fertilisers, 2021) and has attracted more than USD 5.59 billion between 2000 and 2019 (FDI India, n.d.). A number of multinational corporations operating in the sector have established their production units across the states. The state earns revenue of more than Rs 15,000 crore annually from this sector and has a huge potential to grow. After Gujarat, Maharashtra, and Himachal Pradesh, it emerged as a hub of the pharma industry in the country (Das, 2018). Out of the 6,000 medicinal plants available in India, more than 424 plants (including the famous Artemisia vulgaris, which is used as an antiseptic) are grown in Sikkim (FDI India, n.d.). The state is covered under the North East Industrial and Investment Promotion Policy 2007, the North East Industrial Development Scheme 2017, and the Transport Subsidy Scheme launched by the Government of India (DPIIT, n.d.). The pharmaceutical sector in the state avails itself of these schemes apart from the facilities and benefits provided by the state.

Sikkim recorded merchandise exports of USD 18.91 billion during the financial year 2022. A majority of these exports included products from the pharmacy sector, including drug formulations, biologicals, and medical and scientific instruments. In the financial year 2022, total exports of drug formulation products recorded USD 11.27 million (IBEF, n.d.).

Educational Institutions

Sikkim has a number of higher educational institutions in both public and private sectors. There is one Central University, one National Institute of Technology fully funded by the Government of India, a State University, and ten colleges owned by the Government of Sikkim, four private universities, and five private colleges (Education Department, n.d.). These institutions are located across the state to cater to the needs of the poor and rural areas and offer specialized programmes as well as courses in subjects like Tibetan studies, medical sciences, engineering, management, computer applications, pharmacy, education, law, vocational studies, science and technology, among others. In a few of these institutions, seats for students from neighbouring countries are specially allocated, and these students can enrol to pursue higher studies. Central University of Sikkim has developed and offers master's programmes in local languages such as Limbu, Lepcha, and Bhutia (Sikkim University, n.d.), which are also attractive among the ethnic communities of neighbouring Nepal and Bhutan. The university also has a special Centre for Endangered Languages and has developed a dictionary and grammar of five endangered languages (Bhujel, Rai, Gurung, Magar, and Sherpa) of the local ethnic and sub-ethnic groups (CEL, n.d.). Under the National Education Policy 2020, the educational institutions also created an additional 25 per cent of seats in various disciplines to accommodate students from foreign countries, and this opportunity is immensely helpful to the students from the neighbouring countries, allowing them to take admissions in the educational institutions of Sikkim without appearing in the entrance examinations (IANS, 2022). At the moment, a small number of Bhutanese and Nepalese students are studying in the various institutions in the state.

Hydropower Generation

Sikkim had a total installed power generation capacity of 965.51 megawatts (MW), of which 154.33 MW was under central utilities, 399.07 MW was under private utilities and 412.11 MW was under state utilities as of November 2019 (FDI India, n.d.). The electricity demand of Sikkim is below 150 MW, whereas the installed generation capacity under state-owned utilities is 412 MW. Through this hydropower potential, Sikkim is exploring options to sell the electricity to Bangladesh from its Teesta III power plant (Dahal, 2016). At the moment, the state's transmission lines are connected to the regional grids, and it sells electricity to many Indian states (CFA, 2019). The same arrangements could also be made with Nepal and Bangladesh, as these two countries suffer from an electricity shortage as well. It could contribute to the Sikkim economy as well as boost the electrification activities of the neighbouring countries (Rahaman and Mamun, 2020). According to the Helsinki Rules of 1966, Bangladesh has priority to import hydropower from Sikkim as both share the Teesta River basin (Helsinki Rules of 1966).

Sikkim and Nepal: Trade and Connectivity

Sikkim shares about 99 km of border with Nepal, and the two are separated by the Singalila range of the Himalayas. Though Sikkim and Nepal share borders, the major road link between them is through the West Bengal–Nepal border at Panitanki–Kakarvitta land border to enter Nepal, which is about 150 km and takes six or seven hours of travel. It has been a major hurdle in terms of goods, services, and the movement of people between the two.

In recent times, initiatives have been taken to address the connectivity problems. In 2021, construction of the Uttarey (Sikkim)–Chewa Bhanjyang (Nepal) road of about 35 km was completed, and the road is now open for tourists and trading activities. Uttarey is located at an elevation of about 6,600 ft, and Chewa Bhanjyang is at a height of about 10,500 ft above sea level. This connectivity is important for the people on both sides because it facilitates an increase of trade, which largely takes place in the form of the barter system with items like salt, sugar, kerosene, vegetables, and other daily needs and other important items like ginger, large cardamom, honey, ghee, and other milk products by travelling deep within each other's territories to benefit local employment and livelihood. The road also improves connectivity between West Bengal in India and Darchula in Western Nepal as the road is also connected to the east–west highway in Nepal, benefiting both the countries and especially the backward interior rural areas in eastern parts of Nepal (Budhakoti, 2021). Trekkers and tourists from India visit the nearest points in Nepal to have a better view of Mount Kanchenjunga, helping the local communities to sustain their livelihood. The Government of India, in principle, approved the construction of a national highway connecting Naya Bazar, Sombaria, Soreng, Dentam, Uttarey, and Chiwabhanzyang, and the work is expected to begin soon. Apart from this, an evaluation study on the economic prospects of the border roads has been done by the Ministry of Development of the Northeastern Region (DoNER). The study has highlighted that opening the borders and developing modern, integrated land ports can boost tourism, health, education, and the trade sector (NET, 2022). Though Gangtok has a seasonal airport at Pakyong, air connectivity to Kathmandu is yet to be established. Although a visa is not required, travellers and vehicles from both sides have to carry identity cards and other required valid documents and have to register at border check posts to enter each other's territories.

In order to explore and encourage economic cooperation and investment opportunities between Nepal and Sikkim, and India's Northeastern Region and Nepal, the PHD Chamber of Commerce and Industry, in collaboration with the India–Nepal Centre (INC) and Sikkim State Development Council (SDC) organized an "India–Nepal Economic Partnership Summit" in June 2019 at Gangtok as part of the Kanchenjunga dialogue. The summit has discussed investment opportunities for the business community of both sides in sectors such as tourism, agriculture, food processing, energy, infrastructure, healthcare, education, skill development and start-ups, and services (AIDIA, 2019). This summit can be seen as an attempt to integrate Sikkim into the sub-regional cooperation initiatives of the Government of India to include border states in the BBIN initiative.

Sikkim–Bhutan: Road Infrastructure

Sikkim shares about 32 km of border with Bhutan. During the British rule in India, the two kingdoms were connected through the Jalep La pass, which touches the trijunction of Sikkim, Bhutan, and Tibet. After the 1962 war, the border points, including Nathu La, were closed. There is no direct road connectivity between Sikkim and Bhutan, and people have to pass through the Jaigaon (West Bengal)–Phuntsholing (Bhutan) border point. National Highways (NH) 10, 31A, and 317A, which connect Gangtok with Siliguri, Fulbari (Bangladesh border), and Phuntsoling (Bhutan border), are the connectivities through which Sikkim is joined to neighbouring Bhutan and Bangladesh, respectively. Through NH 10 and 31A, Sikkim is also connected to the cross-border connectivity initiatives like Asian Highways 1 and 2. Both these highways provide land corridors between the countries of BBIN at the sub-regional level and from Portugal to Japan and from Iran to Indonesia, respectively. A large number of infrastructure development projects are part of these corridors, and once completed, these corridors can change the trade and development prospects of the region. Under Bharatmala Pariyojna, the Ministry of Road Transport and Highways, Government of India is constructing an alternative NH 717 between Melli Bazar to Gangtok via Lava, Kalimpong, and Rhenock (Bhattacharya, 2021). This road can provide connectivity between Gangtok and Phuntsoling, facilitating faster transportation of goods and increased tourist movement (Sinha, 2018). Another important project connecting Sikkim with land corridors is the Rangpo–Sevoke railway line. This first phase of connecting Siliguri to Nathu La in the subsequent phases is expected to be completed very soon. Once in operation, the line may result in economical transportation of goods between Sikkim and other places (PTI, 2021).

All these connectivity projects emphasized the participation of Sikkim in the larger regional integration initiatives within India and with neighbouring countries. Given the topographical and geographical conditions of landlocked Sikkim, and the strategic significance attached to the state, it is imperative for it to be connected to gain the benefits of regional integration. The state possesses substantial potential in various sectors and considerable experience in sectors such as tourism and organic farming. Locating Sikkim in the sub-regional cooperation with neighbouring countries must bring in the Darjeeling hills and needs to be looked into in terms of greater geographical affiliation. It is important to include the Darjeeling hills in the sub-regional context not only because of the shared commonalities but also because the region facilitates the physical connectivity between Sikkim and these countries as the state does not have direct border points for interactions, though it shares borders with its neighbours. Thus, Sikkim is physically dependent on the Darjeeling hills for interactions and connectivity.

Sikkim, Nepal, and Bhutan: Revitalizing the Natural Partnership

Any sub-regional cooperation has the potential to create regional value chains, expand economic linkages, and integrate markets (Hasran, 2018). This can lead to further integration of the socio-cultural practices and a greater understanding of shared ideas and goals. Such integration is particularly relevant in regions such as Sikkim, Nepal, and Bhutan, where demographic and ethnic commonalities can serve as a foundation for deeper sub-regional cooperation. It necessitates a shift from geographic determinism to an emphasis on cultural embeddedness and trans-local connectivity. The demographic and ethnic compositions of Sikkim, Nepal, and Bhutan share many similarities. The population composition of Sikkim is largely mixed, comprising communities such as Nepali, Bhutia, Limbu, Lepcha, Sherpa, Tamang, Rai, Bihari, Marwari, and Bengali. These communities are also predominant in the population configuration of neighbouring Nepal, Bhutan, and Tibet. Sikkim has a history of exchanges of territories back and forth with the neighbouring countries in the span of hundreds of years to the early twentieth century, resulting in exchanges and the shifting of population between these three territories. Although the modern concept of the nation state has created hard boundaries, the commonalities in terms of language and ethnicity between Nepal and Bhutan, as well as the Tibetan Autonomous Region of China, reflect the proximity that the Sikkim state shares with these countries. Sikkim, along with the Darjeeling hills, makes the region of Eastern Himalayas from Nepal to Bhutan complete in terms of commonalities in addition to the geographical features.

The ethnic relationship with Nepal and Bhutan can be categorized into two groups based on the communities. The dominant Nepali ethnic communities in Sikkim (Sikkimese of *Nepali* origin) have similar cultural and religious linkages with Nepal. They share similarities with Bhutan in terms of other ethnic groups such as Bhutia and Sherpa. What connects these three regions are the religions (both Hinduism and Buddhism) as the sacred places of these religious beliefs are located in all three places.

These shared cultural practices, religious traditions, and transnational social networks transcend political borders. While the Himalayan terrain offers spatial proximity, it is cultural flows and socio-religious affiliations that have more decisively shaped Sikkim's regional identity. The presence of Nepali-speaking populations and the influence of Tibetan Buddhism across these regions have fostered enduring linguistic, religious, and institutional continuities (Subba, 1999; Aris, 1979; Mullard, 2011). Overlapping ethnic identities, such as those of the Lepchas and Bhutias, further reflect longstanding patterns of mobility and integration (Denjongpa, 2002). These cultural affinities position Sikkim not merely as a geographical periphery but as an integral node within the trans-Himalayan socio-cultural landscape.

Centuries of migration, pilgrimage, and shared religious practices have created a web of cross-border linkages that continue to shape informal modes of cooperation. The persistence of Tibetan Buddhist networks and the linguistic cohesion enable everyday interactions that transcend state boundaries (Balikci, 2008; Subba, 1999). These dynamics illustrate the relevance of "everyday regionalism", where people-to-people linkages form the soft infrastructure for sustainable sub-regionalism (Soderbaum, 2015). Incorporating this perspective, challenges relating to state-centric paradigms highlight the historical and relational geographies underpinning Eastern Himalayan cooperation.

A multi-scalar approach, combining state initiatives with grassroots participation, is essential. Sub-regional groupings like BBIN and BIMSTEC should institutionalize "cultural corridors" that promote cross-border exchanges in heritage, religion, and the arts (Acharya, 2012; Aris, 1979). People-to-people diplomacy can be furthered through joint conservation efforts, academic collaborations, and cultural tourism circuits linking historically significant sites. Local governments and civil society must be integrated into decision-making processes to reflect vernacular cosmopolitanism and lived cultural affinities (Appadurai, 1996; Soderbaum, 2015). Embedding such efforts within a relational geography, grounded in shared memory and belief systems, could reimagine Sikkim as a cultural conduit for inclusive and resilient regionalism.

Realizing this vision requires India, Bhutan, and Nepal to collectively adopt a "Himalayan Cultural Compact", a normative framework for preserving shared heritage, facilitating cultural flows, and institutionalizing regional cooperation. Civilizational ties, expressed through Buddhist networks, ethnolinguistic continuities, and indigenous traditions, offer a robust foundation for trust-building (Acharya, 2012; Denjongpa, 2002). Initiatives such as cross-border cultural commissions, inter-monastic dialogues, and regional heritage circuits could align cultural diplomacy with existing sub-regional mechanisms like BBIN and BIMSTEC (Söderbaum, 2015). Educational exchange and collaborative research on Himalayan knowledge systems could help build a shared epistemic community (Appadurai, 1996). A sustainable vision must rest on multi-level governance, wherein national, sub-national, and civil society actors co-produce regional agendas. Such an approach reconceptualizes the Eastern Himalayas not just as a strategic space but as a pluralistic and culturally integrated sub-region offering a model for human-centred cooperation in South Asia.

In order to highlight the sub-regional initiatives from the people-centric dimensions of cooperation, a Trans-Himalayan Cultural and Eco-Tourism Circuit model could be adopted. This model provides a platform for shared cultural capital, environmental stewardship, and inclusive development (Soderbaum, 2015; Acharya, 2012). By linking sacred geographies, ecological zones, and vernacular cultural economies through coordinated tourism policy, joint circuits, and community engagement, such a model can strengthen people-to-people diplomacy while fostering sustainable livelihoods across borders. It thus positions tourism as both an instrument of regional integration and a means of articulating an alternative vision of South Asian cooperation rooted in historical continuity and socio-cultural affinities (Appadurai, 1996).

The Trans-Himalayan Cultural and Eco-Tourism Circuit Model

The Trans-Himalayan Cultural and Eco-Tourism Circuit model provides a framework for sub-regional cooperation through integrated tourism development across the region. The shared Buddhist heritage, mountain ecologies, and rich cultural landscapes connect cities such as Gangtok, Paro, and Kathmandu through thematic linkages like pilgrimage, heritage conservation, and adventure ecotourism. By leveraging complementarities in each country's tourism focus, like Sikkim's eco-heritage routes, Bhutan's sustainable high-value tourism, and Nepal's mountaineering and cultural assets, the circuit has the potential to create a cohesive, impactful tourism experience while reinforcing regional connectivity and cultural diplomacy. The core components of the circuit are presented in Table 9.5.

Table 9.5 Core components of the Trans-Himalayan Cultural and Eco-Tourism Circuit

Country	Tourism focus	Key destinations	Thematic linkage
Sikkim (India)	Eco-tourism, Buddhism, heritage	Gangtok, Rumtek Monastery, Nathula Pass, Yuksom	Buddhist circuit, adventure trekking, Indo-Tibetan culture
Bhutan	High-value, low-impact tourism	Paro, Thimphu, Punakha, Tiger's Nest Monastery	Buddhism, Himalayan culture, architecture
Nepal	Cultural tourism, mountaineering	Kathmandu valley, Lumbini, Pokhara, Namche	Buddhist heritage, trekking, Gorkha history

Source: Author.

However, the circuit needs policy alignment and facilitation:

- **Visa integration**: this is the most important step towards the implementation of the circuit. This step calls for a sub-regional visa or simplified tourist permit under BBIN or BIMSTEC.
- **Transport connectivity**: the successfulness of this circuit requires coordinated road and air links (e.g. Bagdogra–Phuentsholing–Kathmandu). Though there is a provision in the BBIN Agreement, more is required.
- **Tourism Boards Alliance**: there is a need for joint marketing under the "Eastern Himalayan Heritage Trail" so that all issues are addressed and all people from different parts of the region can benefit from the circuit.
- **Eco-tourism standards**: the governments of the circuit should develop equally acceptable eco-tourism standards and guidelines. There is also a need for shared sustainability guidelines to protect fragile ecosystems.

The successful implementation of a trans-Himalayan tourism circuit involving Sikkim, Bhutan, and Nepal necessitates the active participation of a diverse range of stakeholders operating across multiple levels. At the governmental level, the tourism ministries of India, particularly Sikkim, Bhutan, and Nepal, must play a central role in policy coordination, infrastructure facilitation, and regulatory alignment. This could help to use the regional platforms like BBIN and BIMSTEC effectively, which would serve as institutional mechanisms for cross-border cooperation, enabling harmonization of visa regimes, joint branding, and capacity building. The private sector, especially eco-tourism operators and heritage-focused travel agencies, would be instrumental in designing and marketing culturally immersive and environmentally sustainable tour packages. Equally critical are local communities, including homestay providers, craft cooperatives, and cultural performers, who ensure the authenticity and inclusivity of the tourism experience. Additionally, Buddhist monastic institutions across the region could serve as custodians of shared heritage, not only offering spiritual depth to the tourism circuit but also acting as cultural bridges that reinforce historical connectivity. A collaborative framework involving all these stakeholders is essential in order to realize a meaningful and sustainable model of sub-regional tourism integration. However, it requires great political will for the success of the BBIN or any sub-regionalism (Kumar, 2015).

Conclusion

Sikkim has much potential and offers many opportunities to its neighbours in the promotion of sub-regional cooperation. The possible areas where contributions could be made are (i) sub-regional branding of tea, (ii) the creation of sub-regional electricity connectivity and building bonds in terms of the green energy corridor with hydro power connectivity, (iii) a sub-regional Himalayan and Buddhist tourism circuit, (iv) a sub-regional Himalayan Organic Mission—to share experiences and expertise, (v) sub-regional education collaborations and exchange programmes, to list only a few. However, these initiatives could be successful if travel restrictions on the movement of people, trade, commerce, and investments were eased.

References

Acharya, Amitav (2012), *The Making of Southeast Asia: International Relations of a Region*, Ithaca, New York: Cornell University Press.

AIDIA (Asian Institute of Diplomacy and International Affairs) (2019), "India–Nepal Economic Partnership Summit Concludes in Gangtok" (https://www.aidiaasia.org/news/india-nepal-economic-partnership-summit-concludes-in-gangtok).

APEDA (Agricultural and Processed Food Products Export Development Authority) (n.d.), "AgriExchange Portal" (https://agriexchange.apeda.gov.in/IndExp/PortNew.aspx).

Appadurai, Arjun (1996), *Modernity at Large: Cultural Dimensions of Globalization*, Minneapolis, MN: University of Minnesota Press.

Aris, Michael (1979), *Bhutan: The Early History of a Himalayan Kingdom*, Warminster: Aris & Phillips Ltd.

Balikci, Anna (2008), *Lamas, Shamans and Ancestors: Village Religion in Sikkim*, Belgium: Brill Academic.

Bhattacharya, Pinak Priya (2021), "New Road to Reduce Travel Time to Sikkim by an Hour", *The Times of India*, 3 September (https://timesofindia.indiatimes.com/city/kolkata/new-road-to-reduce-travel-time-to-sikkim-by-an-hour/articleshow/85879501.cms).

Brunet-Jailly, Emmanuel (2022), "Cross-Border Cooperation: A Global Overview", *Alternatives: Global, Local, Political, SAGE*, 47 (1), pp. 3–17.

Budhakoti, Arun (2021), "Border Roads Bring India and Nepal Closer", *The Diplomat*, 27 September (https://thediplomat.com/2021/09/border-roads-bring-india-and-nepal-closer).

CEL (Centre for Endangered Languages) (n.d.), "Centre for Endangered Languages", Sikkim University (https://cel.cus.ac.in).

CFA (Centre for Financial Accountability) (2019), "Controversies of 1200 MW Teesta III HEP in Sikkim" (https://www.cenfa.org/uncategorized/controversies-of-1200-mw-teesta-iii-hep-in-sikkim).

Chakma, Bhumitra (2020), *South Asian Regionalism: The Limits of Cooperation*, Bristol: Bristol University Press.

Dahal, C.K. (2016), "Sikkim Eyes Bangladesh for Hydroelectric Power Export; PTC Exploring Possibility", *The Economic Times*, 18 December (https://energy.economictimes.indiatimes.com/news/power/sikkim-eyes-bangladesh-for-hydroelectric-power-export-ptc-exploringpossibility/56045357).

Das, Sanjiv (2018), "Sikkim's Tryst with Pharma Sector", *Express Pharma*, 4 October (https://www.expresspharma.in/sikkims-tryst-with-pharma-sector).

Denjongpa, Anna Balikci (2002), "Kangchendzönga: Secular and Buddhist Perceptions of the Mountain Deity of Sikkim among the Lhopos", *Bulletin of Tibetology*, 38 (2) (https://lib.icimod.org/records/tnr8z-c2x74#:~:text=Denjongpa%2C%20A.%20B.%20(2002).%20Kangchendz%C3%B6nga%3A%20Secular,the%20Lhopos.%20In%20Bulletin%20of).

DPIIT (Department for Promotion of Industry and Internal Trade) (n.d.), "Department for Promotion of Industry and Internal Trade" (https://dpiit.gov.in).

Ecotourism & Conservation Society of Sikkim (2020), "Scheme on Pradhan Mantri Formalisation of Micro Food Processing Enterprises: Report on One District One Product for Sikkim State", Director, Micro, Small, and Medium Enterprises (MSME), Department of Commerce, Government of Sikkim.

Education Department (n.d.), "Higher Education in Sikkim", Government of Sikkim (https://sikkim.gov.in/departments/education-department/higher-education-in-sikkim).

FDI (Foreign Direct Investment) India (n.d.), "Sikkim: The Country's First Fully Organic State" (https://www.fdi.finance/states/sikkim).

Gambhir, Mohak (2020), "Evolution of Regional and Sub-Regional Cooperation in South Asia", Delhi: Center For Land Warfare Studies (CLAWS).

Guha, Pradyut (2018), "Organic Tea Farming and Its Performance in Sikkim", *Indian Journal of Economics*, 98 (391), pp. 621–37.

Hasran, V.P. (2018), "Regional Cooperation in South Asia", *Indian Foreign Affairs Journal*, 13(3), pp. 195–208.

Helsinki Rules (1966), "Helsinki Rules on the Uses of the Waters of International Rivers", International Law Association, 52nd Conference, Helsinki.

Hosen, S. (2019), "Sub-regional Cooperation in South Asia: Issues, Challenges and Policy Implications", *Bangladesh Institute of International and Strategic Studies Journal*, 40(3), pp. 291–310.

IANS (Indo-Asian News Service) (2022), "25% Additional Seats, No Entrance Tests for Overseas University Students", *Deccan Herald*, 21 August (https://www.deccanherald.com/national/25-additional-seats-no-entrance-tests-for-overseas-university-students-1137938.html).

IBEF (India Brand Equity Foundation) (n.d.), "Sikkim" (https://www.ibef.org/states/sikkim-presentation).

Kumar, A. (2015), "BBIN: Sub-regionalism in the SAARC", Indian Council of World Affairs.

Ministry of Chemicals and Fertilisers (2021), "Details of Number of Pharmaceutical Drug Manufacturers in States/UTs", 27 July (https://www.pib.gov.in/PressReleasePage.aspx?PRID=1739466).

Ministry of Statistics and Programme Implementation (2024), "Sikkim Economy" (https://statisticstimes.com/economy/india/sikkim-economy.php).

Mullard, Saul (2011), *Opening the Hidden Land: State Formation and the Construction of Sikkimese History*, Leiden: Brill.

Murthy, Padmaja (2008), "SAARC and BIMSTEC: Understanding their Experience in Regional Cooperation", Briefing Paper No. 12, Consumer Unity & Trusts Society (CUTS) International, Jaipur.

NET (Northeast Today) (2022), "Centre Evaluates Indo-Nepal Border Trade Prospects via Sikkim; High-Level Delegation Submits Report to CM Golay", *Northeast Today*, 27 June (https://www.northeasttoday.in/2022/06/27/centre-evaluates-indo-nepal-border-trade-prospects-via-sikkim-high-level-delegation-submits-report-to-cm-golay).

Palit, Amitendu and M. Shahidul Islam (2011), "Sub-regional Cooperation under SAARC: An Economic Analysis", in S.D. Muni (ed.), *The Emerging Dimensions of SAARC*, Cambridge: Cambridge University Press, pp. 113–31.

PTI (Press Trust of India) (2021), "Sevoke–Rangpo Railway Line to Spur Socio-Economic Development in Sikkim: Minister", *Business Standard*, 22 November (https://www.business-standard.com/article/current-affairs/sevoke-rangpo-railway-line-to-spur-socio-economic-devpt-in-sikkim-minister-121112200624_1.html).

Rahaman, M.M. and A.A. Mamun (2020), "Hydropower Development along Teesta River Basin: Opportunities for Cooperation", *Water Policy*, 22 (4), pp. 641–57.

Sarmah, Dipika (2019), "Status of Floriculture in Sikkim", *International Journal of Applied Research*, 5 (10), pp. 249–52.

Shukla, Ashish (2019), "Sub-regional Cooperation under BBIN Framework: An Analysis", *Issue Brief, Indian Council of World Affairs*, 1 (4).

Sikkim University (n.d.), "School of Languages and Literature" (https://cus.ac.in/index.php/en/schools-e/languages-and-literature).

SIMFED (Sikkim State Co-operative Supply and Marketing Federation Ltd) (n.d.), "*Tea*" (https://simfed.in/business/products-services/tea).

Sinha, Avijit (2018), "New Highway to Link Sikkim", *The Telegraph*, 28 May (https://www.telegraphindia.com/west-bengal/new-highway-to-link-sikkim/cid/1456942).

Soderbaum, Fredrik (2015), *Rethinking Regionalism*, London: Palgrave Macmillan.

Subba, T.B. (1999), *Politics of Culture: A Study of Three Kirata Communities in the Eastern Himalayas*, Hyderabad: Orient Longman.

Tea Board of India (n.d.), "Sikkim Tea" (https://www.teaboard.gov.in/TEABOARDCSM/MjIwOQ).

Tourism and Civil Aviation Department (n.d.), "About Sikkim", (https://www.sikkim.gov.in/departments/tourism-civil-aviation-department).

10

Sub-regional Cooperation between India and Bangladesh

A Driving Force for Tripura's Development

*Ashish Nath**

Introduction

Growth and development of the Indian economy in the past two decades was made possible largely by the opening up of the economy to foreign investments. After the reforms of 1991, foreign capital inflows played an important role in the growth and development of states like Gujarat, Maharashtra, Karnataka, and Delhi. These states have initiated policy reforms and succeeded in attracting investment flows both domestically and internationally. In fact, Maharashtra, Karnataka, Gujarat, and Delhi received 81 per cent of the total foreign direct investment (FDI) equity inflows in India from October 2019 to March 2025 (FDI Statistics, 2025).

The Northeastern states of India are land-locked states and are connected to the rest of India by a narrow strip of land (called the "Chicken's Neck"), measuring 22–35 km in width (Ghosh, 2025) that borders Bangladesh on one side and Nepal on another side. The region shares 98 per cent of its boundary with East, South, and Southeast Asian countries.[1] The structure of income of the states in the region is characterized by low levels of manufacturing (except Sikkim) and non-governmental activities, with a large proportion of the population dependent on the agriculture sector. Poor infrastructure and governance, along with low

* This chapter would be incomplete if I did not express my sincere thanks to Prabir Ghosh and other friends and colleagues who helped me in informal trade data collection.

Ashish Nath, *Sub-regional Cooperation between India and Bangladesh* In: *Sub-Regional Cooperation for Trade, Investment, and Employment in North-East India*. Edited by: Ashish Nath, Oxford University Press.
 DOI: 10.1093/9780197908938.003.0010

productivity and poor market access, are the major reasons for the underdevelopment of the region and its inability to attract investment. There has been little investment inflow into the Northeastern states of India. Assam, Arunachal Pradesh, Meghalaya, Tripura, Nagaland, and Manipur received rupees (Rs) 252.27 crore (0.0108202 per cent) as FDI equity inflows during the period October 2019 to March 2025 (FDI Statistics, 2025). Again, among the eight Northeastern states of India, the per capita net state domestic product (NSDP) at constant prices (base 2004–05) of only three states (namely, Arunachal Pradesh, Mizoram, and Sikkim) was above the All India per capita net national income of Rs 99,404 during the year 2022–23 (RBI, 2024). The noteworthy point is that the contribution of the construction sector is substantially high in the gross state domestic product (GSDP)_ of all the Northeastern states except Sikkim.

Tripura is the only state which is surrounded by Bangladesh from three sides (84 per cent of total border area) and the foreign trade of Tripura is mainly with Bangladesh. Tripura shares 856 km of border area with Bangladesh, 109 km with Mizoram (India) and 53 with Assam (India). Thus the state shares border more with a foreign country than with the Indian Union. Majority of population of the state depends on agriculture for livelihood. The situation is more prone in rural and border sharing areas. This is true for people living in either side of the countries sharing border. Thus, the state depends more on Bangladesh to accelerate its development process. This chapter posits that facilitating trade and investment relations with neighbouring countries, in particular Bangladesh, with whom the state share a vast common border, could help accelerate the economic growth and development process of the state. The district map of Tripura is shown in Figure 10.1 and the map shows that all the eight districts of the state share a geographical border with Bangladesh.

The economy of Tripura is agrarian and is characterized by geographical isolation, poor infrastructural facilities, low capital formation, low industrial activity, communication bottlenecks, poverty, and high unemployment. The state is industrially backward and heavily dependent on central assistance (Bhowmik and Nath, 2016). The 2022–23 budget estimates shows that out of total receipts of Rs 19,306.90 crore, the state received Rs 14,906.98 (77.21 per cent) as grants from the centre (Budget at a Glance 2024–25, Finance Department, n.d.). The almost isolated geographical location of the state and lack of infrastructural and

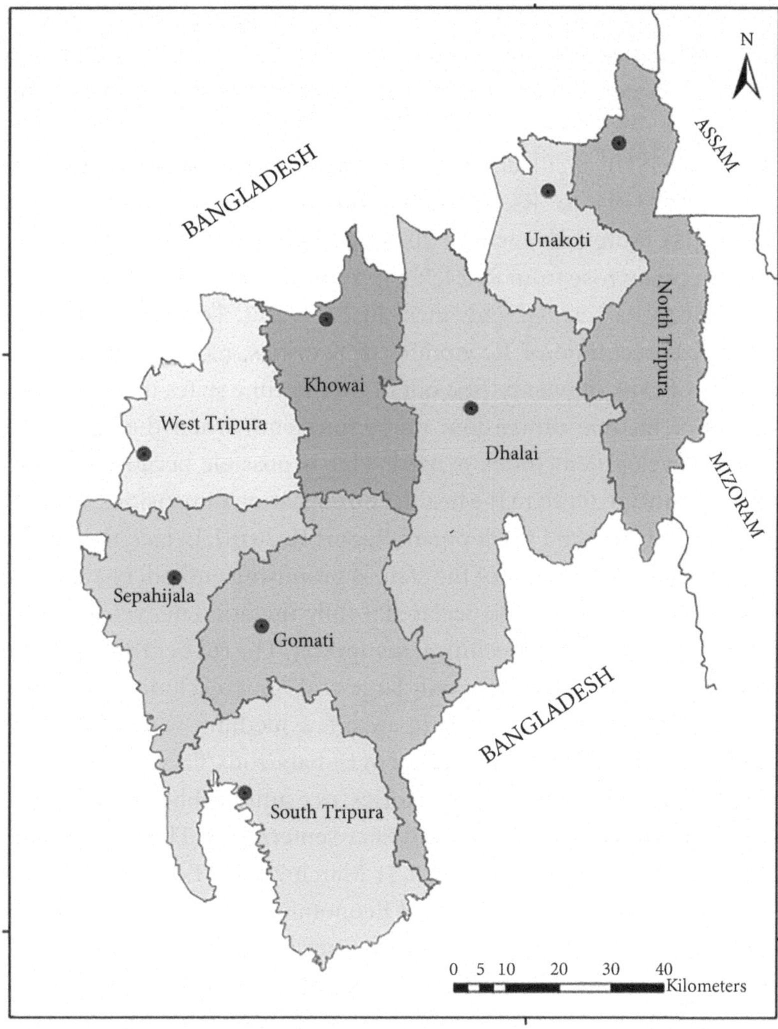

Figure 10.1 District boundary map of Tripura
Source: Prepared by Tripura Space Applications Centre DSTE, Government of Tripura.

communication facilities have proved to be major handicaps to the state's industrial development. The majority of population (73.8 per cent in 2011) of Tripura lives in rural areas and consequently depends on the primary sector for its livelihood. The services sector is the driving force of economic growth of the economy and grew at a rate of 18.1 per cent in its gross value added (GVA) at current prices during 2022–23. On the other hand, agriculture and allied sectors and the secondary sector grew at a rate of 7.1 per cent and 8.6 per cent, respectively, in GVA during the same period.

Tripura's GSDP at current prices increased from a meagre Rs 1,777.23 crore in 1993–94 to Rs 5,270.07 crore in 2000–01 and finally to Rs 89,681.81 crore (advance) in 2024–25. The state's per capita income at current prices rose from Rs 24,394 in 2004–05 to Rs 84,267 in 2015–16 and finally to Rs 1,92,842 (advance) in 2024–25 ("Tripura at a Glance, 2024–25", Directorate of Economics & Statistics, n.d.b). Tripura, despite its poor rank of twenty-first out of twenty-nine states in the country in terms of income dimension, ranks thirteenth when the composite Human Development Index is used. This is possible because the state ranks seventh and tenth in the health and education dimensions, respectively (Tripura Human Development Report II, 2018). In fact, the human development achievement of the state is promising and offers a hopeful picture. Though the state is declared a fully literate state, yet there is a dearth of managerial and technical manpower. The rubber thread unit at Bodhjungnagar, Agartala is the only large-scale unit (excluding the power sector) in Tripura. However, there are a few medium-scale units, such as a thermo-mechanically treated (TMT) bars/rods/flats unit, bamboo floor units, some tea processing factories, rice mills, rubber-based industries, etc. and a number of small and micro enterprises. The total number of registered units was 34,885 as of 31 March 2023 ("Economic Review of Tripura, 2022–23", Directorate of Economics & Statistics, n.d.a). The share of manufacturing sector in the economy is very low and has hovered around 3–4 per cent of the GSDP over the years. The formal foreign trade of Tripura with Bangladesh has a very low impact on the economy as this constituted only 1.24 per cent of GSDP in 2019–20. The labour force participation rate (LFPR) in usual status for all ages in Tripura was 44.5 per cent in 2022–23, while for rural areas, the rate was 45 per cent and, for urban areas, it was 42.4 per cent. The unemployment rate of all ages in Tripura was 1.4 per cent in 2022–23, while this was 1.1 per cent in rural areas and 3 per cent in urban areas (Economic Review of Tripura, 2022–23, Directorate of Economics & Statistics, n.d.a).

In order to analyse how improving trade relations with Bangladesh could help Tripura's development, the rest of the chapter is organized as follows. We first look at the overall trade between India and Bangladesh. This is followed by an analysis of the amount of trade flows between Tripura and Bangladesh and the factors that have resulted in low trade volumes, despite Tripura's proximity to Bangladesh. Since the present pattern of trade between Bangladesh and Tripura does not really offer much scope in terms of its becoming an instrument to accelerate the state's growth rate, the following section looks at the natural resource endowments of Tripura and outlines sectors that hold the potential for substantial growth. This is then mapped to the demand for products from Tripura in Bangladesh to outline the sectors in which investment would be needed to both increase trade and to ensure higher growth in the state. The final section looks at the measures needed to realize growth benefits from increased trade.

India–Bangladesh Trade Relations

Relations between India and Bangladesh have not always been smooth, but there has been an improvement in relations after the Awami League came to power in Bangladesh. A number of bilateral agreements have been signed between the two sides to strengthen the relationship (Ministry of External Affairs, 2024).

Bangladesh is India's biggest trade partner in South Asia, and India is the second biggest trade partner of Bangladesh in Asia (Ministry of External Affairs, 2024). The value of exports from India to Bangladesh increased from USD 1,664.36 million during 2005–06 to USD 3,242.90 million in 2010–11 and finally to USD 11,065.87 million in 2023–24. The share to total exports from India increased from 1.30 per cent in 2010–11 to 2.71 per cent in 2022–23 and finally to 2.54 per cent in 2023–24. Similarly, the value of imports from Bangladesh to India increased from USD 127.03 million during 2005–06 to USD 446.75 million in 2010–11 and to USD 1,844.76 million in 2023–24. Accordingly, the share to total imports by India increased marginally to 0.12 in 2010–11 to 0.28 per cent in 2022–23 and finally to 0.27 per cent in 2023–24. This is depicted in Figure 10.2.

The figure shows that though exports from India to Bangladesh and share of Bangladesh to total exports increased at an increasing rate,

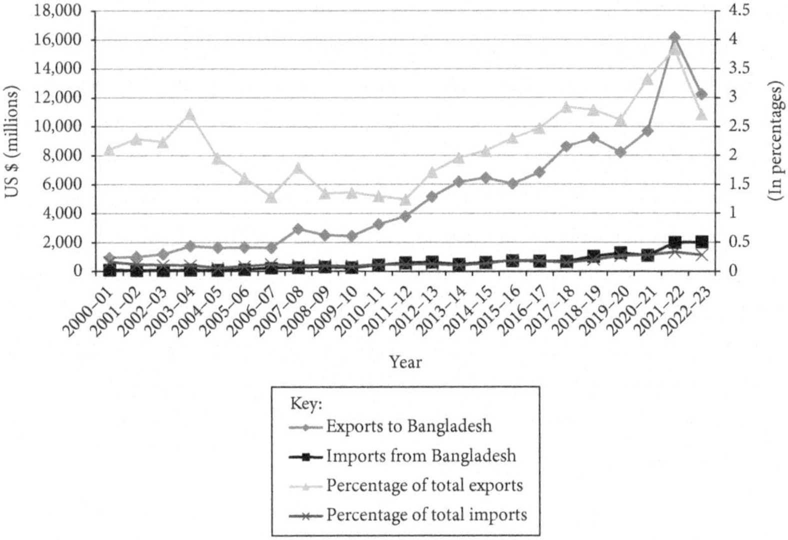

Figure 10.2 Trade between India and Bangladesh, 2000–01 to 2022–23
Note: share to total exports and imports are measured in the secondary axis.
Source: Export Import Databank, Ministry of Commerce and Industry, Government of India.

especially after 2011–12, but imports and its share did not increase substantially over the years. According to the Export–Import Databank (Ministry of Commerce and Industry, n.d.), the major items imported from Bangladesh during 2022–23 were fish and crustaceans, molluscs, and other aquatic invertebrates; animal or vegetable fats and oils and their cleavage products, pre-edible fats, and animal or vegetable waxes; plastic and articles thereof; articles of leather, saddlery and harness, travel goods, handbags and similar, and articles of animal gut; other vegetable textile fibres, paper yarn, and woven fabrics of paper yarn; articles of apparel and clothing accessories, knitted or crocheted; articles of apparel and clothing accessories, not knitted or crocheted; other made-up textile articles, sets, worn clothing and worn textile articles, and rags; footwear, gaiters and the like, parts of such articles. The major items exported to Bangladesh during the same period were edible vegetables and certain roots and tubers; coffee, tea, and mate and spices; cereals; sugars and sugar confectionary; residues and waste from the food industries; prepared animal fodder; salt, sulphur, earths and stone, plastering materials, lime, and cement; mineral fuels, mineral oils and products of their distillation, bituminous substances, and mineral waxes; organic chemicals; tanning or dyeing extracts, tannins and their deri, dyes, pigments and other colouring matter, paints, putty and other mastics, and inks; miscellaneous chemical products; plastic and articles thereof; cotton; man-made filaments; man-made staple fibres; iron and steel; articles of iron or steel; aluminium and articles thereof; nuclear reactors, boilers, and machinery and mechanical appliances and parts thereof; electrical machinery and equipment and parts thereof, sound recorders and reproducers, and television image and sound recorders and reproducers and parts; vehicles other than railway or railway rolling stock and parts and accessories thereof.

The economy of Bangladesh grew at the rate of 4.2 per cent during 2024 and is expected to grow 4 and 5 per cent in 2025 and 2026, respectively (ADB, 2025). Gross domestic product (GDP) at current prices increased from USD 154.1 billion in 2011 to USD 233.69 billion in 2015 and to USD 475.01 billion in 2025 (International Monetary Fund, 2025). The GDP per capita at current prices increased from USD 311.09 in 1980 to USD 2.73 thousand during 2025. Exports increased from USD 10.53 billion in 2005–06 to USD 22.92 billion in 2010–11 and to USD 3.78 billion in 2020. The major export items during 2019 were clothing, knitwear, and leather footwear. The major export partners in 2019 were the United States (15 per cent), Germany (14 per cent), the United Kingdom (8 per cent), France (7 per cent) and Spain (7 per cent) (CIA, 2022). There are eight export-processing zones in Bangladesh. Chittagong port, the biggest port in Bangladesh, carries about 92 per cent of the country's sea trade. Imports increased from USD 15 billion in 2005–06 to USD 34 billion in 2010–11 and to USD 57.26 billion in 2020. The major import items in 2019 were refined petroleum, cotton, natural gas, scrap iron, and wheat, and the major partners were China (31 per cent), Singapore (5 per cent), and India (15 per cent) (CIA, 2022). Bangladesh's exports exhibited strong growth and doubled their world market share between 1995 and 2012, owing to success in garments, catering largely to the European Union and the United States (Kathuria and Malouche, 2016). FDI plays an important role in the economy of Bangladesh. According to the World Investment Report (2023), Bangladesh FDI inflows increased from USD 1,136 million in 2011 to USD 2,152 million in 2017 and finally to USD 3,480 in 2022. One of the major sources of foreign exchange earnings are the remittances from Bangladeshis working overseas, mainly in the Middle East. Thus, in spite of neighbours, India and Bangladesh are never major trade partners.

Tripura's Trade with Bangladesh

In the past, Tripura had excellent transportation links with the erstwhile East Bengal (now Bangladesh). The radial distance between Agartala and Kolkata is only about 350 km, and many large cities of Bangladesh are within 150 km from the towns in Tripura (Agartala–Dhaka 150 km, Agartala–Brahmanbaria 25 km, Sabroom–Chittagong 75 km, Sonamura–Comilla 25 km, Kailashahar–Sylhet 90 km). The foreign trade of Tripura is mainly with Bangladesh, and officially, the trade was started in 1995–96. The improvement in bilateral ties between India and Bangladesh and the relatively robust growth rate in Bangladesh can be used to strategize growth plans for the Northeastern Region in general and Tripura in particular.

At present, as Table10.1 indicates, Tripura's contribution to both exports to and imports from Bangladesh represents a miniscule portion of India's total exports to and imports from Bangladesh. This is despite Tripura's proximity to major towns in Bangladesh.

The important conclusions that can be drawn from Table 10.1 are as follows:

- Bangladesh's trade balance with India has always been negative, whereas that with Tripura through integrated check posts (ICPs)/ land customs stations (LCSs) is positive.
- The negative trade balance between Tripura and Bangladesh has increased over the years.
- The value of export from Tripura to Bangladesh was always less than 0.07 per cent of total exports (except for 2021–22) from India during the period under study.
- The value of imports by Tripura from Bangladesh varied between 6 and 13 per cent of total imports by India.
- The ratio of exports from Tripura to Bangladesh is less than 5 per cent (except for 2021–22 and 2022–23) of the value of imports from Bangladesh to Tripura.

Table 10.1 Export and import: India/Tripura and Bangladesh (value in rupees crore)

Year-wise	Export from India to	Export from Tripura to	Import from Bangladesh by		Trade balance between India and Bangladesh	Trade balance between Tripura and Bangladesh
	Bangladesh		India	Tripura	–	–
2007–08	11,743.21	1.49	1,034.68	134.34	10,708.53	–132.85
2008–09	11,317.21 (–3.63)	0.31 (–79.19)	1,418.46 (37.09)	129.16 (–3.86)	9,898.75	–128.85
2009–10	11,501.07 (1.62)	0.41 (32.26)	1,205.28 (–15.03)	162.89 (26.11)	10,295.79	–162.48
2010–11	14,752.48 (28.27)	1.71 (317.07)	2,031.39 (68.54)	256.01 (57.17)	12,721.09	–254.30
2011–12	18,386.69 (24.63)	1.55 (–9.36)	2,796.36 (37.66)	329.05 (28.53)	15,590.33	–327.50
2012–13	27,982.57 (52.19)	0.41 (–73.55)	3,467.93 (24.02)	342.65 (4.13)	24,514.64	–342.24
2013–14	37,411.26 (33.69)	0.41 (0.00)	2,903.33 (–16.28)	229.83 (–32.93)	34,507.93	–229.83
2014–15	39,440.38 (5.42)	1.02 (148.78)	3,794.41 (30.69)	357.65 (55.62)	35,645.97	–356.63
2015–16	39,527.26 (0.22)	1.96 (92.16)	4,767.07 (25.63)	381.76 (6.74)	34,760.19	–379.80
2016–17	45,740.44 (15.72)	4.60 (134.69)	4,707.73 (–1.24)	300.23 (–21.36)	41,032.71	–295.63
2017–18	55,536.99 (21.42)	6.46 (40.43)	4,419.98 (–6.11)	384.22 (27.98)	51,117.01	–377.76
2018–19	64,391.52 (15.94)	14.66 (126.93)	7,338.69 (66.03)	522.42 (35.98)	57,052.83	–507.76
2019–20	58,176.61 (–9.65)	30.34 (106.96)	8,975.14 (22.30)	644.78 (23.42)	49,201.47	–614.44
2020–21	71,509.30 (22.92)	16.39 (–45.98)	8,053.48 (–6.93)	716.87 (11.18)	63,455.82	–700.48
2021–22	1,20,534.73 (68.56)	241.40 (1372.85)	14,749.50 (83.14)	767.00 (6.99)	1,05,785.23	–525.60
2022–23	1,97,784.51 (64.09)	121.37 (–49.72)	16,245.26 (10.14)	636.72 (–16.99)	1,81,539.25	–515.35

Sources: Ministry of Commerce and Industry (n.d.), "Export Import Data Bank", Government of India (https://tradestat.commerce.gov.in) and Economic Review(s) of Tripura.

(. . .): Growth rate.

There has been a sharp increase in both exports from and imports to Tripura from Bangladesh in the years 2009–10 and 2010–11. The growth rate of export from India and Tripura shows that exports from India to Bangladesh increased steadily over the years except for the year 2019–20. On the other hand, exports from Tripura also increased but declined in the years 2020–21 and 2022–23. Similarly, the growth rate of import also showed a positive trend both for India and Tripura except for the year 2020–21 for India and 2022–23 for Tripura.

The relationship between Bangladesh and Tripura is beyond boundaries,[2] and consequently, the trade between the two sides take place through the following channels:

- formal channel of trade,
- informal channel of trade, and
- border *haats*.

Formal Trade

Tripura has road and water connectivity with Bangladesh. However, regular trade between Tripura and Bangladesh is undertaken only through land ports, that is, ICPs and LCSs. There are five LCSs and three ICPs in Tripura. They are

1. Agartala (West Tripura district) ICP
2. Muhurighat (South Tripura district) LCS
3. Srimantapur (Sepahijala district) ICP
4. Khowaighat (Khowai district) LCS
5. Dholaighat (Dhalai district) LCS
6. Manu (Unakoti district) LCS
7. Old Ragnabazar (North Tripura district) LCS and
8. Sabroom (South Tripura district) ICP.

The formal Tripura–Bangladesh trade is carried out through four LCSs and two ICPs, and the bulk of the total trade is carried through Agartala ICP followed by Srimantapur, Muhuripur, and Manughat LCSs. In all the LCSs, including ICPs, the value of imports is more than exports, except in 2015–16, where the value of exports was more than that of imports for Old Ragnabazar LCS (Appendix 10.1). The volume and composition of trade between Bangladesh and Tripura showed a manifold increase over the years. The total volume of trade increased from a mere Rs 4.12 crore in 1995–96 to Rs 758.09 crore in 2022–23 (an increase of 183 times over a span of 29 years), though the rise in imports by Tripura has been much sharper than that of exports to Bangladesh. This is mainly because Tripura does not have any manufacturing industry that can spearhead the export potential of the state. In fact, the regional specialization index showing comparative advantage for the products of the state also failed to create demand for a substantial amount for exports (Ministry of DoNER and NEC, n.d.). Again, the Sabroom ICP has all infrastructural facilities to undertake trade through the Ramgarh LCS of Bangladesh using "Maitri Setu" bridge but is yet not functional due to the prevailing situation in Bangladesh. A Special Economic Zone (SEZ) is also sanctioned in the area to facilitate trade. Similarly, the Dholaighat LCS, situated in the Dhalai district of Tripura, has no infrastructural facilities to support movement of goods between the two sides and, as such, is used for movement of passengers only.

Tripura imports from Bangladesh through all the functional LCSs and ICPs, and imports from Bangladesh consist of both low value-added and medium value-added manufactured products. The bulk of imports consists of a variety of fish, including hilsa, small fish, dry fish, etc. (always more than 30 per cent) followed by food items, including soft drinks, from Bangladesh. Thus, Tripura imports various products ranging from broken stone to manufactured products to perishable goods. However, no raw material or semi-finished products were imported for value-added manufacturing and export to other countries including Bangladesh. The composition of imports (Figure 10.3) shows that a very limited number of items is imported from Bangladesh through LCSs/ICPs, and the trade volume increased over the years, though it declined during 2022–23.

On the other hand, the value of exports from Tripura to Bangladesh (Figure 10.4) is very low, and a very small number of items are traded through ICPs and LCSs. Again, the figure shows that primary and perishable commodities like fruits and food items are also exported to Bangladesh. However, it is observed that during the past two financial

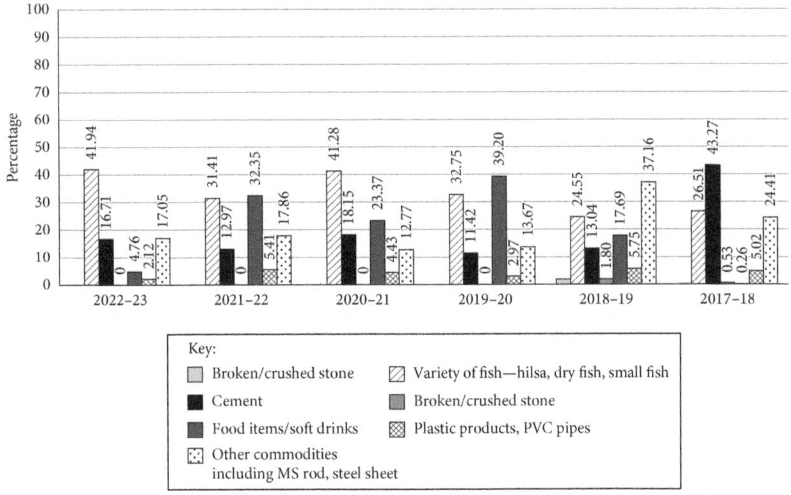

Figure 10.3 Import of major commodities (through LCSs/ICPs) from Bangladesh by Tripura (percentage share of total import value)
Source: Economic Review (s) of Tripura, 2017-18:2022-23 (https://ecostat.tripura.gov.in).

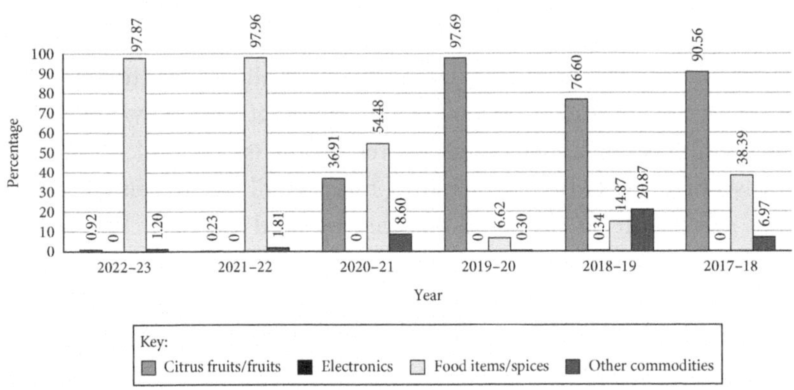

Figure 10.4 Export of major commodities (through LCSs/ICPs) by Tripura to Bangladesh (percentage share of total export value)
Source: Economic Review (s) of Tripura, 2017-18:2022-23 (https://ecostat.tripura.gov.in).

years, Bangladesh imported wheat of more than 85 per cent of its import value from Tripura, and the value increased substantially from 2021–22 to 2022–23. Tripura does not have noticeable manufacturing units based on products with comparative advantage which can be used to strategize the state.

A look at the composition of trade between the two sides shows that exports from Tripura to Bangladesh consist of both manufacturing and agricultural products and are very low in number, whereas the state imports a variety of items from Bangladesh worth crores of rupees.

One reason for the relatively small amount of formal trade between Tripura and Bangladesh is the existence of tariff and non-tariff barriers. In the case of India and Bangladesh too, there exist many tariff and non-tariff barriers. In South Asia, both nature and man have contrived to fragment the region, denying countries and people the benefits of proximity (Kathuria and Mathur, 2018). Although tariff barriers came down drastically between India and Bangladesh after the agreement on the South Asian Free Trade Area, non-tariff barriers continue to exist. Personal communication with Bangladeshi traders indicates the following kinds of barriers to trade:

1. Any product from Bangladesh is subjected to laboratory tests. This is time-consuming and affects the timely delivery of products.
2. Bangladesh citizens' movements are subject to visa restrictions, and this affects interaction with local people.
3. Loading and unloading of goods/vehicles near the shipment place across the border area is restricted and has many hurdles due to the presence of informal intermediaries, etc.
4. The infrastructure in and around the land ports of Tripura is very poor, which affects the movement of goods, including warehousing. Akhaura–Agartala ICP is the busiest trade route, but this is only a two-lane route on both sides of the border.
5. There is a labour and vehicle syndicate in almost all centres on the Indian side of the border. Therefore, importers cannot use their own labour and vehicles to carry goods from the landing centre(s) to the warehouse.
6. There is no Bangladeshi bank in Tripura and this causes transaction problems. Transactions are done mainly through letters of credit through the nationalized banks of the two countries.
7. Road connectivity between Bangladesh and Tripura is poor, leading to high transport costs.
8. Bangladesh has a list of negative products, which Indian exporters find it difficult to sell to their Bangladeshi counterparts.

The foregoing discussion on formal trade between Bangladesh and Tripura shows that though the trade volume and composition are at low level, the overall trade has increased substantially over the years. Bangladesh dominated the overall trade, but due to the sharing of large portions of border between the two sides, a substantial portion of the formal trade gets diversified towards the informal channel of trade.

Informal Trade

Informal trade is the most important component of trade between Bangladesh and Tripura, both in terms of composition and volume. Informal trade is defined as cross-border trade carried out without the approval of the competent authorities. There are eight districts in Tripura, and all the districts share a border with Bangladesh. As such, informal trade between Tripura and Bangladesh is undertaken through all the districts sharing an international border with Bangladesh. Many villages and gaon panchayats of Tripura have common borders with Bangladesh. Many towns and markets of Bangladesh are also located close to these villages, leading to trade opportunities. This is particularly attractive given the high unemployment and under employment in the border areas of rural Tripura.

The informal channel of trade shows that large numbers of products go to Bangladesh through various trade points (Appendix 10.2). The trade points were identified through personal contacts and through interaction with local knowledgeable persons. The products traded informally can be categorized into three groups:

1. products consisting of cows, foreign liquor, drugs (Phensidile, Corex, tablets for addiction, and other drugs used for addiction), and ganja/cannabis;
2. semi-sophisticated products;
3. horticultural and agricultural products.

Informal trade is the most important channel of trade between the Northeastern states of India and the neighbouring countries sharing boundaries because there are many factors that fuel the informal channel.

Pohit and Taneja (2000) also pointed out that informal trade is preferred because of various barriers to official trade and inadequate infrastructure. In the case of Bangladesh–Tripura trade as well, the following factors seems to have contributed to this informal channel:

- Informal trade saves the transaction costs involved in formal trade, including custom duty, as well as avoiding the unfriendly behaviour of government officials responsible for border trade.
- Formal trade is time-consuming, and it is difficult to supply goods within the stipulated time period due to official procedures.
- Many towns and markets in Bangladesh are close to Indian villages.
- Cheap labour is available for carrying goods.
- There is harassment and delay in supplying/receiving goods in formal trade, and through informal trade, they can save "transport cost" because of easy mobility across the borders.
- There is no LCS in or around Shimna (West Tripura). The traders of Shimna are petty businessmen who find it easy to trade informally because the Mohanpur–Shimna road is close to Bangladesh (approximately 2 km) and the Sahapur railway station (Bangladesh) is very close. This is true for Mohanpur (West Tripura) also.
- The traders of Khowai (Khowai district) said that the "Balla" railway station in Bangladesh and the "Khowai" river helps their trade.
- In Belonia (South Tripura), "fencing" has not been done on several parts of the border, and this facilitates informal trade. The Muhari river helps to move material and elephants are used to carry wooden logs between the two sides.
- Tripura and Bangladesh share many rivers, and on many occasions, these rivers are also used by traders to informally export bamboo from Tripura to Bangladesh.

Thus, many factors fuel the informal channel of trade between Bangladesh and Tripura. Here, it is to be pointed out that the value of exports and imports undertaken by the traders of both sides is not significantly high in many cases, and hence, they want to save transaction costs involved in the formal channel of trade.

Alongside this informal export of goods, there is also informal import of goods from Bangladesh through various trade points. The importable product basket consists of a variety of items ranging from perishables to manufactured products. The informal channel of trade dominates the formal channel between Bangladesh and Tripura for a number of reasons. One of the important reasons is the low opportunity for livelihood along the international border areas, and this situation has played a significant role in the governments of neighbouring countries establishing "border *haats*".

Border *Haats*

Border trade can take many forms. Border trade takes place formally through notified LCSs/ICPs and informally as well as through "border *haats*". "Border" means sharing area, "*haat*" means market, and a "border *haat*" is a market at the zero-point area of the two countries, where people (called "vendors") from the local designated areas of the two countries come and sell local products in an exchange of currencies of the respective countries. The idea is to improve the well-being of the people dwelling in remote areas across the border areas because people living along the international border areas are prone to abject livelihood and opportunities for a better livelihood are also low. The governments of border-sharing countries (India, Myanmar, and Bangladesh) have coined the idea of "border *haats*" (Ministry of Commerce and Industry, 2010, 2012). The Government of the Republic of India and the Government of the People's Republic of Bangladesh established four border *haats* along the borders of Bangladesh and India:

1. Kamalasagar (Sepahijala district, Tripura, India)—Tarapur (Brahmanbaria district, Bangladesh),
2. Srinagar (South Tripura district, Tripura, India)—Chagalnaiya (Feni district, Bangladesh),
3. Kalaichar (*West Garo* hills, Meghalaya, India)—Baliamari (Kurigram district, Bangladesh), and
4. Balat (East Khasi hills, Meghalaya, India)—Lauwaghar (Dalora, Sunamgang district, Bangladesh).

The border *haats* are managed by "*haat* management committees (HMCs)", and the committee comprises five members, including one representative each from the police, customs, border security agency, and village-level local government. The size of the border *haats* are 75 x 75 m on the zero line, and no passport is required to enter the *haat.* The *haats* have two points for entry and exit—one from the Indian territory for Indian citizens and another from the Bangladesh territory for Bangladeshi citizens. The committees are guided by their respective border security agencies for the functioning of the *haats.*

Initially, the following commodities produced in India and Bangladesh are allowed to be traded in the border *haats* only by the residents as vendors of the area living within a 5-km radius from the location of the *haat*:

- vegetables produced locally, food items, fruits, spices;
- minor products of the forest, such as bamboo, bamboo grass, and broom stick (excluding timber);
- cottage-industry products, such *as gamcha* (a small, traditional towel), *lungi* (a draper round the waist for men), *saree*, and any other handloom products, etc;
- small household and agricultural implements, e.g. the *dao* (a traditional cutter made with iron), plough axes, spades, chisels etc;
- garments, melamine products, processed food items, fruit juice, toiletries, cosmetics, plastic products, aluminium products, cookeries, stationery;
- indigenous products specifically produced in and around the area of the border *haats*, subject to mutual consent.

The list of items allowed for trade in designated border *haats* can be modified and expanded by mutual consent of the committee. The number of vendors from both sides is regulated with the objective of ensuring that border *haats* will not be overcrowded. Again, only residents (called "vendees"[3]) of the area living within a 5-km radius from the location of border *haats* will be allowed to buy products from the border *haats*, and the number will be regulated in such a way that the *haats* do not get overcrowded. Border *haats* are held on a fixed day of the week as mutually decided between the HMCs. Vendors and vendees are issued identity cards to enter border *haats* for both the countries.

The commodities sold in the border *haats* are free from the payment of custom duties, including other duties or taxes levied by the concerned authorities of both countries. The idea of the *haats* is that tariff and non-tariff measures should not hinder the working of the *haats*. It is also advocated that custom officials and health officials will invoke restrictions in the event of infringement of custom regulations or outbreak of any disease dangerous to public health. The commodities are allowed to be exchanged in local currency and/or on a barter basis. Each individual is allowed to purchase a limited quantity of the commodities produced in Bangladesh or India, which can be used for personal or family consumption. The value of such purchases should not be more than the respective local currency equivalent of USD 200 for any particular day. However, the limit may be re-fixed by mutual consent (Nath, 2018a).

Kamalasagar (Tripura, India)—Tarapur (Brahmanbaria, Bangladesh) border *haat* came into operation on 11 June 2015, and the *haat* operated weekly on every Sunday from 9:30 am to 3:30 pm (Indian Standard Time, IST). The basic idea of the *haat* is to enhance the livelihood of the local people through the traditional system of marketing local produce. The *haats* have sheds with a "ceiling" and four sides open for both sides of the vendors. The vendors sit on the floor, which is made up of cement coverings, to sell their goods. It is to be noted that the "*haat*" not only ensures sale and purchase of goods but also acts as a meeting place for families from both countries with blood and other relationships as well. Thus, all sections of society participate in the *haat* and carry out their own business.

The *haats* have provision for "visitors" other than the local people. All individuals who enter the *haat* with a valid identity proof can purchase goods from vendors of both countries using either Indian rupees or Bangladeshi "*taka*" or both types of currencies. There is a huge demand for Indian products among the Bangladeshi people, especially for grocery items, toiletries, etc. Similarly, Indians are more interested in purchasing dry fish, plastic products, etc. at least in the Kamalasagar–Tarapur border *haat*. The Kamalasagar–Tarapur border *haat* has been successful in improving the economic status of the people engaged in the activities of the *haats* (Nath, 2018a). Table 10.2 shows the sale and purchase by

Table 10.2 Sale and purchase by Indian and Bangladeshi vendors at Kamalasagar border *haat*

Financial year	Sale by Indian vendors (value in rupees crore)	Sale by Bangladesh vendors (value in rupees crore)	Total amount (value in rupees crore)
2015–16 (w.e.f. 11 June 2015)	2.96	0.55	3.51
2016–17	5.88	0.59	6.47
2017–18	4.25	1.21	5.46
2018–19	3.17	0.91	4.08
2019–20	8.39	0.98	9.37

Note: w.e.f: with effect from.

Source: "Economic Review of Tripura 2021–22", Directorate of Economics & Statistics.

Indian and Bangladeshi vendors at Kamalasagar–Kasba border *haat*. The table shows that sale by Indian vendors is substantially more than that by the Bangladeshi vendors. This is mainly because of the huge demand for Indian fast-moving consumer goods, including cosmetics and toiletries, in Bangladesh. On the other hand, Indians mainly demand local Bangladeshi products, including fish, dry fish, and plastic products, the price being substantially lower than the Indian products. This, to a great extent, explains the disparity in sale volume by the vendors of the two countries.

The major commodities sold on the Indian side are fruits, tea leaf, steel, garments, bakery items, masala (spices), baby foods, toiletries, and cosmetics, etc. Similarly, the major commodities sold by the Bangladeshi vendors are fish, dry fish, bakery items, plastic goods, fruits such as green apples, watermelons, local vegetables, etc. The establishment of this border *haat* not only helped the local vendors to improve their financial status but also improved human relationships across the border as well.

The second Srinagar (India)—Chagalnaiya (Bangladesh) border *haat* is located across the international border of India and Bangladesh in Srinagar and Chagalnaiya under South Tripura district (India) and Feni district (Bangladesh). The border *haat* was inaugurated on 13 January 2015. The Srinagar–Chagalnaiya border *haat* has been successful in increasing the income not only of the designated vendors but also of non-licence holders. The composition of products in

Table 10.3 Sale and purchase by Indian and Bangladeshi vendors at Srinagar border *haat*

Financial year	Sale by Indian vendors (value in rupees crore)	Sale by Bangladesh vendors (value in rupees crore)	Total amount (value in rupees crore)
2014–15	0.18	0.09	0.27
2015–16	1.81	0.70	2.51
2016–17	7.39	3.81	11.20
2017–18	4.28	3.29	7.57
2018–19	0.94	0.63	1.57
2019–20	0.83	4.61	5.44

Source: "Economic Review of Tripura 2021–22", Directorate of Economics & Statistics.

Srinagar–Chagalnaiya border *haat* is more than that of the Kamalasagar–Tarapur border *haat*. Except for 2019–20, the sales by the Indian vendors were always more than their counterparts (Table 10.3).

There were no sales in both the border *haats* during the 2020–21 and 2021–22 due to the COVID-19 pandemic. However, though a process was started to re-open the *haats* after the pandemic, the recent turmoil in Bangladesh has stopped the development, and consequently, the border *haats* stopped functioning. The functioning of two border *haats* between Tripura (India) and Bangladesh show that though the *haats* function weekly for one day, there is sufficient scope for the *haats* to function more than one day in a week.

The establishment of two border *haats* between Tripura in India and Bangladesh has been successful in improving the economic condition of the villages in general and of the vendors in particular (Nath, 2018a). The success of the existing border *haats* has encouraged the Governments of India and Bangladesh to establish six more border *haats* (for the state of Meghalaya and Tripura) along the India and Bangladesh border. These border *haats*, if properly function could go a long way to increasing the economic condition of the vulnerable groups of people.

The foregoing paragraphs show that trade between Bangladesh and Tripura takes place through three channels (formal, informal, and border *haats*). In addition, recently, cross-border railway lines between Agartala and Akhaura Upazila in the Brahmanbaria district of Bangladesh was established, and it is expected that this link will help Tripura to bypass the "Chicken's Neck", by reducing not only the distance from 1,600 km to 500 km but also the time duration from thirty-one hours to ten hours. All these things are made possible because Tripura shares not only a long international border but also ethnic, cultural, cordial, and blood relations with Bangladesh. There are many places along the border where demarcation of land between the two countries is difficult to implement. This has boosted informal trade not only for commercial purposes but also for the daily needs of the local households. At the same time, the widespread presence of unemployment in the rural areas has fuelled the informal channel of trade. After interaction with border traders, Bhattacharya (2015) also opined that illegal trade between Bangladesh and Tripura is unaccountable. Understanding that informal trade is not only illegal but also a loss to the state exchequer, the government has started to fence the international border between Tripura and Bangladesh. This fencing has drastically reduced the intensity of the informal trade between the two sides. But due to the non-completion of the fencing in many dispute areas and unearthing loopholes in the fencing by the people involved in the informal channel, this method of trading, though at a lower scale, has continued.

It is noteworthy that though a trial run for an inland waterways project to send consignments from Daudkandi, Chattogram, Bangladesh to Sonamura, Tripura was successfully conducted on 3–5 September 2020 (Ministry of External Affairs, 2020). The new protocol route is yet to be used regularly for movement of consignments between the two countries.

The Advantage of Tripura

As the analysis of formal and informal trade between Tripura and Bangladesh indicates, the volume of formal trade remains miniscule, while informal trade is dominated by items that cannot be legally traded. More importantly, there is a need to strategize Tripura's development taking into account its natural resource endowments and the sectors in which it enjoys a clear competitive advantage. The location of Tripura is strategic in the international context, being between Bangladesh on one side and Southeast Asia on the other. The location and resource advantages of Tripura, along with socio-economic linkages with Bangladesh, could make Tripura a potential hub for trade with and through Bangladesh for the entire North-East of India. In order to prioritize Tripura and set it on the path of growth, the Government of Tripura, with support from the Union government, has initiated a number of connectivity projects as well as identification of potential products that will be drivers of growth.

In order to promote trade and investment in the states of the Northeastern Region of India, the Government of India announced the Uttar Poorva Transformative Industrialization Scheme on 24 March 2024 for fostering industrial growth and economic transformation (Department for Promotion of Industry and Internal Trade, 2024). Again, the Government of Tripura has notified thrust-sector (manufacturing-sector[4] and service-sector[5]) industries that are eligible to get additional subsidy under the state incentive scheme called "Tripura Industrial Investment Promotion Incentives Scheme, 2022" in the form of capital investment subsidies, industrial promotion subsidies, power subsidies, partial reimbursement of interest on term loans, reimbursement of fees for obtaining technology know-how, employment cost subsidies, subsidies on fees paid for credit guarantee trust funds for micro and small enterprises, export promotion subsidies, and transport subsidies (Department of Industries and Commerce, n.d.).

The state has rich natural resources, gas, and forests. Tripura is the second largest producer of natural rubber in India, and this is the most important crop of the state. The state government has identified rubber plantation as the priority area for livelihood generation and, consequently, declared rubber-based industries as a "thrust sector" for investment. The total area under rubber plantation is 85,453.63 hectares and the yield is 1,350 kg/hectare. There is approximately one lakh rubber growers, and the total rubber production was 1,02,989 metric tonnes during 2022–23. In Tripura, it is estimated that 99 per cent of the natural rubber produced is processed into different marketable forms such as rubber sheet, Indian standard natural rubber/block rubber, and centrifuged latex. A rubber park and an industrial area were set up near

Agartala to provide infrastructural facilities for setting up rubber-based industries. There are two central processing units (Downstream Partner and Manimalayar Rubbers) and 208 group processing units in the state. The state-run corporations (namely, Tripura Forest Development and Plantation Corporation Limited and Tripura Rubber Plantation Corporation Limited) have fifty-eight and fifty-four group processing centres, respectively. Thus, there is vast potential for sectors like auto parts, footwear, vulcanized rubber, rubber bands, latex thread, textile fabrics, etc in the state. Here, it is important to note that the necessary facilities are made for the processing of field latex and the smoking of sheet rubber in order to increase the quality of graded sheet (Department of Industries and Commerce, n.d.).

Bamboo is the principal non-timber forest produce in Tripura. Tripura is home to 21 species of bamboo out of 130 species available in India. The cane and bamboo industries of Tripura are considered to be among the best in the country as per the report of the Department of Industries and Commerce, Government of Tripura. The state meets 60 per cent of the requirement of the entire country for bamboo sticks for *agarbatti* (Indian incense sticks) making. This sector has great export potential. Industrial products like bamboo tiles, laminated products, ply boards, corrugated sheets, etc. can be produced and used as building materials for furniture manufacturing, etc. The Tripura Bamboo Mission was established in 2007 for the integrated development of the bamboo sector. The total turnover of the sector increased from Rs 27.90 crore in 2006–07 to Rs 96.53 crore in 2016–17. The Tripura Bamboo Mission established more than 1,000 self-help groups and 60 producer societies/cooperatives and community owned institutions, along with bamboo farmer's groups for the promotion of the sector. This initiative is mainly to develop bamboo as an alternative to timber. A bamboo park has also been established to facilitate the setting up of bamboo-based industries. The sector is gradually transforming from a manual stick producer to a mechanized stick producer in the form of the introduction of *agarbatti* rolling machines, etc. through value addition with the help of foreign technology (Department of Industries and Commerce, n.d.). *Mutha* Industry Pvt. Ltd, a Mumbai-based company, has already come up with a plan to add value to raw bamboo produce and bamboo-made products in Tripura, including marketing the product outside the country. *Mutha* industries introduced "Epitome"—a premium range of *bamboowood* flooring. *Bamboowood* is produced in a sprawling state-of-the-art manufacturing facility spread over ten acres in the bamboo park by using fifteen species of bamboo (Epitome, n.d.).

The agro-climatic conditions of Tripura are suitable for tea plantation, and this industry is the only organized industry. Tea plantation in Tripura started in 1916 and is the sixth largest, among the sixteen tea-producing states in India. The state has fifty-four tea estates, twenty-three tea-processing factories, and more than 2,755 small tea growers, having 1,398 hectares of land under cultivation of tea, producing over 73 lakh kg of tea every year. In order to recognize the tea of Tripura at the national and global level, the Tripura tea logo was launched in 2018. Tripura Tea Development Corporation Limited has developed the brand of "Tripureswari tea" as the tea made in their factory and the average sale price realized by Tripura tea in auction market is about Rs 200 per kg. The industry has also taken steps to set up more tea-processing factories for green tea, orthodox tea, and crush, tear, curl (CTC) tea (Department of Industries and Commerce, n.d.). There is considerable scope for increasing productivity through investment in the tea sector in the state, especially for blending units.

Tripura has a suitable agri-climate condition for agricultural products. There is plenty of scope for food-processing industries in the field of rice, pineapple, oranges, jackfruit, and bananas. Major spices found in the state are ginger, turmeric, chillies, black pepper, cinnamon, and bay leaves. There is ample scope for developing the spices sector. The development of agro- and food-processing industries would not only ensure better returns to the farmers but also would create employment opportunities in the rural areas as well. A food park has been set up to provide the infrastructural facilities required for food-processing industries. Similarly, a mega food park has been approved with the help of the Ministry of Food Processing Industries through a private developer. Pran Beverages India Private Limited started its manufacturing business in Tripura in 2017 in the food park at Bodhjung Nagar, Agartala, based on local resources. The products manufactured by the company include crispy rusk, bakery products, a lichi drinks plant, an ice pop drinks plant, a cup jelly plant, and a tetra pack juice plant, and it is successfully supplying and trading its products.

Tripura has vast reserves of natural gas as well. Although the state government is encouraging private-sector investment in gas-based industries, natural gas is at present used mainly for the generation of power and in the domestic, industrial, and transport sector. The gas reserve of Tripura is estimated at 400 billion cubic metres (BCM). Since 1962, the Oil and Natural Gas Corporation Limited (ONGC) has been engaged in the exploration of the gas reserves of Tripura and, again in 2005, took the initiative to generate electricity using natural gas as raw material. OTPC (ONGC Tripura Power Company Private Limited), the largest gas-based combined thermal power plant of North-East India, was set up in Tripura with an installed power generation capacity of 726.6 megawatts. This has improved the opportunities for setting up of industries in the state of Tripura. The surplus electricity power is exported to Bangladesh as well. Bangladesh had already agreed to allow India to use its waterways to transport heavy machines for ONGC power projects.

Tripura has a rich history, archaeology, and cultural heritage and traditional art and music, also affluent flora and fauna. By using its locational advantage, the state could become an attractive tourist location. There are a number of historical Hindu and Buddhist sites. There is huge potential in the state in terms of eco-tourism and rural tourism, including the opportunity for the state to develop a tourism network involving all the Northeastern states and the neighbouring countries. There is also potential to develop industries based on human capital as Tripura is considered the second-best information technology destination after Guwahati.

The capital of Tripura, Agartala, is India's third internet gateway after Chennai and Mumbai. Consequently, Bharat Sanchar Nigam Limited (BSNL) leased ten gigabits per second (Gbps) bandwidth from Bangladesh Submarine Cable company Limited (BSCCL). The import of internet bandwidth will help India to strengthen telecom services and connectivity in the underdeveloped and sparsely connected Northeastern Region of India. Again, in 2022, a second 10Gbps link was added and the total increased to 20Gbps. This connectivity will not only revolutionize the Northeastern Region but also neighbouring regions as well. However, this third international internet gateway at Agartala has been non-functional since October 2025.

Realizing the importance of trade and investment in growth and development, a number of initiatives have been taken at the level of government as well as the business community to improve trade and cultural links between Tripura and Bangladesh. The Bangladesh government has set up a visa office at Agartala. There have been regular visits by the chambers of commerce of both countries. The Bangladesh government has already agreed to allow India to use Chittagong international port, which is about 75 km from southern Tripura's border town Sabroom, situated on the bank of the Feni river. The "Maitri Setu" over the Feni river would make it easier to transport goods between the Northeastern states and the rest of the world via the Chittagong sea port in Bangladesh through Sabroom–Ramgarh ICP. Since Agartala is the nearest Indian city to this international seaport, Tripura would have the opportunity to become the gateway to North-East India. The transportation cost of raw materials, consumer goods, and finished industrial produces would come down greatly, increasing the investment potential of the region. It is believed that this port is the key driver of trade relations between North-East India and Bangladesh. In this context, an SEZ has been notified by the government of India to be set up at Jalefa, Sabroom, in the South Tripura district. The SEZ will focus on four sectors, including agro-based processing such as food processing, rubber, bamboo, and textiles.

Ashuganj has been declared as a port of call fulfilling a long-pending demand of Tripura (MDoNER, 2011). Ashuganj in Bangladesh was declared a "port of call" for this purpose in June 2016, and under the agreement, vessels carrying Indian cargos would unload at Ashuganj port, from where Bangladeshi trucks would carry the goods to Tripura to be delivered at the Akhaura checkpoint. This substantially reduces the distance between Kolkata and Agartala from about 1,600 km to 500 km (CUTS International and FICCI, 2017). By allowing Ashuganj port, over the Megna river in Comilla district to carry consignments for Tripura, the Bangladesh government has not only strengthened the economic cooperation between India and Bangladesh but will also go a long way towards transforming North-East India by making it the gateway to the Act

East Policy. Again, Delhi airport started a facility to export fresh fruits such as oranges, pineapples, kiwi, and bananas as well as chillies and cut flowers from the Northeastern states to Dubai in an effort to help the locals take their produce to international markets (Haidar, 2017).

In 2015, the Bangladesh, Bhutan, India and Nepal (BBIN) Motor Vehicles Agreement was signed by the Governments of the People's Republic of Bangladesh, the Kingdom of Bhutan, and the Republic of India and Nepal for closer and enhanced regional connectivity through road transport, including promoting cross-border road transportation for increased intra-regional and inter-regional trade. Tripura could become a gateway for the entire Asian region by using this corridor not only for the transportation of goods and services but also to enhance the value chain.

Similarly, the Agartala–Akhaura railway project is the first railway project between the Northeastern states of India and Bangladesh (PIB, 2023). The railway link will connect Gangasagar under the Akhaura subdivision of Brahmanbaria district of Bangladesh with Nischintapur in India and Nischintapur to Agartala railway station. The alignment of the project has a length of 5.46 km in India and 6.78 km in Bangladesh. The railway link will not only provide additional connectivity between India and Bangladesh by encouraging trade but also will boost passenger traffic.

The bilateral relationship between Tripura and Bangladesh developed immensely during the past two decades because of the positive initiatives of the two governments as well as the signing of various agreements to boost trade relations between the two countries (India–Bangladesh Bilateral Relations, 2024). Trade volume increased, and this has affected the overall business environment. The Neighbourhood First Policy and the Act East Policy of the Government of India have greatly helped to increase infrastructural facilities and connectivity in the Northeastern Region of India during the past decade. Consequently, many agreements and proposals were initiated for the Northeastern region to play a greater role in the sub-region in terms of trade and investment.

The recent turmoil (since August 2024) in Bangladesh and the sudden exit of Sheikh Hasina from Bangladesh has severely affected the economic and political relations between India and Bangladesh in general and Bangladesh and the Northeastern Region of India in particular. The cordial relations developed over the years between the two countries reduced drastically after the interim government headed by Muhammad Yunus took charge in Bangladesh. As a result, trade (exports from India declined to USD 11.4 billion and imports to USD 2 billion during 2024–25) declined not only for India and Bangladesh but also for the entire border-sharing Northeastern states with Bangladesh. Bangladesh has restricted import of yarn from India through its land ports, and this will impact cotton yarn exports and increase logistics costs (Preetha, 2025). Similarly, the Government of India allowed the import of readymade garments only through Nhaya Sheva and Kolkata seaports and not from any other land ports. The imports of fruit/fruit-flavoured and carbonated drinks, processed food items, cotton and cotton yarn waste, plastic and PVC finished goods, and wooden furniture have been discontinued through LCSs/ICPs in Assam, Meghalaya, Mizoram, and Tripura (PIB, 2025). In fact, India has formally revoked the transshipment facility that allowed Bangladesh to export goods to third countries through Indian land custom stations, ports, and airports (Singh, 2025), effective from 8 April 2025. The volatile political relationship between the two countries has started to affect the economic relationship as well. Given the geographic location and history of Bangladesh, a healthy relationship between the two countries is crucial for the development of both sides. The role of Bangladesh could be a driving force for the development of border-sharing Northeastern states of India, especially Tripura in the same manner as India's role in boosting the growth process of Bangladesh. Though many countries (Japan, South Korea, and now China) are becoming engaged in the upliftment of the region through various projects, without India's involvement, the chances of success are very low. However, recent positive gestures shown by both the governments towards each other (such as the sending of mangoes to the Chief Minister of Tripura by the Bangladesh government on 10 July 2025 and the Government of India's reaching out to Bangladesh offering assistance to deal with the aftermath of the tragic aircraft crash of 21 July 2025) show that there is still hope of good days in the near future. Again, for the first time since the collapse of the Sheikh Hasina government in August 2024, a top diplomat of Bangladesh (M. Riaz Hamidullah, the high commissioner of Bangladesh to India) arrived in Tripura on 1 August 2025 for a three-day visit to review bilateral issues related to Tripura (Bhattacharjee, 2025).

The Way Forward

The trade between Tripura and Bangladesh is miniscule compared to the overall trade between India and Bangladesh. However, the proximity and potential of Tripura calls for a larger volume and more varied composition of trade between the two sides. Despite the positive developments that have taken place in terms of fiscal and other policy measures to exploit the potential for trade with Bangladesh to stimulate Tripura's industrial growth, bottlenecks remain that militate against the state becoming a favoured trade and investment destination.

This chapter shows that Tripura has many advantages from connectivity to resources, both within the state and with the neighbouring countries, especially with respect to Bangladesh, to propel its growth process. The resource advantage of the state, mainly based on bamboo, rubber, tea, and gas, is not reflected in the trade strategy, and the export basket shows that some of the natural products are exported without any value addition. This means that Tripura's trade with Bangladesh runs more on need-based requirements than on resource advantage. There is an urgent need to reorientate the trade strategy of the state so that the advantage in resources with necessary value addition can be mapped into the export basket for making trade an engine of growth.

The analysis above indicates some of the areas where action needs to be taken to give a fillip to boost trade and investment in Tripura, especially with reference to Bangladesh. The government should expedite the process of opening a branch of the Bangladesh Bank in Tripura. Agartala–Akhaura ICP needs to be upgraded into at least a four-lane route on both sides of the border for the smooth movement of vehicles and loading–unloading of products on both sides as this is the busiest land port for trade between Tripura and Bangladesh. Labour and vehicle syndicates create problems in land ports and increase transaction costs in both countries. This increases the cost of commodities imported or exported. Law enforcement agencies of both countries need to deal with this issue to boost trade. There is an urgent need to improve the infrastructure facilities of the functional and non-functional LCSs of the state for greater cross-border movement of commodities.

The Government of Tripura should explore the possibility of setting up industries to manufacture potential products for which there is high import demand in Bangladesh but where Tripura and/or India has not been able to capture all of the opportunity available. The "Maitri Setu" and the Sabroom ICP can play a key role in this respect through facilitating raw materials from different countries at lower transportation costs. The government could set up growth poles through investments in many sectors to support self-sustaining industrialization of the state. The state has a Central University, and there are regular flows of students from Bangladesh. Similarly, one of the private hospitals set up in Agartala had accepted significant numbers of patients from Bangladesh before the turmoil. Again, the state has already established a Buddhist University in South Tripura district. So, it could think of building a hub with the necessary logistic support for health and education sectors for the South and Southeast Asian region.

The policy and strategy for increasing the competitiveness of products have changed, and the value chain or cross-border intra-industry production networks have gained importance in enhancing the value of the products (Nath, 2018b). Asia's success during the last one-and-a-half decades can be attributed to a large extent to intra-industry production networks of the regional supply chain. The value chain view of global economic integration highlights that, for many, industries access to international markets is not achieved merely through designing, making, and marketing new products but involves gaining entry into international design, production, logistics, and marketing networks consisting of many different firms (Brunner, 2010). However, in spite of sharing borders with foreign countries, the Northeastern Region (NER) of India (especially Tripura) remained aloof from the fruits of development due to non-utilization and/or under-utilization of resources along with its inability to engage itself in the inter-industry production network. Spices, processed foods, and rubber are examples of products in which the Northeastern states could participate in some of India's comparative strengths in world markets (Brunner, 2010). The state is endowed with plantation crops, horticultural products, spices, and medicinal plants and enjoys a competitive advantage in some of these products. In fact, Taneja, Das, and Bimal (2018) also pointed out that imports from Bangladesh are dominated by resource-intensive manufacture and non-fuel primary commodities, and the same category dominated exports from India to Bangladesh, indicating possibilities of intra-industry trade in their bilateral economic relations. There is already an India–Japan initiative for strengthening the bamboo value chain in North-East India. The advantages of Tripura in natural and other resources will help the industrial development of the state. The state could focus on organic industry as a key industry for exports. India's growing economic engagements with South, Southeast and East Asian countries tend to increase the international demand for goods produced in the NER (De and Majumder, 2014). Therefore, identifying the products of Tripura with competitive advantage and engaging those in the intra-industry production could help the state in boosting not only productivity but also markets for the products and growth process.

Under the Bay of Bengal Industrial Growth Belt (BIG-B) initiative, Japan is developing the deep sea port (DSP) in Chattagong in order to develop connectivity between Bangladesh and its neighbouring countries such as Bhutan, Nepal, and India's NER. The India–Japan–Bangladesh trilateral partnership will help in realizing a prosperous and vibrant Indo-Pacific region. The enhancing cooperation with Bangladesh may provide the NER and other parts of India with access to three active seaports (Chattogram, Mongla and Payra) and the upcoming Matarbari DSP (Asian Confluence, 2023). The access to the DSP will help in overcoming the land-locked status of the state by connecting it to other parts of the world.

Tripura's development to a large extent depends on cooperation and connectivity with Bangladesh. The past few years have witnessed a cordial relationship between India and Bangladesh, and consequently, a number of trade and connectivity projects were initiated to increase the trade and investment. The recent turmoil witnessed in Bangladesh after 4 August 2024 has severely downsized the relationship between India and Bangladesh. However, given the geographical and historical relation between these two countries, it is expected that political and economic relations will be established again in the near future.

Appendix 10.1 ICP/LCS-wise: Value of exports and imports between Tripura and Bangladesh (value in rupees crore)

Name of the LCS/ICP	2022–23			2021–22			2020–21			2019–20	
	Import Value	Export Value	Total Trade Value	Import Value	Export Value	Total trade value	Import value	Export value	Total trade value	Import value	Export value
Agartala ICP	339.80	99.31	439.11	642.24	134.73	776.97	580.17	1.46	581.63	585.60	0.38
Srimantapur LCS/ICP	151.62	20.61	172.23	68.27	104.69	172.96	73.52	7.30	80.82	23.97	0.40
Muhuripur LCS	45.78	0.52	46.30	13.42	Nil	13.42	35.59	0	35.59	8.81	Nil
Manughat LCS	86.72	0.0074	86.7274	28.81	0.02	28.83	24.29	2.77	27.06	23.05	21.46
Khowaighat LCS	1.65	0.0009	1.6509	3.61	0.01	3.62	1.98	0	1.98	1.53	Nil
Old Ragnabazar LCS	11.15	0.0093	11.1593	10.65	1.95	12.60	1.32	4.86	6.18	1.82	8.10

Source: "Economic Review of Tripura", Directorate of Economics & Statistics, various issues (https://ecostat.tripura.gov.in).

	2018–19			2017–18			2016–17			2015–16		
Total trade value	Import value	Export value	Total trade value	Import value	Export value	Total trade value	Import value	Export value	Total trade value	Import value	Export value	Total trade value
585.98	355.10	0.57	355.67	235.24	0.27	235.51	189.66	0.64	190.30	282.20	0.24	282.44
24.37	95.93	0.47	96.4	93.18	0.12	93.30	56.42	2.45	58.87	47.85	0.59	48.44
8.81	45.42	0	45.42	40.06	00	40.06	43.55	0	43.55	38.62	0	38.62
44.51	14.58	10.05	24.63	10.42	5.24	15.66	9.37	1.40	10.77	11.57	0.07	11.64
1.53	2.18	0.24	2.42	02.45	0.04	2.49	0.80	0.04	0.84	1.32	0	1.32
9.92	9.21	3.33	12.54	2.87	0.79	3.66	0.43	0.07	0.50	0.20	1.06	1.26

Appendix 10.2 The informal trade of Tripura

Districts of Tripura	Informal exports from Tripura to Bangladesh	Informal imports to Tripura from Bangladesh	Subdivisions/ block/ places of the district (s)	Trade points
West Tripura	Cows and buffaloes, ganja (i.e. opium), liquor (country and foreign), drugs (Fensidil, Correx, tablets, etc), kerosene, fertilizers (potash, urea, etc.), jackfruit-(seasonal), ginger, bicycle and bicycle spare parts, cosmetics, blades, steelware, chocolate, sarees, fish, spare parts of vehicles (including bikes), coins, tea, truck tyres, milk powder, wood/ logs, paper, pens, sugar, DDT, Hilton pesticides (for use as poison), betel leaf, bamboo, bananas, rubber sheets, potatoes, tobacco, rice, flour, *biri* (Indian cigarettes), cloth, glassware, dry fish, onions, aluminiumware, cumin seeds, furniture fittings, broken glass, imitation ornaments, scrap iron, etc.	Fish, dry fish, garlic, ready-made garments, plasticware, furniture, chips/cold drinks/juice/ jelly/pickles, tortoises, eggs, cosmetics, diesel/petrol, "Jamdani" sarees, palm/ refined oils, goats, nylon thread/rope, electronic goods, gold ornaments, toys, grocery items, chowmein, rubber (Malaysia), milk powder, peas, betel nut, soaps, vegetables, melamineware, cinnamon, dry grapes, onions, domestic birds, china made clay ware, pillows/ mattresses, bags/umbrellas, food for poultry farms, chicken, etc.	Shimna	1. Katlamara 2. Brammakunda 3. Panchabati 4. Kalagachia

Appendix 10.2 Continued

Districts of Tripura	Informal exports from Tripura to Bangladesh	Informal imports to Tripura from Bangladesh	Subdivisions/ block/ places of the district (s)	Trade points
			Mohanpur	1. Bijoynagar 2. Gougagatipur 3. Gopalnagar 4. Kalkalia 5. Bamutia
			Sadar	1. Akhaura Golachakhar 2. Lankamura 3. Narshinghar 4. Ashiwani Market 5. Charipara 6. Camparbazar
Khowai			Khowai	1. Paschim Singichhara 2. Gournagar, Paschim 3. Bachaibari, Paschim 4. Laxmichhara 5. Paharmura
Sipahijala			Sonamura	1. Durgapur 2. Boxanagar 3. Kulubari 4. Kamalanagar 5. Matinagar 6. Kalamchhara 7. Rahimpur 8. Kalshimura 9. Rabindhanagar 10. Dhanpur 11. Santinagar 12. Sobhapur 13. Sanapur 14. Bolardhepa 15. Srimantipur 16. Bhugmanasahapur 17. Kathalia 18. Machima 19. Durlavpur 20. Katrikrishnanagar

(continued)

Appendix 10.2 Continued

Districts of Tripura	**Informal exports from Tripura to Bangladesh**	**Informal imports to Tripura from Bangladesh**	**Subdivisions/ block/ places of the district (s)**	**Trade points**
			Kamalasagar/ Kasba	1. Debipur 2. Madhupur 3. Konaban
South Tripura			Belonia	1. Muharighat 2. Bankarghat 3. Joychandrapur 4. Hrishyamukh 5. Sarasima 6. Abhoynagar 7. Amzadnagar 8. Rajnagar, Srirampur (Puran Rajbari) 9. Krishnapur 10. Anandapur 11. Prakashnagar
			Sabroom	1. Amlighat 2. Harbatali 3. Doulbari 4. Brajendranagar 5. Alimara 6. Magrum 7. Kaptali
Unakoti			Kailashasahar	1. Chandipur 2. Unakoti 3. Tilagoan 4. Samrurpar 5. Halaichhara
North Tripura			Dharmanagar	1. Ragna 2. Mashpur 3. Banuakamdi 4. Bhagyapur 5. Sanala 6. Sanashpur
Dhalai			Kamalpur	1. Ganganagar 2. Uttar Bilashchera 3. Bishnupur
Gomati			Amarpur	1. Korbook 2. Tirthamukh 3. Matribari 4. Chakpur

Source: Author's field survey, 2012.

Notes

1. The Northeastern Region shares 5,437.15 km of international boundary with Bangladesh, Bhutan, China, Myanmar and Nepal, the highest being 1,880 km with Bangladesh.
2. Tripura is one of the Indian states that helped Bangladesh in fighting her "War of Liberation" in 1971 by expanding all sorts of support not only in the form of shelter to refugees and political personnel but also with food and military personnel.
3. Local people living within 5 km of the border *haat* are authorized to buy goods from the *haat*.
4. Industrial units that use bamboo, rubber, agriculture and horticulture produce and gas as their major raw materials during production; tea manufacturing; the agar oil extraction industry; the rubber wood processing industry; industrial units using plastic waste/e-waste as a major raw material during production; municipal waste processing; packaging material manufacturing activity; the agro waste processing industry; industries manufacturing/using bio-degradable plastics; industries making cutlery items using areca nut leaves or bamboo.
5. Tourism promoting activities, hospitals/nursing homes with minimum investment of Rs 3 crore (excluding land) and a minimum capacity of twenty-five beds.

References

Asian Confluence (2023), *Assessing Connectivity between Northeast India and Bangladesh: Towards a Prosperous Bay of Bengal Region*, New Delhi: Asian Confluence and SANEM.

ADB (Asian Development Bank) (2025), "Asian Development Outlook", Manilla, September (https://www.adb.org/sites/default/files/publication/1085061/asian-development-outlook-september-2025.pdf).

Bhattacharjee, Biswendu (2025), "Bangladesh High Commissioner in Tripura to Review Bilateral Issues", *The Times of India*, 1 August.

Bhattacharya, Rakhee (2015), *Northeastern India and Its Neighbours: Negotiating Security and Development*, New Delhi: Routledge.

Bhowmik, Indraneel and Ashish Nath (2016), "State Finances of Tripura—A Critical Assessment", *Assam Economic Review*, 09, pp. 18–37.

Brunner Hans-Peter (ed.) (2010), *North East India—Local Economic Development and Global Markets*, New Delhi: SAGE Publications India Pvt. Ltd.

CIA (Central Intelligence Agency) (2022), *The World Factbook*, Langley, VA: Central Intelligence Agency.

CUTS (Consumer Unity & Trust Society) International and FICCI (Federation of Indian Chambers of Commerce and Industry) (2017), *Harnessing the Potential for Cross-Border Trade between North East India and its Neighbouring Countries*, Jaipur: CUTS International and FICCI.

De, Prabir and Manab Majiumder (2014), *Developing Cross-Border Production Networks between North Eastern Region of India, Bangladesh and Myanmar—A Preliminary Assessment*, New Delhi: RIS (Research and Information System for Developing Countries).

Department for Promotion of Industry and Internal Trade (2024), "Uttar Poorva Transformative Industrialization Scheme", Government of India (https://unnati.dpiit.gov.in).

Department of Industries and Commerce (n.d.), "Government of Tripura", 23 October 2025 (https://industries.tripura.gov.in/).

Directorate of Economics & Statistics (n.d.a), "Economic Review of Tripura: Various Issues", Government of Tripura (https://ecostat.tripura.gov.in/).

Directorate of Economics & Statistics (n.d.b), "Tripura at a Glance 2024–25", Government of Tripura (https://ecostat.tripura.gov.in/sites/default/files/publications/Tripura%20At%20a%20Glance%202024-25.pdf).

Epitome (n.d), "Bamboowood Products" (https://bamboowood.in).

FDI (Foreign Direct Investment) Statistics (2025), "Quarterly Factsheet on Foreign Direct Investment Inflow", Department for Promotion of Industry and Internal Trade, Ministry of Commerce and Industry, Government of India.

Finance Department (n.d.), "Budget at a Glance 2024–25", Government of Tripura (https://finance.tripura.gov.in/sites/default/files/Budget%20at%20a%20Glance%202024-25_0.pdf).

Ghosh, Dwaipayan (2025), "17 Security Drills to Be Held in Chicken's Neck", *The Times of India*, 8 May.

Haidar, Faizen (2017), "Fruits from Northeast Will Now Reach Dubai, Thanks to Delhi Airport", *Hindustan Times*, 13 October.

International Monetary Fund (2025),"World Economic Outlook", Bangladesh, October (https://www.imf.org/external/datamapper/NGDPD@WEO/BGD?zoom=BGD&highlight=BGD).

Kathuria, Sanjay and Mariem Mezghenni Malouche (2016), "Toward New Sources of Competitiveness in Bangladesh", World Bank Group.

Kathuria, Sanjay and Priya Mathur (2018), "Overview", in Sanjay Kathuria (ed.), *A Glass Half Full—The Promise of Regional Trade in South Asia*, Washington, DC: The World Bank, p. 26.

Ministry of Commerce and Industry (n.d), "Export Import Data Bank", Government of India (https://tradestat.commerce.gov.in).

Ministry of Commerce and Industry (2010), "Memorandum of Understanding for 'Establishing Border Haats across the Border between India and Bangladesh", Government of the Republic of India, 23 October (http://commerce.nic.in/trade/MOU_Border_Haats_across_Border_India_and_Bangladesh2010.pdf).

Ministry of Commerce and Industry (2012), "Memorandum of Understanding for 'Establishing Border Haats across the Border between India and Myanmar", Government of India, 28 May (https://www.commerce.gov.in/wp-content/uploads/2020/05/MoU_on_Estt_of_Border_Haats_with_Myanmar.pdf).

Ministry of DoNER (Development of North Eastern Region) (2011), "Look East Policy and the North Eastern States", 15 February.

Ministry of DoNER and NEC (North Eastern Council) (n.d.), "North Eastern Region Vision 2020", Shillong, 13 May (https://necouncil.gov.in/sites/default/files/about-us/Vision_2020.pdf).

Ministry of External Affairs (2020), "Tripura Receives First Ever Inland Shipping Cargo from Bangladesh", Government of India, 3 September (https://www.mea.gov.in/press-releases.htm?dtl/32927/Tripura).

Ministry of External Affairs (2024), "India–Bangladesh Bilateral Relations", Government of India (https://www.mea.gov.in/Portal/ForeignRelation/Bilateral-Brief-Bangladesh-February-2024.pdf).

Ministry of Finance (n.d.), "Economic Survey: Various Issues", Government of India (https://www.indiabudget.gov.in/economicsurvey).

Nath, Ashish (2018a), "Border Haats: New Dimensions in Cross-Border Trade", *Economic & Political Weekly*, 53 (11), pp. 14–17.

Nath, Ashish (2018b), "Integration with Regional Blocks through Intra-Industry Production Network: Boosting the Growth Prospects of NE India", in Atul Sarma and Saswati Choudhury (eds), *Mainstreaming the Northeast in India's Look and Act East Policy*, Singapore: Palgrave Macmillan, pp. 177–209.

PIB (Press Information Bureau) (2023), "Agartala–Akhaura Railway Project", 7 December (https://www.pib.gov.in/PressReleaseIframePage.aspx?PRID=1983579&reg=3&lang=2#:~:text=The%20Agartala%2DAkhaura%20railway%20project%20is,project%20of%20immense%20national%20importance).

PIB (2025), "Port Restriction on Import of Certain Goods from Bangladesh to India", 17 May (https://www.pib.gov.in/PressReleaseIframePage.aspx?PRID=2129380&reg=3&lang=2).

Pohit, Sanjib and Nisha Taneja (2000), "India's Informal Trade with Bangladesh and Nepal: A Qualitative Assessment", Indian Council for Research on Internation Economic Relations, New Delhi, Working Paper No. 58, July.

Preetha, M. Soundariya (2025), "Bangladesh Restricts Import of Yarn from India by Land", *The Hindu*, 16 April.

RBI (Reserve Bank of India) (2024), "Handbook of Statistics on the Indian Economy 2023–24", Mumbai (https://data.rbi.org.in).

Singh, Rimjhim (2025), "India Ends Transshipment for Bangladesh Exports: What It Means for Trade", *Business Standard*, 10 April.

Taneja, Nisha, Deb Kusam Das, and Samridhi Bimal (eds) (2018), *Sub-Regional Cooperation between India, Myanmar and Bangladesh—Trade, Investment and Connectivity*, New Delhi: Academic Foundation.

Tripura Human Development Report II (2018), "Pratichi Institute Pratichi (India) Trust" (https://www.pratichi.org/research-reports).

World Investment Report (2023), "World Investment Report", United Nations Conference on Trade and Development, New York.

11

Shaking Hands with Neighbours

The Border *Haats* between India and Bangladesh

Indranil Bose

Introduction

India shares with Bangladesh a border that stretches almost 4,097 km. In fact, India's Northeastern states and Bangladesh have coexisted as natural neighbours, and people inhabiting these regions have traded freely between themselves over decades. Recognizing the years of symbiosis that characterized the lives of these people who inhabited geographically contiguous areas across generations, the Governments of India and Bangladesh decided to create for them an institutional space where they would be able to meet from time to time and freely trade their goods without having to go through official and cumbersome documentation procedures that are usually required when people cross borders between countries. Apart from helping the people living in remote border areas to market their local produce, these mechanisms would also serve as a confidence-building measure among the citizens of the two countries. The result was "border *haats*".

"Border *haats*" are rough-and-ready markets that enable local residents to trade with locally grown agricultural and manufactured products. These markets are located on the zero line of the border that separates India and Bangladesh and allow people from both sides of the border to purchase each other's products. According to the Memorandum of Understanding (MoU)[1] signed between the two countries, on 23 October

Indranil Bose, *Shaking Hands with Neighbours* In: *Sub-Regional Cooperation for Trade, Investment, and Employment in North-East India*. Edited by: Ashish Nath, Oxford University Press.
 DOI: 10.1093/9780197908938.003.0011

2010, the border *haats* or *bazaars* were to be established within 5 km on either side of the international border. The border *haats* were to be operated as per modalities that would be agreed upon between the two countries and would be established on a "pilot" basis.

Instances of such institutional mechanisms to facilitate trade and exchange among people across the borders are visible across the world (Schoenberger and Turner, 2008). The World Bank Report (2008)[2] draws attention to the complementarities that cross-border trade facilitate between people living on the two sides of a border. In order to illustrate this point, the report draws upon the case of the potato growers in the Osh region of Kyrgyzstan; since the production of potatoes in Kyrgyzstan far exceeds the local demand, these potato growers prefer to sell their produce in Uzbekistan, where the selling price is higher. Similarly, those cultivating tomatoes and cucumbers in Uzbekistan prefer to sell their produce in Kyrgyzstan rather than in their own country.

The border *haats* between India and Bangladesh allow sale of locally produced agricultural and horticultural products, small agriculture and household goods (e.g. spices), minor forest products (excluding timber), fresh and dry fish, cottage-industry items, wooden furniture, handloom and handicraft items, etc. The basic idea was to buttress the livelihood opportunities of the local residents by offering them a forum where they could market their "local produce", and that is why the commodities were specified. Subsequently, however, the list of commodities has been expanded and the stipulation of "local produce" removed from the guidelines. No local taxes are imposed on trading, and both Indian rupees and Bangladeshi taka are accepted in these markets. This chapter argues that border *haats* help in improving the standards of living of poor people living adjacent to international border areas and contribute in positive ways to ensuring peace, security, stability, and prosperity in the border areas.

Border *Haats* between India and Bangladesh: A Positive Experience

Four such *haats* were initially envisaged at the Indo-Bangladesh border: two of these were in Tripura (namely, Kamalasagar–Kasba and

Srinagar–Chagalnaiya), and the other two *haats* were in Meghalaya (namely, Balat–Dolora and Kalaichar–Baliamari). The first border *haat* was made functional from 23 July 2011 at Kalaichar (India)–*Kurigram* (Bangladesh) in the West Garo hills of Meghalaya. The three other *haats* that followed are located at Balat (Meghalaya, India)–*Dolora* (Bangladesh) in 2012, Srinagar (Tripura, India)–*Chagalnaiya* (Bangladesh) and Kamalasagar (Tripura, India)–*Kasba* (Bangladesh) in 2015.

The border *haats* between India and Bangladesh yield economic benefits for the local people in a number of ways (CUTS International, 2018). People living in remote border areas are able to procure items of day-to-day necessity and preference. For example, at the Kamalasagar–Kasba *Haat* between Tripura (India) and Bangladesh, one could see Bangladeshi vendors displaying an incredible variety of dried fish, which is greatly fancied by fish lovers from the Indian side. These *haats* promote several cottage industries of Bangladeshi manufacturers producing items such as *gamcha* (a small, traditional towel), *lungi* (a draper round the waist for men), garments, and mats. Plastic and melamine products, processed food items, juices, agricultural produce, and household tools (such as spades, axes, ploughs, sickles, etc.) are greatly in evidence. The rules and regulations of border *haat* trade require sellers and buyers to reside within the proximity of a 5-km radius of a particular border *haat*. This is mainly for securing improved standards of living and economic development of the local residents. However, in practice, people residing well beyond the stipulated distance manage to travel to the *haat* and participate as buyers. Traders get a trading permit (locally known as a vendor card), which is usually valid for one year, and they are required to carry photo identity cards. For several vendors who have regular shops in their villages, the border *haat* serves as an additional venue where they are able to augment their incomes. In fact, for some vendors, the income reaped on *haat* days sometimes exceeds their average monthly incomes. These vendors are beginning to look at the border *haats* as the primary source of their incomes. The customs officials, local police, and border security personnel are present during the days of trading in the *haats* to oversee smooth conduct of trade and business. What is noteworthy is that commodities sold in these *haats* are exempt from customs duties. Thus the local people get commodities at low prices, incur lower transaction and transportation costs, and enjoy better availability of items of everyday necessity.

Apart from trading opportunities for villagers around the area, border *haats* also create employment opportunities for the local youths, who have emerged as providers of various services: transporters, labourers, and food stall owners. Transporters do not just carry visitors or vendors to the *haats*; they also carry goods for vendors who trade in large quantities. Several people have found employment as labourers. Cultivators growing seasonal fruit and vegetables, particularly those not engaged in their fields round the year, find an alternative or an additional means of sustenance. This is also true for several women folk who manage to earn modest sums on *haat* days after finishing with their household chores. They could be seen doing odd jobs such as offering assistance to vendors in setting up stalls at the *haat* or carrying *headloads* for a buyer. Border *haats* are thus seen to impact gender issues in a positive way. It goes without saying that wider participation of women on one side of the border will have ripple effects in a positive way on the other side of the border (Dutt et al., 2018). There were several women vendors in the Meghalaya *haats*, and they drew attention to the growing enthusiasm among tribal women to engage themselves in the border trade as most of them are working for their livelihoods either on the fields as cultivators or as local traders and want their products to be sold on the Bangladeshi side, where there is a higher demand for their goods. In fact, there has been a persistent demand on the part of women in the border regions of Meghalaya for reservation of more vendorships in favour of women. By contrast, one witnessed a paucity of women vendors in the Tripura *haats*, probably because of more entrenched patriarchal values among families residing in Tripura. In fact, even in Bangladesh, one encountered such socio-cultural constraints towards involvement and participation of women. On the Bangladesh side, women were seen to participate at the border *haats* more in the capacity of buyers. However socio-cultural factors are not the only deterrents to women's participation; inadequate infrastructure at the *haats* is also responsible (CUTS International, 2019).

The opening up of such livelihood opportunities for the rural folk inhabiting remote border locations merits further appreciation in view of the fact that these folk have low levels of literacy, and educational institutions are also feeble in the region. Given this backdrop, people in this region responded to the institution of border *haats* with enthusiasm and fervour. In fact, border *haats* offered them a much-needed forum for exchange of their local produce. Border *haat* trade has subsequently been consolidated to include not merely trade of items that are locally produced but also other commodities and items that have gradually assumed the proportions of regular business. This has immensely benefited buyers and sellers from both sides of the border and has also provided opportunities of earning to other incidental stakeholders such as labourers and transporters. The institutionalization of trade in such formal mechanisms has also lessened the scope for trade between the concerned people through informal channels. Border Security Force (BSF) personnel confirmed that with the erection of the fence along the border, problems of dacoits and theft have been reduced perceptibly. The smuggling of forbidden items like drugs and opium have also decreased by an appreciable measure.

No wonder, then, that a worldwide trend is discernible among countries to look upon their international borders no longer exclusively in terms of military security but rather as meeting points where two adjacent communities can interact and exchange (Chalfin, 2001; Elsing, 2018; Troshin et al., 2019). Not that security is unimportant, or even secondary, but such meeting grounds can facilitate people-to-people connect and foster cultural exchange, which can contribute to improved relations at the grass-root levels between people and communities inhabiting geographically contiguous areas. The more under-developed border areas are, the more vulnerable they become and the more prone to harbouring an illegal activity, which exacerbates the insecurity of such remote regions (Rippa, 2018).

Yet another interesting instance of such cross-border trade is highlighted by Awang et al. (2013) in their article on Malaysian–Indonesian cross-border trade. The location of their research is a small town named Serekin in Sarawak, Malaysia. The town is located about 5 km from the border of West Kalimantan in Indonesia. Previously, most of the communities living in the border region took recourse to trails or "mousepaths" (locally called "*jalantikus*") for purposes of cross-border labour immigration, smuggling various commodities, and also visiting friends and relations. But in 1967, a "Basic Agreement" was signed between the

Governments of Malaysia and Indonesia, on the basis of which they agreed that communities living in the immediate border areas on either side would be permitted to cross the border for short, non-work-related visits. For this purpose, "Border Crossing Passes" would be issued by the respective governments to enable Indonesians and Malaysians to cross the international border without official documents or passports. These passes, however, limited movement to 30 km of the border areas. Facilitation of cross-border trade in the case of Malaysia–Indonesia helped people in border areas to emancipate themselves from the vicious cycle of poverty that fraught their lives and improved the socio-economic conditions and status of their families by providing them with a vital source of livelihood. Indeed, cross-border trade can be a veritable instrument for boosting the local economy and elevating the living standards of the local communities (Lesser and Moise-Leeman, 2009; Peberdy, 2000).

Since the whole idea of border *haat* trade revolves around the notion of providing an enabling environment for people who reside in the vicinity of the Indo-Bangladesh border to engage in trading activities between themselves, the importance of adequate infrastructural facilities can hardly be exaggerated. Better infrastructure—such as well-structured stalls with sufficient protection from sun and rain, the availability of electricity, water (particularly drinking water), proper and separate toilets for men and women—would help the residents on the two sides of the border to eagerly engage in border *haat* trade. Such infrastructural facilities would also boost women's participation. Infrastructure is largely the responsibility of the concerned state government. Some of the infrastructural inadequacies are *haat*-specific. Major infrastructural inadequacies across the *haats* include poor toilets, unavailability of regular drinking water, lack of currency exchange booths, and absence of electricity. Several vendors and buyers suggested the need for a separate body to look into infrastructural facilities and their maintenance at each *haat*.

The Northeastern states of India and Bangladesh have coexisted as natural neighbours, and communities inhabiting in these regions have traded freely between themselves in the past (Bhattacharjee and Barman, 2019). This relationship was suppressed by political boundaries, and the institutionalization of border *haat* trade signifies the revival of the earlier relationship. Local people need these delinked markets for trade. One of the perceptible benefits of border *haat* trade is the opportunity that it provides for people on both sides of the border to connect with each other. One encountered numerous instances when people have come to the border *haat* with the additional incentive of meeting up with friends, families, and acquaintances from whom they have become distanced (sometimes for more than decades) as a result of political barriers. It was heart-warming to see vendors from Bangladesh carrying goodies to the *haat* for their fellow vendors in India on the occasion of Id, or an Indian vendor carrying a special dish prepared in his home for his Bangladesh friend. One did encounter at the border *haats* visibly emotional scenes of reconnecting (Dutt et al., 2018). As Shirin Akhter, MP from Bangladesh opined, "Border *haats* can, therefore, be viewed as a platform at the grassroots level where the bilateral relations of India and Bangladesh can be cemented." Indeed, border *haat* trade should be looked at from the broader perspective of Indo-Bangladesh relations, not simply as an economic institution, for it has as many political and social implications as it has economic content. In that sense, the border *haats* could well be likened to some kind of a stethoscope in the hands of the governments for feeling the pulse of ground realities and for gauging what is happening at the border. Following a revision of the MoU in April 2017 (an addendum had been signed in 2012), six more *haats* were promised under the agreement. Both addition and revision have expanded the scope for trade and economic activity in the region (Dutt et al., 2018). Four of these new border *haats* were functionalized in Meghalaya at Bholaganj (East Khasi hills), Nalikata (South-west Khasi hills), Shibbari (South Garo hills) and Ryngku (East Khasi hills).

Keeping in mind the success of border *haats*, India and Bangladesh mutually agreed to open several more border *haats*. These were envisaged in Tripura at Kamalpur, Ragna Palbasti, Kathaliya (Sipahijala district) and Khowai (Belchara). Although the infrastructure of all these sanctioned border *haats* had largely been put in place, the COVID-19 pandemic of 2020 impeded their operationalization. In the post-COVID phase, the Governments of both India and Bangladesh intervened to expedite the reopening of these border *haats*. The border *haats* started to function regularly at Balat and Kalaichar in Meghalaya and Srinagar in Tripura. The encouraging outcomes of the border *haats* in Meghalaya and Tripura also ushered in proposals for the establishment of new *haats* in other regions of Assam, Mizoram, and West Bengal.

The Department of Border Management, Ministry of Home Affairs of the Government of India has been implementing the Border Area Development Programme (BADP) through the state governments as part of a comprehensive approach to border management. The programme aims to meet the special development needs of the people living in remote and inaccessible areas situated near the international border and to saturate the border areas with the essential infrastructure through convergence of central/state/BADP/local schemes and a participatory approach. The BADP was initiated in the border areas of the Western region during the Seventh Five-Year Plan period for ensuring balanced development of border areas through development of infrastructure and promotion of a sense of security among the border population. The programme now covers 394 border blocks of 111 border districts in 17 states, which includes 167 border blocks in 55 districts of eight Northeastern states (including Sikkim) of India, located along the international land border. The states covered are Arunachal Pradesh, Assam, Bihar, Gujarat, Himachal Pradesh, Jammu & Kashmir, Manipur, Meghalaya, Mizoram, Nagaland, Punjab, Rajasthan, Sikkim, Tripura, Uttar Pradesh, Uttarakhand, and West Bengal. Under this programme, priority is given to the areas closer to the border.[3] The BADP is an important intervention of the central government to bring about the development of border areas by supplementing the State Plan Funds to bridge the gaps in socio-economic infrastructure, on the one hand, and improving the security environment in border areas, on the other. It follows that development of border areas is a top priority of the Government of India.

Therefore, given the historical relationship and synergies between the border residents, the conceptualization and establishment of the border *haats* represented a pragmatic, people-sensitive, inclusive (involving local communities) border management approach by both governments. These border *haats* contributed in positive ways to ensuring peace, security, stability, and prosperity in the border areas between India and Bangladesh.

The value of the border *haats* is indispensable for the people, especially among the poor and vulnerable sections, living along the international border areas. In addition to the personal benefits, the *haats* offer the following benefits:

- **Exploring peace**: border *haats* have entrusted the local people with greater decision-making powers in implementing various developmental plans meant for their areas. They have also secured people-to-people connect between the two sides of the border by facilitating socialization and cultural exchange. The fact that people are keen to re-connect and strengthen their bonds across the border that separates them is borne by instances like the "*Milan Mela*". This was a fair organized jointly by India and Bangladesh once a year to the north of West Bengal, which enabled Bangladeshis and Indians to meet their relatives across the barbed wire fencing. Thousands of residents from nearby villages flocked along their respective sides of the fence and managed to exchange greetings and gifts (sweets, sarees, hilsa, soap, home-made goodies, etc.).
- **Enhancing security**: it needs to be reiterated that one of the professed advantages of border *haats* lies in respect to the reduction of informal trade. The decline in informal trade post establishment of border *haats* was primarily due to the creation of local employment opportunities and the permission subsequently granted for trade in commodities through border *haats*, which was earlier done through informal and often risky informal channels.

Informal trade was earlier rampant along the Meghalaya and Tripura border, even after the erection of fencing. For example, prior to the commencement of Kalaichar–Baliamari *haat*, trade between the Indians and the Bangladeshis flourished through the well-known channel of Mankachar, situated at a distance of 15–20 km from Kalaichar. The goods that used to flow through Mankachar included cows, wine, local tobacco products like *biri* (Indian cigarettes), spices like *jeera* (cumin seeds), sarees and garments, sugar, and tea. The goods that flowed into India from the Bangladesh side included biscuits and bakery items, local fruits, vegetables, and fish.

Subsequent to the establishment of this *haat*, the volume of goods that flowed to Mankachar decreased substantially, whereas, in other places (like Dalu, where there was no border *haat*), informal trade continued to flourish. The institutionalization of trade through formal channels like border *haats* alongside the diminution of informal channels indicated that trade of unwelcome commodities such as drugs and explosives was substantially diminished, if not eradicated altogether.

- **Instilling stability**: in all the locations where border *haats* were established, agriculture is the main source of livelihood of the residents. The landless either used to work as labourers or they migrated to towns and cities in search of livelihood opportunities. Border *haats* ushered in the welcome creation of different avenues of income for these poor and marginalized people by offering them employment as vendors, transporters, labourers, and support service providers.

Border *haats* have also created earning opportunities for the buyers who purchase products from the *haats* and sell them in their local markets and thereby manage to earn some profit. These border *haats* have been instrumental in not only boosting trade but also generating livelihood opportunities for residents in these remote border areas. Many of these stakeholders associated with border *haats* are the sole income earners for their families, and the border *haat* is the only source of livelihood for them.

In the Balat–Dolora border *haat*, the Indians got fresh vegetables and fish from Bangladesh at half the price, and on the other hand, Bangladeshis got spices, fruits, and other items at affordable prices. For example, while *jeera* cost around USD 5.31 per kg in Bangladesh, the buyers could purchase the same product at USD 3.30 per kg at this *haat*. Border *haats* thus instilled stability in the lives of border residents by ensuring them steady incomes, a reliable market for their produce, and access to essential products at affordable prices (CUTS International, 2019).

- **Ensuring prosperity**: it has been observed that the incomes derived by women through participation at the *haats* has allowed them to invest in health and education, which has raised their standard of living. Border *haats* have also buttressed income-earning opportunities for the people, particularly women traders, by serving as marketplaces for various local handicrafts. Women self-help groups (SHGs) are engaged in home-based manufacture of items like traditional dresses, bags, and cane and handicraft items: mats, caps, bags, flower vases, etc. using stems of the Water hyacinth plant (*Kochuripana*), which are handcrafted by women in Satrasal (Assam). All these products can find markets in the border *haats.*

A Changing Landscape

The outbreak of COVID-19 forced governments of many countries to enact stringent measures such as national lockdowns, suspension of international trade, etc. Closing of border *haats* along the international border between India and Bangladesh, during the period of the COVID-19 pandemic from March 2020 until the recent past was a measure adopted by the Governments of India and Bangladesh to contain the spread of this virus. After a brief period that witnessed the revival of border *haats*, once again they have faced closure as a result of political turmoil in Bangladesh.

Given the significance of the border *haats* and their positive impact on the local communities, prolonged closure of border *haats* would be detrimental to the interests of border residents of both India and Bangladesh as it may force many people below poverty level due to a decrease in income opportunities and the non-availability of essential commodities that were available at the border *haats* at affordable prices. Additionally, this could result in the migration of border residents as income opportunities are limited in these border areas. The situation will be even more critical for women as their mobility is restricted, given their domestic responsibilities and security concerns—a consequence of occupational segregation due to socio-cultural norms prevalent in a patriarchal society like Tripura on the Indian side and the villages in Bangladesh that are adjacent to the border *haat*. It is logical to be apprehensive that the pangs of unemployment and hunger might even drive a few towards unwelcome forms of informal trade, which was predominant in these areas before the establishment of the *haats*. Given these inevitable adverse consequences of the suspension of border *haats*, it is crucial to re-open border *haats* and explore the possibility of more such platforms.

The Northeastern region has been long plagued by developmental inadequacies (Chatterjee, 2017). Inclusive development in the region demands a shift in the development strategy and the planning process towards designing and implementing people-centric programmes based on harnessing the natural resources of the region. Only such a strategy as this could ensure inclusive development, help in poverty alleviation, and raise the standards of living of the inhabitants of the region (Rao and Brunner, 2010).

The impact of border *haats* on the income and livelihood of the local communities is immense. The operationalization of border *haats* has led to the generation of alternative employment opportunities and reduced out-migration; provided additional income support; and in the process, contributed to a significant decline in the informal trade between India and Bangladesh that was earlier happening across these border points. Further, the border *haats* are also important for promoting cross-border value chains in agri-horti products and spices at the local level.

The envisioning and establishment of the border *haats* was also complemented by other initiatives of the Government of India. One such significant initiative is the Government of India's decision to implement the Shekatkar Committee recommendations[4] relating to the creation of border infrastructure. The government has accepted and implemented three important recommendations of the Committee of Experts (CoEs) under the Chairmanship of Lt General D.B. Shekatkar (Retd) relating to border infrastructure. These were related to speeding up road construction, leading to socio-economic development in the border areas. On the matter related to creating border infrastructure, the government has implemented the recommendation of CoEs to outsource road construction work beyond the optimal capacity of the Border Roads Organization (BRO). It has been made mandatory to adopt Engineering Procurement Contract (EPC) mode for execution of all works costing more than rupees (Rs) 100 crore. Such complementary initiatives may facilitate the journey of vehicles to and from the border *haats* and also prevent congestion of traffic at the approach to border *haats*.

Conclusion

The existence and examples of cross-border trade across the world confirm that informal mechanisms of trade, border markets, and such other instances of regionalism and localism are compatible with liberalization and decentralization (Schoenberger and Turner, 2008). Institutional innovations like border *haats* can thus be viewed as instruments to address local needs and livelihood concerns of large numbers of unemployed youths, women, and others inhabiting remote corners of large countries like India. One can only hope that restoration of political stability in Bangladesh, and the region in general, will enable the Governments of India and Bangladesh to work constructively towards mutually beneficial ends and revive the border *haats* in the interests of the border residents of both the countries.

In a world where nation states are proliferating rather than diminishing, it may seem utopian to sing out as did John Lennon, "Imagine there are no countries"! But that is no reason why countries and individuals cannot mend their fences and reach out to each other in amity and goodwill. That is also no reason why thinking minds across the globe should abandon the quest for transforming our world into a better place to live in. As Amartya Sen (2010) reminds us, while it may seem impossible to achieve a perfectly just world, we can always take small steps to remove clear injustices to the extent we can. As such, men and women across the globe live in miniature worlds of their own—worlds that are ridden with poverty and hunger, strife and feuds, dilemmas and deficiencies. These need to be understood and addressed. The case of the Indo-Bangladesh border *haats* reveal that prudent measures on the part of governments can go a long way in transforming the worlds of people living in often neglected and remote border regions. And it will be the responsibility of informed citizens, think tanks, and civil society organizations to sensitize governments in regard to domains such as this and other such domains.

Notes

1. See http://commerce.gov.in/writereaddata/trade/MoU_on_Estt_of_Border_Haats_with_Myanmar.pdf.
2. Ahmed, Sadiq and Ejaz Ghani (2008), "Making Regional Cooperation Work for South Asia's Poor",Policy Research Working Paper No. 4736, The World Bank, South Asia Region, South Asia Regional Progams Unit, September (http://documents.worldbank.org/curated/en/554791468101961794/pdf/WPS4736.pdf).

3. https://badp.mha.gov.in.
4. Insightsias (n.d.), "Shekatkar Committee Recommendations" (https://www.insightsonindia.com/2020/05/19/shekatkar-committee-recommendations).

References

Awang, Abd Hair, Junaenah Sulehan, Noor Rahamah Abu Bakar, Mohd Yusof Abdullah, and Ong Puay Liu (2013), "Informal Cross-Border Trade Sarawak (Malaysia)–Kalimantan (Indonesia): A Catalyst for Border Community's Development", *Asian Social Science*, 9 (4), pp. 167–73.

Bhattacharjee, Abhigyan and Mridul Barman (2019), "Pattern of Cross-Border Commodity Transactions through Kalaichar Border Haat", *Indian Journal of Economics and Development*, 7 (3), pp. 1–7.

Chalfin, Brenda (2001), "Border Zone Trade and the Economic Boundaries of the State in North-East Ghana", *Africa*, 71 (2), pp. 202–204 (http://journal.cambridge.org).

Chatterjee, Aneek (2017), *Neighbours, Major Powers and Indian Foreign Policy*, Hyderabad: Orient Blackswan Pvt. Ltd.

CUTS (Consumer Unity & Trust Society) International (2018), *Connecting Corridors beyond Borders—Enabling Seamless Connectivity in the BBIN Sub-region*, Jaipur: CUTS International.

CUTS International (2019), *Bordering on Happiness – An Assessment of Socio-Economic Impacts of Bangladesh–India Border Haats*, Jaipur: CUTS International.

Dutt, Mohini, Prithviraj Nath, Indranil Bose, and Sayandeep Chattopadhyay (2018), "Bangladesh–India Border Markets", in Sanjay Kathuria (ed.), *A Glass Half Full—The Promise of Regional Trade in South Asia*, Washington, DC: World Bank Group, pp. 189–227.

Elsing, S. (2018), "Navigating Small-Scale Trade across Thai–Lao Border Checkpoints: Legitimacy, Social Relations and Money", *Journal of Contemporary Asia*, 49 (2), pp. 216–32 (https://www.tandfonline.com/doi/full/10.1080/00472336.2018.1551559, https://doi.org/10.1080/004723362018.1551559).

Lesser, C. and E. Moisé-Leeman (2009), "Informal Cross-Border Trade and Trade Facilitation Reform in Sub-Saharan Africa", Organisation for Economic Co-operation and Development (OECD) Publishing, Paris, OECD Trade Policy Papers No. 86, 18 February (http://dx.doi.org/10.1787/225770164564).

Peberdy, Sally Ann (2000), "Border Crossings: Small Entrepreneurs and Cross-Border Trade between South Africa and Mozambique", *Tijdschrift voor Economische en Sociale Geografie*, 91 (4), pp. 361–78 (https://onlinelibrary.wiley.com/doi/epdf/10.1111/1467-9663.00124).

Rao, Govinda M. and Hans-Peter Brunner (2010), "Economic Governance in the North East", in Hans-Peter Brunner (ed.), *North East India: Local Economic Development and Global Markets*, New Delhi: Sage Publications India Pvt. Ltd, pp. 83–105.

Rippa, Alessandro (2018), "Cross-Border Trade and the 'Market' between Xinjiang (China) and Pakistan", *Journal of Contemporary Asia*, 49 (2), pp. 254–71 (https://

www.tandfonline.com/doi/full/10.1080/00472336.2018.1540721, https://doi.org/10.1080/004723362018.1540721).

Schoenberger, Laura and Sarah Turner (2008), "Negotiating Remote Borderland Access: Small-Scale Trade on the Vietnam–China Border", *Development and Change*, 39 (4), pp. 667–96 (https://onlinelibrary.wiley.com/doi/epdf/10.1111/j.1467-7660.2008.00500.x).

Sen, Amartya (2010), *The Idea of Justice*, London: Penguin Books.

Troshin, A.S., S.V. Kupriyanov, and I.S. Sandu (2019), "Features of the Economic Development of Border Regions", *Proceedings of the International Conference on Sustainable Development of Cross-Border Regions: Economic, Social and Security Challenges, Advances in Social Science, Education and Humanities Research*, Atlantis Press, 364 (https://www.atlantis-press.com/proceedings/icsdcbr-19/125922237, https://doi.org/10.2991/icsdcbr-19.2019.2).

Index

For the benefit of digital users, indexed terms that span two pages (e.g., 52–53) may, on occasion, appear on only one of those pages.

Tables and figures are indicated by an italic *t* and *f* following the page number.

The manufacturer's authorised representative in the EU for product safety is Oxford University Press España S.A. of El Parque Empresarial San Fernando de Henares, Avenida de Castilla, 2 - 28830 Madrid (www.oup.es/en or product.safety@oup.com). OUP España S.A. also acts as importer into Spain of products made by the manufacturer.
Printed and bound by CPI Group (UK) Ltd, Croydon, CR0 4YY
14/09/2026
02216308-0003